Destination:
The World
Volume One

AN NCPA ANTHOLOGY

A collection of fiction and nonfiction
travel/vacation stories
by NCPA authors and poets.

Elaine Faber, Kathy Lynne Marshall, Steve Pastis, Barbara A. Barrett, M.L. Hamilton, A.K. Buckroth, Bob Irelan, Bonnie Coleman, Betty Staley, Loy Holder, Denise Lee Branco, Anita Kando, Barbara Klide, Amy Rogers, Emma Clasberry, Charlene Johnson, Jackie Alcade Marr, Sharon S Darrow, Ellen Osborn, Dorothy Rice, Carolyn Radmanovich, Norma Jean Thornton, Judith Vaughan, Barbara Young, Christine "Chrissi" L. Villa, Linda Villatore, Sandra Simmer, L.D. Markham, Ron Javor, Dierdre Wolownick, Roberta "Bert" Davis, Tom Kando, Kimberly A. Edwards, Patricia E. Canterbury, & RoseMary Covington Morgan

DESTINATION: THE WORLD Volume One

A collection of fiction and nonfiction travel and vacation stories by NCPA writers and poets.

Published by
Samati Press
P.O. Box 214673
Sacramento, CA 95821
www.sharonsdarrow.com

This book is independently published by Samati Press in arrangement with individual members of Northern California Publishers & Authors: www.norcalpa.org.

Printed in the United States of America

ISBN: (paperback) 978-1-949125-16-0
        (ebook) 978-1-949125-17-7
        Library of Congress Control Number: 2020916342

Table of Contents

CAMPING WITH THE KIDS
ELAINE FABER

I recall the day I picked up the magazine and read *Camping with Your Children Brings Families Together.* The full article described a family sitting around a roaring fire roasting marshmallows, making S'mores, and it guaranteed such activities created bonds with children. I set the magazine in my lap. *That's what my family needs. More bonding and less bickering.* I tossed the magazine and phoned my husband. "I have a wonderful idea. Let's take the kids camping."

By the time he got home, I had made arrangements for the neighbor to feed the cat, borrowed a tent, a kerosene lantern, sleeping bags, a campstool, camp cots, cooking gear, kerosene cook stove, and an ice chest. Hubby capitulated when I promised him a fishing trip with his buddies later that summer.

It took the promise of a Barbie doll and roller blades to secure the children's cooperation.

The smooth-talking Outdoorsman salesman sold me dehydrated ham and eggs, powdered potatoes, canned beef stew, dried prunes, beef jerky, and powdered applesauce. He guaranteed it was enough to cook, stew, puree, and heat over a cheery campfire to create gourmet meals for a family of four for two days. The picture on the can of dehydrated ham and eggs showed a mom on a hillside with the breeze blowing through her hair. The picture on the canned beef stew showed Daddy snoozing in a camp chair with his dog at his feet. It guaranteed memories of camp side dinners to last a lifetime. I knew it had to be true; it said so, right on the front label.

We set off for a campground in the Sonoma County redwoods about an hour away.

As we neared the campsite, we traversed a steep,

narrow, winding road. With no guardrails on the side, the car crept around hairpin curves as rocks rolled over the canyon edge.

We found our assigned campsite about a half-a-block's distance from the outhouse and 50 feet from a pipe with a faucet on top, surrounded by 263 bees. Thus, we learned the true meaning of the phrase: dry camp. No running water, no electricity, and the aforementioned outhouse.

After successfully pitching our tent, Hubby started to assemble the camp cots, only to find the poles on the end of each cot were missing. Our sleeping bags would lie on the hard ground. My thoughts strayed to my own bed with fourteen inches of cotton batting, memory foam and bedsprings. Ah, well, I reasoned, the promised *family togetherness* was worth it.

The children chased around the camp, and then my seven-year-old daughter requested I accompany her to the *facilities*. Imagine our amazement as we walked past other campsites and noticed folding chairs, down comforters, portable record players, and Porta-Potties. What did they know that I didn't know? The answer soon became clear.

Within fifteen feet of the outhouse, all that we previously thought we knew about outhouses didn't hold a candle to the reality. An indescribable smell hung overhead like a rancid cloud. The hinges on the outhouse door were sprung and defied latching. We held our noses and rushed the door. All bodily urges disappeared at sight of the contents and we raced back to our campsite. The bushes held more promise.

Overhearing conversations from nearby and better prepared campers, we learned of a washhouse up the road with real toilets. We made a plan to do a washroom run after dinner.

The forest ranger at the gate had informed us of a recent restriction on open fires in the fire pits. No problem. We had the little kerosene stove to cook our instant and dried foods. Hubby unpacked the stove. Flip this, fold that, click in the burners, attach the kerosene tank, pump it up and light with a match. *Easy-peasy!* He pumped and pumped vigorously–it would not light. The *sssssssssheoshee* emanating from the kerosene tank could mean only one thing...a minute hole in the tank. Thus, no hot water for a dried, vacuum-sealed, gourmet meal.

"Don't worry," I assured my disappointed family. "We can eat the canned beef stew cold." I reached for the can opener. "It must be here somewhere." No can opener. *"Um...*I must have left it on the kitchen counter."

Like all survival conscious men, Hubby always carried a pocket knife. He attacked the can with a vengeance. The children sat with tin plates in their laps, looking like hungry waifs from a Charles Dickens novel, waiting for their daily gruel.

My daughter's shriek interrupted my fascination with the jagged hole Hubby was gouging into the beef stew can. She danced around the cold campfire, beating her chest and tore at her tee shirt, which I pulled over her head. A flattened kamikaze bee dropped to the ground, twitched and lay still. Several inflamed bumps swelled on my daughter's chest. We painted her upper torso with a mud poultice, having failed to consider bringing along any emergency medical supplies.

By now the ragged hole in the top of the stew can revealed its contents. Unfortunately, it was all too reminiscent of the contents in the outhouse. The anticipated hopes of the family gathered around the fire, eating a gourmet meal, tumbled into the dirt next to the stew. The children tossed their tin plates beside the mutilated can and ripped open a bag of dried prunes.

"Ah well," I mused, as I bit into a dried prune, "family togetherness...."

At 5:45 P.M., the sun disappeared behind the towering pine trees and darkness crashed around us. "We can sit around the fire pit by lantern light and pretend we have a roaring fire. We'll tell stories," I cheerfully suggested. (You can see this coming, can't you?) A few pumps on the kerosene lantern should have blossomed into a soft and romantic glow...but didn't. "Please don't tell me the tank is empty," I squeaked, barely able to distinguish the features of my amazingly quiet children, actually holding hands in the darkness. My long-suffering husband pumped furiously on the lantern to no avail. Telling stories by lantern light joined the beef stew, oozing into the mountain dirt, casting an ominous green glow.

I munched on another dried prune as we drove down the road to the washhouse where we thankfully used the facilities. Returning from the washroom, Hubby turned off the headlights and we sat in total disillusionment and despair for about five minutes, staring at the sagging tent, dark fire pit, and useless accoutrements. Should we give up and go home or stay? Going home meant driving down *death hill* at risk of plunging over the canyon, or going to bed at 6:30 P.M. in the hot tent.

My husband wanted to chance the hill and sleep in his own bed. I insisted it was only twelve hours till dawn when we could strike camp and get out of this hellish nightmare. From the barely discernible expression on Hubby's face, I knew he would never forgive me.

Our four sleeping bags touched on the canvas tent floor. An enormous lump pressed into the small of my back. Counting on the camp cots, we hadn't cleared the rocks off the ground before we set up the tent. We could only wiggle and squirm and try to sleep. Blackness...hot air...kids snoring... Was that a bear? No clock... I heard a mosquito. Mosquitoes find me the way bears find honey. I had to get inside the sleeping bag or be eaten alive.... *Oh Lord, what time is it?* I poked my husband. "Honey, what time is it?"

He groaned and looked at his watch with a luminous dial. "9:30 P.M.," he growled.

I would not survive the night. I would go insane before dawn. The strains of *Kum Ba Yah* drifted faintly from another campsite. I hated those well-prepared campers.

Within a few hours, the unbearable heat turned into a freezing mountain chill. 895 hours later when I could faintly see Hubby's scowling face, I punched him. "Are you asleep?"

"You're kidding, right?"

We struck the tent, wadded and pitched it into the station wagon. We tossed our still unconscious children on top of the tent. The sun cast a faint glow across our neighbors, dreaming of last night's gourmet meal cooked over a functioning camp stove and memories of bonding with their kids, before crawling into sleeping bags on tripod camp cots. We roared out of the campground and hurtled down the hill, spewing rocks over the canyon wall. We did not look back.

By 7:45 A.M. we were home at our worn kitchen table, eating bacon and eggs. We laughed about the camping disasters until tears rolled down our faces. That breakfast is a memory we talk about to this day. It is a memory that will last a lifetime.

Elaine Faber is a member of Sisters in Crime, Cat Writers Association, Northern California Publishers & Authors, and volunteers weekly with the American Cancer Society Discovery Shop. She has published seven cozy cat mystery novels, three humorous WWII mystery adventures, and an anthology of cat stories. Elaine's short stories have appeared in national magazines, won multiple awards, and are included in 14 anthologies. She leads two critique groups in the Sacramento area.

Elaine's Published Novels & Awards:
Black Cat's Legacy
Black Cat and the Lethal Lawyer
Black Cat and the Accidental Angel
Black Cat and the Secret in Dewey's Diary
Mrs. Odboddy Hometown Patriot * 1st Place: 2017 Fiction (NCPA)
Mrs. Odboddy Undercover Courier * 3rd Place: 2018 Cover and Design (NCPA)
Mrs. Odboddy And Then There was a Tiger * 2nd Place: 2019 General Fiction (NCPA)
All Things Cat

FINALLY A PRIORITY
KATHY LYNNE MARSHALL

'm frugal. Cheap. Thrifty. *Discerning…* There, I said it.

You won't catch me in fancy clothing stores, at the hair dresser, or in nail salons. I won't even pay $3.00 for colored water at a restaurant. I was raised that way by my Depression-era mother. If you can't pay for it with cash, you don't buy it.

In 1998, I became the sole breadwinner for myself and my two young sons after my ex-husband was killed by a drunk driver. Frugal suited us just fine … until my accomplished boys became adults and I retired from my day job with the State of California. My pension, good benefits, and thirty years of investing have allowed me to become Auntie Mame to live, Live, LIVE my dream of traveling the world.

Since 2012, my boyfriend, Michael, and I have cruised the Mediterranean, delighted that I could finally use my Bachelor of Arts degree *en Français* (French), experiencing historical places we had only read about. I thought my head would explode with delight, walking on centuries-old cobblestones in Provence in the ground below crenelated homes built in the 1500s. Stepping further back into time found us standing atop the Acropolis where Homer and Socrates discoursed. The pristine blue and white structures on the island of Santorini and the startling, intact "ruins" of Pompeii and Turkey brought wonder to our eyes, as did Antonin Gaudi's whimsical architectural works in Barcelona. Seeing the underground hallways from which wild animals bounded into the Colosseum in Rome, and almost getting arrested in Florence for buying a toy from a street vendor, were memories we shall never forget.

My favorite way to see Europe, though, is on a Rick Steves tour through the "back door"—meaning, skipping some of the most touristy sights and focusing instead on the marvels one block *off* the beaten path. In 2015, I spent three days by myself in Paris, the City of Love, then ten glorious sunrises exploring France with a small group of intrepid travelers. We've enjoyed Rick Steves' "Best of Europe" and "Southern Villages of England" tours, having incredible adventures in Rome, Cinque Terre, Florence, France, Switzerland, Germany, Austria, and England.

We've cherished two intimate Viking River Cruises: our first along the Danube, floating to historic Budapest, open air shops in Slovakia, elegant Vienna, delightful villages and walled-cities in the Czech Republic, bucolic Bavaria, and an extended trip to study the mixed-architecture of Prague. The second Viking cruise was to the South of France. Yes, I was getting good use of my forty-year-old French degree *enfin* (finally).

I've also visited my son and grandkids in lush Okinawa, Japan, which is heavily-impacted by American military bases, but is still charming in its own way. *Arigato!* (Thank you!)

Numerous genealogy-related trips took me to states I had never before visited, like Louisiana, Mississippi, Alabama, Maryland, Virginia, West Virginia, and the capitol of the United States while the first Black President still presided.

I've taken thousands of photographs and videos, and created numerous photo books from my daily journals in order to commemorate the sites and my feelings from those varied trips.

Each of those memorable journeys found us constrained into tiny economy seats on overbooked planes. The interminable nine-hour flights over the Atlantic left us stiff, sore, and tired upon arrival at our fantasy destinations. Each time we vowed to fly Business Class the next trip. Each time I balked at the extreme cost.

So I amazed myself in 2019 by handing over $3,000 for a Business Class plane ticket *upgrade* for our second

Viking cruise to the South of France. The total cost of that ten-day trip was $10,000, nearly one-fifth the cost of my first house, but was it ever worth it!

If you've never had the pleasure of flying Business or First Class, let me give you a glimpse into the luxury that will make you question whether you can *ever* fly economy again.

The heightened experience begins as soon as you enter the airport. Our Delta One ticket allowed us access to their private Sky Club Lounge, which offered complimentary snacks, fresh foods and spirits in an upscale setting. We got accelerated check-in, security, and baggage handling service. Once it was time to board, upper class patrons enter the plane first.

The flight from Sacramento to Minneapolis afforded us seats at the front of the plane, which offered plenty of leg room. Our Delta One cabin included elevated dining—the freshest regionally-sourced foods and chef-curated meals, and a selection of fine wines, served on beautifully designed serving trays. How does cucumber, tomato and olive salad, ciabatta roll with butter, vegetarian lasagna, cheesecake, and red wine sound for lunch? Michael had a large piece of salmon over a bed of lettuces, Sungold tomatoes, grilled vegetables sprinkled with feta cheese, and wine. Tiny geodesic salt and pepper shakers were a nice memento. Excited that we could order whatever we wanted—Pringles, granola bars, candy, and too much wine—we slept two hours upright, in bliss.

Flying over Minnesota toward the airport, I marveled at the number of lakes in the *State of Nice*. Once landed, we visited the Sky Lounge designated for First and Business Class passengers, where we sampled BBQ ribs, chicken and pasta, and more wine.

For the long flight from Minneapolis to Amsterdam, we were boarded first. Imagine entering the plane through a different portal than the other passengers, into a separate section of the fuselage. Individual beige and khaki-colored "suites" or pods were situated along the side windows with two pods separated by a privacy screen in the center aisles. On the shared table between Michael and me sat bottles of water and noise-cancelling headphones. On our seats were leather-bound amenity kits which contained eyeshades, the airline's signature electric blue socks, slippers, lotion, lip balm, toothbrush, toothpaste, and a nail file. A packaged blanket and a fluffy pillow also lay on our seats. The 15" adjustable monitor and remote control gave us easy access to movies, TV shows, and music. One could sit back and relax in an adjustable 90-to-180-degree seat. In the fully reclined position, I felt like I was wrapped in a cozy cocoon of warmth and restrained luxury. Beaming, we adjusted and readjusted our seats and monitor, and took dignified photos of ourselves sitting in the lap of opulence, as though we were someone special ... because we now were.

The plane fully loaded, the engines began whirring, then it backed out of the terminal, onto the tarmac, and sped down the runway. Still grinning from ear to ear in our personal suites, we sailed into the air, wondering what additional treats were in store for Business Class patrons. We did not have to wait long.

The stewardess came around with a tray of steamy, aromatic, rolled-up white washcloths. We pulled up a food tray next to our arm rests, accepted the washcloth from her silver tongs, then sanitized our hands with the scented cloths. This prepared us for the first of what would be many appetizing bites over the next nine hours.

First, was an aperitif, like Kirsch. Then we perused the fancy dinner menu. I ordered everything. The appetizer consisted of salad, cylindrical roll, prawns with lemon, corn chowder, and wine. The next course was grilled chicken breast and vegetables, rice pilaf, soup, and more wine. The dessert tray consisted of gourmet crackers, fine sliced cheeses, fig spread, a Meyer lemon curd cream pie, and sweet wine. My motto remained for the rest of the trip, "I'm NOT going to think about the weight scale back at home. This is a once-in-a-lifetime experience and I want to enjoy every morsel of it."

We watched a couple of inane movies on the big screen, but the food and wine made us drowsy. Spending so much money, it was hard to justify sleeping, but I *forced* myself to s-t-r-e-t-c-h out my limbs languidly like a lazy cat, as I never could on previous flights. Wrapped in the quilted blanket, eyeshades and slippers on, fluffy pillow behind my neck, I dropped into a deep sleep.

The smell of a caprese quiche breakfast woke me from a restful slumber. Landing in Amsterdam, we observed people from all corners of the world, as we made our way through the crowds to ... yes, you guessed it ... another lounge, with more scrumptious treats to eat and drink. I was so stuffed that I only ate a thin, sliced egg and spinach sandwich from the extensive buffet. Michael hadn't eaten anything since dinner for he vowed to exercise restraint ... unlike me.

We napped for a couple of hours in a cozy seat in the lounge before it was time to catch our flight to Marseille, located at the edge of the French Riviera. Our gate was crowded, but Michael noticed a sign that delineated where Sky Priority passengers were to stand. We boarded first, ahead of a very long line. It was only an hour flight, and my overworked stomach pleaded, "No more food," but I took the offered plate of smoked salmon over grilled veggies with chocolate pudding on the side. The cute little red Dutch shoe salt and pepper shakers became another of our treasures. I was milking this trip for all it was worth.

At Marseille, we waited downstairs at the baggage claims area. Michael's sturdy blue luggage was among the first to appear, but where was my purple suitcase? Oh ... a familiar bag wrapped in duct tape appeared on the circular conveyer belt. Yes, my suitcase had been chewed somewhere between Sacramento and Marseille. What now? Viking Cruise Lines had assigned a representative to pick us up from the airport, along with other cruisers, to drive us 45 minutes away to the awaiting ship. I had to hurry to the Claims Office in an adjacent building to show my mutilated bag and seek their assistance. Because I was flying Business Class, they gave me a brand new, firm-sided suitcase, of much higher quality than my inexpensive cloth version. Lucky me!

Our cruise to the south of France was enjoyable, but bittersweet, because it would likely be our last to France; there are far too many other places in the world to keep coming back to one country. We had paid in advance for several food tours, which entailed shopping in an indoor fresh food market, and hands-on learning how to make focaccia bread and choux pastry in a renovated chateau. Local guides encouraged us to taste olive products and various sweets, in addition to sampling Beaujolais and Pinot Noir at several home vineyards and wine caves. We also spent a day in Arles learning how to paint like Vincent Van Gogh, and visited many of his haunts.

Moonlit nights were spent walking through centuries-old towns, or floating down the Rhone. We passed through a dozen locks, ate outdoors on the ship's Aquavit Terrace, and practiced drawing and painting from our personal balcony on the ship. We awoke to the quiet that is a longship meandering through a still river at sunrise. It was Heaven.

After the cruise, we spent three extra days in Dijon—where mustard is King—for more tasting, smelling of fragrant lavender fields, walking paths which bore witness to numerous historical events, and learning about different people, customs, and places.

When it was time to travel back home, we left the ship early in the morning, hopped into a Viking van, and were driven to the small airport in Lyon. We got help figuring out how to check our bags, then we were off to ... yes, another comfortable lounge, to wait an hour to board our flight. By then, after ten days of savoring *everything* I wanted to taste, thoughts of the weight scale limited my appetite, so I only ate a small pastry that time. The commuter plane took us to Charles De Gaulle Airport in Paris where we were first to board an Air France plane at 12:45 PM.

The color scheme in this long flight from Paris to Seattle, was light and dark gray. Like the trip to Europe, we were given another amenities bag—fancier than the first—

but with a slimmer pillow, and a thinner blanket. Immediately, I donned my electric blue socks and slippers for the trip home, relaxing like I had *always* traveled this way ... now that I was one of the beautiful people ... at least for that day.

The one-page menu was simple, yet elegant. The stewardess placed a white linen tablecloth and rolled napkin on each of our built-in dining trays. The first serving was bright-green watercress, a fragrant olive ciabatta roll, carpaccio atop a cream sauce, and a ball of mixed grains adorned with julienned yellow squash. Light, healthy, and yummy. The next course was white fish, spinach polenta, peas, and butternut squash soup. Three movies, a brief snooze, more food, more wine. Wait! Slow down! I was dismayed that the flight back home passed *so* quickly ... part of me wanted more time, more pampering, more *joie de vivre* (zest for life), more ...

We landed in Seattle where their lounge had a charcuterie buffet of high quality cold cuts, cubes of cheese, fresh fruits, steamed broccoli with grilled onions, bacon, and Haagen Dazs ice cream. Sigh. The dream was nearly over.

Spoiled, we were on the last leg of our trip from Seattle to Sacramento. Sitting in the first rows of the commuter plane, our legs extended comfortably. We *expected* a meal even though the trip was only 90 minutes long. The steward was very friendly, chatting, and joking with the passengers, but he didn't seem to understand that we wanted our meal. Someone behind me asked where our lunch was. The steward said, tongue-in-cheek, that he would check with the chef to see what he had in the kitchen. The steward was the chef, of course. He took our food orders and worked to service his upper class customers. We got *our* food—watermelon soup and a pale steak-fried chicken something or other, but to our horror, no wine. Many passengers were upset they did not get their meal at all before the plane began descending into Sacramento. Ah well, you can't please everybody.

Now we know what richer folk experience on a regular basis and we loved it. Frankly, I was shocked at how demanding we had become, how much we began expecting top-notch service and accommodations, now having tasted the lifestyle of the almost-rich and famous. Will I start having my nails done and hair coiffed, and shop for clothes in Nordstrom for our next overseas trip? It's doubtful. I'm not a girly-girl or Queen Grimhilde who preens in front of a mirror every day.

Still, my friends have asked me the hundred-thousand dollar question many times since hearing our extraordinary tale of luxury: Will I choose to be a Priority traveler on future trips? What do you think?

 Kathy Lynne Marshall's lifelong infatuation with African culture was challenged when a DNA test revealed her diverse ancestry. Her dual-award winning *Finding Otho: The Search for Our Enslaved Williams Ancestors* is a part-research, part-story, part-guide book that contains a "Solve Your Mystery" chapter, extensive research and sleuthing techniques, and a four-chapter DNA analysis section to help others find their relatives too. *The Ancestors Are Smiling!* contains life stories about the descendants of Otho Williams. *Finding Daisy: From the Deep South to the Promised Land* explores Marshall's paternal grandmother, who lied about her beginnings, but became a powerhouse in Cleveland, Ohio. Marshall's books are in libraries across the United States, as well as at Underground Books, Amazon, and her website: www.KanikaMarshall.com. She also published "Wolf Song" in NCPA's *Birds of a Feather* Anthology, many photo books, and articles in various genealogy journals.

Marshall lives in Elk Grove, California..

LANCE'S TOBOGGAN OF MIRACLES
STEVE PASTIS

Zenith heard her Jeep's left rear tire explode and she knew it wouldn't be long before the rhinos would overtake her. Her life flashed before her. She remembered her parents telling her not to go. She pictured her girlfriends begging her not to go. She thought about Meldwich the butcher telling her to change perfumes.

Now this.

She heard the approaching rhinos and wondered how to spend her last moments on Earth. Suddenly, she heard a "Ho, ho, ho." She knew that could only mean one thing. She looked up and there it was – Lance's Toboggan of Miracles.

"Climb aboard and hurry," said Lance who was standing in the spectacular toboggan. He was holding its steering wheel in one hand and releasing the rope ladder with the other.

"No time to lose, Zenith," he said. "We are needed elsewhere."

In Midway City, Hector looked over the reports placed on his desk by the grinning police detective. There would be no avoiding the consequences now. He was going to jail. Even after turning over so many of his friends to the police to avoid this fate over the years, he was going to jail. He feared what awaited him there, surrounded by so many angry ex-friends.

"Isn't there something you could do?" Hector inquired as he took off his Rolex and placed it in front of the detective. The detective picked up the watch and studied it before placing it into his pocket.

"No," was all he said.

"Ho, ho, ho," was all Lance said as he stopped the Toboggan of Miracles outside the window of the fifteenth-floor office. Lance carefully cut a large square in the window as the policeman smiled and waved. Hector climbed out into the toboggan and they were off. The policeman stuck his head and shoulders through the hole in the window, still waving.

"Hector, this is Zenith, Zenith, this is Hector," said Lance. "It's time for burgers."

The Toboggan of Miracles touched down in front of an In-N-Out and they all went inside to order. This one was more than a simple drive-through. No one said much and whatever may have been said wasn't responded to. Soon they were back in the sky.

They flew around for a while. They stopped for more burgers and flew around again. Hours became days. Days became weeks. Flying, stopping for burgers, flying, stopping for burgers, flying, stopping for burgers. At about the same time, both Zenith and Hector cracked.

"We can't take this anymore!" they shouted in unison as if they had that moment well-rehearsed. "Please take us back where you found us!"

Hector's office was the closest, so Lance's Toboggan of Miracles headed there first. Hector got out and climbed back through the same window he had used for his escape. He promised to write even though he never would.

Inside he found the same police detective sitting in his office waiting for him. Sitting in the chairs on each side of him were the detective's children.

"They want to hear all about Lance and his Toboggan of Miracles," he said.

Hector told them all about the flying and the stops for burgers as the children and the detective sat transfixed.

"You know, Hector, you may be a crook but you're really not a bad sort of guy," said the detective when it was clear that Hector's story had adequately covered both aspects of the journey. "How about if you turn in somebody you know for another crime and I'll pretend like I never saw these reports?"

Hector pulled out a photograph of his brother Wally leaving a gas station while waving the large block of wood attached to the bathroom key. Wally was thrown into prison. Hector lived happily ever after on the money he had embezzled.

The Toboggan of Miracles soon descended next to where Zenith's Jeep had blown out a tire. The Jeep was nowhere to be seen. In its place, however, was a brand-new Pontiac Firebird that had recently been stolen. Some car thieves had decided to trade it for the Jeep. They figured that the Jeep owner was probably trampled to death in the rhino stampede and if they stayed in the bright red Firebird, they would be arrested for sure.

Zenith got into the Firebird, claiming it as her own and Lance tossed pieces of cardboard off the Toboggan of Miracles. Each landed perfectly over a different window of the car. The toboggan hovered over the Firebird as Lance poured bright blue paint over the car. When all the red had been covered, Lance's Toboggan of Miracles flew away. The wind created by the toboggan's departure swirled around the now-blue car, blowing off the cardboard and drying the paint.

Zenith drove across three continents until she was back home. She changed her perfume and married Meldwich, the butcher.

At this very moment, Lance is out flying somewhere in his Toboggan of Miracles. Then again, he may have stopped for burgers.

Steve Pastis has written for the *Valley Voice, The Good Life, Greek Accent, Farm News, Custom Boat & Engine, Baseball Cards, Circus, Rock Fever, Occidental Magazine, Destination Visalia, South Valley Networking, Hellenic Calendar,* and *Cool and Strange Music.* His stories have been published in *The Journal of Experimental Fiction, Signs of Life,* and *Gargoyle.* Three of his short story collections, *Fables for the Clarinet, Ten Good Reasons to Fix that Airplane,* and *Elk and Penguin Stories,* are available on Amazon.

QUALITY OR QUANTITY
BARBARA A. BARRETT

"I would rather die!"

The words hung in the room. My cardiologist's eyes widened but he didn't comment.

"I've been waiting 50 years to go to Europe."

I took a deep breath "When I retired, I was going to travel. For the first time, I had the money and I wasn't working or going to school. All that changed when my mother needed caregiving. I took care of her for five years. And, now when I'm free to travel again, you're telling me I need open heart surgery?"

He nodded "Your echocardiogram shows your aortic valve has to be replaced immediately."

I had come so close. A month ago, I saw *Eat Pray Love* and cried as I watched Elizabeth Gilbert living my dream life. After the movie, I bought her book. A few days later, I was eating dinner in front of the TV when I realized I wasn't getting any younger. The next day, I started booking reservations for Europe.

Liz Gilbert spent three months each in Italy, India and Bali. I didn't have that kind of money and my interests were different. I decided on England, Greece and France. I'm not fond of big cities but I wanted to see London, and Paris has been a dream since high school. Most of all, I wanted to visit the Greek Isles and relax on a beach that literally reeked of history. After extensive research, I made airline and hotel reservations online - three days in London, four weeks on the island of Naxos in Greece, and four nights in Paris. With travel time, I would be gone almost six weeks. At least, that was the plan. Now, two weeks before my departure, I was sitting in my cardiologist's office getting the bad news.

Desperately, I told him, "I've already booked my trip."

"You can postpone it until next year."

I had been hearing, "You can always go next year," for far too many decades. I knew "next year" never came. There wouldn't be a next year. Something always came up and it was happening again. Even worse, I was almost 70 and there might not be another next year for me.

My doctor scheduled a cardiac catheterization. Afterwards, he told me it confirmed the diagnosis. When my eyes filled with tears, he and the nurse pulled the curtain so I could have privacy. The thought of not going hurt so bad it took a few minutes to realize I was still in control of my life. I meant it when I said I would rather die. Enough is enough. Life is about quality, not quantity. I evaluated my options. It had been a month between the echogram test results and the doctor appointment. If the operation was an emergency, there would not have been any delay. I decided to go ahead with my trip. Once I made that decision, my doctors supported me. I was given baby aspirin, an inhaler and antibiotics.

The British Airways flight was uneventful. I didn't sleep much on the plane; I was too excited. The next morning, I checked into my London hotel. After following the bellboy down a series of narrow corridors with creaky floors, I stepped into my room. I had asked for a single and it definitely was that. The room was barely larger than my master bathroom. Everything was squished together, but I didn't mind. I was in London.

I went for a walk in my new neighborhood. It was a mixture of multi-storied homes, pubs, hotels and stores. Things that were familiar at home were unfamiliar here. The local Burger King advertised a Texas burger with toppings I'm sure were unknown to anyone in the Lone Star State. The tables inside though were just as crowded.

My first stop would cross two items off my travel list and I headed for one of the world's largest, luxury department stores. Harrods has seven floors and over 300 departments. I was only interested in their High Tea.

To get there, I went down a steep and very long escalator to the underground commuter train. I was prepared. I had a map and knew where to exit. I changed shoes at a nearby bus stop; Harrods didn't allow tennis shoes, or trainers, as they are called in Europe.

The British novels I love were right about the elegance. When I was seated in the Tea Room, I looked around. The waiters wore formal wear. On my table was a full bouquet of fresh flowers and greenery, silver tableware and fine crystal and china. The food was served on a three-tiered stand with appetizing choices on each level. Soft piano music added to the grandeur of the meal. The tea, small sandwiches, scones and *petit fours* were the best I ever tasted, but I'm still not sure whether it was the ambiance or the pastry chef.

The rest of that day and the next I walked the streets of London (getting lost a lot but everyone was so helpful). Somehow, I found the Thames and winding my way through the maze of streets, I found *beaucoup* bookshops! Eating at a gourmet buffet with a tiny stomach perfectly described my dilemma. So many books and so little luggage space. I bought a couple of paperbacks and headed back to my hotel.

I was having a cup of tea in the lobby when an American woman approached me. She came to London often on business. We shared travel stories. Mine was very short because it was my first day. She suggested we have dinner at a nearby pub. It was crowded and we had to wait for our food, but it was delicious.

The next day I flew to Athens.

It was off season, so my flight to Naxos didn't leave until the following morning. Since I had been warned that women traveling alone in Athens were pickpocket targets, I stayed overnight at an airport hotel.

It was a small plane, just 40 passengers. After almost an hour over water that sparkled in the sun, I stepped into the warm Greek air. What a beautiful place. Even the Spiros Hotel exceeded my expectations. I had a spacious room with a small kitchen, and a shower. The floors were a beautiful off-white marble and there were enough beds and couches for 6-8 people. Outside the large patio windows, were two balconies. The sheer curtains blew gently in the wind. Best of all was the view of the Aegean Sea. Yes! That...Aegean...Sea.

The hotel was owned and operated by a local family who went out of their way for guests. I was really grateful for the language lessons I had before I left. A priest from a nearby Greek Orthodox church helped with my accent and taught me about three dozen idiomatic Greek phrases which I practiced until they came easily.

I asked the owner, Stelios, where the local people ate. He suggested Maro's Taverna. It wasn't far and I ate there often during my stay. I sat on the restaurant patio that first time, and watched the waiters deliver food to other customers. Finally, I ordered spaghetti. It came on a big platter topped with meat sauce about an inch thick. Delicious and enough for two more meals.

The staff and customers were welcoming and friendly. During another visit, I asked the waiter about a platter of food he delivered to a nearby table. Delighted, the men insisted I share their spinach greens and mushrooms. Salads on Naxos and in Athens consisted of fresh chopped tomatoes and cucumbers, red onion, feta cheese and kalamata olives. I never saw any lettuce. Later, I bought everything I needed and made a salad every day. The dressing I concocted was made with local olive oil, garlic powder and retsina, a Greek white wine. When I got home, even with the same ingredients, it tasted different, but then I was no longer sitting on a balcony overlooking the Aegean Sea.

Breakfast was my favorite meal. It was part of my room charge so every morning I walked down the three flights of stairs to the lobby. The buffet style meal offered cereals, fresh fruit, hard boiled eggs, bacon, sausage, toast and some wonderful rolls. My favorite was the Greek yogurt. It was light, fluffy and indescribably delicious. I could have taken the tray to my room or sat by the pool, but then I would have missed the international ambiance.

Eating my yogurt with cereal and fruit, I heard many different languages: Greek, Spanish, Italian, French,

Swiss, and German. Even English came in a variety of accents: Canadian, Australian, American and British. There were couples, families and lone travelers like myself. Against the wall were a couple of local, elderly Greek men who sat in the same chairs every morning. They were straight out of Central Casting. The cafe had WiFi so I brought my laptop with me. I didn't write much. Mostly, I reveled in being Barbara Barrett, international traveler.

After breakfast, sometimes I walked to the port area of Chora (Naxos City) about a mile away. "*Kalimera!*" I said good morning to everyone I met. Most of the residents were sweeping the sidewalks and streets in front of their homes. Everything was so clean. They smiled back at me. The people on Naxos were so helpful. When I needed an alarm clock, a store owner who spoke little English, called to a shop owner across the narrow street and accompanied me around the corner to be sure I found the right place. During a downpour, I ducked into a cafe for shelter and an elderly man bought my tea. His only English was "no problemo." Whenever lightning flashed, thunder crashed or hail pounded on the roof, we looked at each other and yelled, "no problemo." It was a fun afternoon.

Almost every day I had a small cup of homemade "killer" chocolate ice cream.

I still have the small souvenirs I bought in another shop as I made my way to the most famous landmark on Naxos: the Portara, a 20 by 11-foot marble gateway that sits atop a small hill, almost completely surrounded by water. It's all that's left of the Temple of Apollo, which was looted to build the local churches. The stone steps leading to it are worn from the feet of Apollo's many worshippers and modern-day visitors. When it first comes into view, nothing can prepare you for the beauty and magic of a monumental gateway that appears to go nowhere and everywhere.

Scattered across the hilltop in various shapes and sizes are the hundreds of discarded segments from the shrine. Sitting on one of those two thousand, five-hundred-year-old pieces of marble and watching the sun sparkle on the Aegean Sea, was the perfect place for me to meditate and contemplate Life. Sometimes I brought along a little retsina wine and poured a libation for Apollo himself.

My only side trip was to Delos, the island of Greek gods and the birthplace of Apollo and his twin sister, Artemis. It was the religious and spiritual center of ancient Greece. When I was booking the ferry, I met another member of what I call, "The Clan of the Laughing Eyes." He remarked that my eyes were filled with laughter too and we talked for quite awhile. I asked if there was someplace on Naxos that had Greek dancing and singing (shades of Anthony Quinn as Zorba.) He said "Yes, right here, after midnight." I laughed and told him I just might show up. A few days later, when I went to pick up my tickets, I was greeted with, "Good morning, my darling."

Did I actually keep that midnight rendezvous? Well, that's a story for another anthology.

It was October and the direct ferries weren't running. I stayed overnight at the Aeolos Hotel on Mykonos. Like Santorini, the city and houses sit on the high surrounding cliffs. The roads to the beaches are long and steep. Very different from the rolling hills on Naxos.

Cars, buses, restaurants and hotels are not allowed on Delos. There are only ruins, legends and ancient memories. It must have been breathtaking to walk streets dedicated to the Twelve Olympian Gods in ancient times when many of the temples had statues over 20 feet high, covered with gold. The rubble I walked over was a sad reminder of the marauders who had sacked this island time and again.

I visited the Avenue of the Lions, an ancient street dating back to seventh century BC, lined with majestic stone lions, seven of which still survive. I walked through the Theatre of Delos, an amphitheater 43 rows high, and wondered whether Homer's *Iliad* and *Odyssey* were ever recited for any of the 6,500 spectators that occupied those seats. I spent hours in the Archaeological Museum that contains vases, statues and other artifacts excavated there. Some so beautiful, it hurt to see they had missing pieces.

I took the last ferry to Mykonos and from there, back to Chora.

The beach wasn't far from my hotel. I loved walking in the warm sea water with my toes digging into the ancient sand. Beneath my feet were thousands of years of crushed relics that had washed up on the shore. Late one afternoon, I explored the Old Town Kastro section: a maze of barely six-foot-wide alleyways. There wasn't much sun because of the high walls, but around every corner I found shops and cafes, all displaying pots of cheerful, bright flowers. Down one passage I found the appropriately named Labyrinth Wine Restaurant, a jewel with small tables and an intimate ambiance. Surrounded with hanging greenery and Greek artwork, I had a delicious dinner by candlelight.

In late October, after a final visit to the Portara, I bid a reluctant farewell to Naxos. Four weeks just wasn't enough. The next morning after eating breakfast at the Athens airport hotel, I boarded a plane, had lunch in London's Heathrow Airport and a short time later, landed at the Charles de Gaulle airport. I rushed to the Hotel du Casino, changed my clothes and went down in an incredibly tiny and slow, wrought iron elevator, to meet my friends.

The five of us took the Metro to the restaurant where we joined more fans of Robert E. Howard, a Texas author and poet (1906-1936) who has an international following. I only know a few French words, but I met everyone at the party before the night was over. Communications were hilarious and fun.

The following morning, two of my French friends took me on a tour of Paris. They asked me to set the itinerary. The first stop was the Musee d'Orsay with its Impressionist art exhibit. We spent most of the day there. I don't think we missed one canvas. Afterwards, we walked to the Seine and had a late lunch on a riverboat. On the spur of the moment, we crashed a weekly Science Fiction fan meeting. Luckily, one of my friends was a member.

Beaucoup beers later, some of us walked to a restaurant and had dinner.

The next morning, one friend had to work so there were just two of us. Again, the itinerary was left to me. At the recommendation of friends I met in Naxos, I suggested the Sacre-Coeur Basilica which sits atop the highest point in Paris. Surrounding it is Montmartre, a unique village that is home to an artists' colony. Colors of every shade and hue, the smell of paint oils and wet canvases, and the chatter of foreign languages assaulted my senses as I walked through the maze of artists and their paintings in the *Place du Tertre*. Much of the artwork was impressive (and expensive). I bought a small painting of the Eiffel Tower. It still hangs in my home.

Like the Portara, Sacre-Coeur is a spiritual *experience*. It reminded me of a rare and exquisite Faberge egg. The outside is a work of art, but the beauty inside takes your breath away. We were there for hours while I explored each nook and cranny and found many treasures. I hated to leave and lit candles for my family, friends and everyone I could think of. Beauty affects me that way.

My friend finally tore me away from Montmartre and we headed across Paris on the Metro to meet another Parisian friend for dinner. We talked for hours and then walked upstairs to see his collection of Robert E. Howard memorabilia. A perfect ending to my days in Paris. I got back to my hotel very late and packed my suitcases for an early morning flight home.

One month later, I had open heart surgery and my aortic valve was replaced without any complications.

* * *

Yes, glitches happened, but it was my *dream* vacation and I didn't allow them to spoil anything. Time proved I was right to go when I did. The trip would not have happened the next year. Greek streets were filled with mobs, rioting over government benefit cuts. I had chosen quality, and it resulted in a European trip beyond my wildest dreams: from High Tea at Harrods and walking narrow London streets that revealed out-of-the-way bookstores, bakeries, and small pubs, to the warm and wonderful people on Naxos, where I immersed myself in ancient Greece at the Portara and on Delos, and finally, to the almost overwhelming beauty and color of the Sacre-Coeur Basilica and the art colony on Montmartre.

During my trip, I met old friends in Paris and made new ones on Naxos and in London. I ate the local food wherever I went and spent time with the local people. One of my favorite cultural differences was the grocery shopping.

European stores are specialized: a meat market, bakery, vegetable stand, and pharmacy. Each has an individual identity and is colorful in its own way. So was each place I visited.

Greece, England and France. During my trip I visited three countries in one day! How great is that? Breakfast in Athens, lunch in London and dinner in Paris. During those decades of longing to see Europe, I never dreamed that big.

Barbara Barrett is a published author and poet who loves and appreciates words. Her many articles have appeared on blogs, websites and in fanzines. Barbara's book, *Moon-Maze, a Collection of Poetry and Prose* was published in 2019. *The Wordbook. An Index Guide to the Poetry of Robert E. Howard* and several of her essays have received awards from the Robert E. Howard Foundation. Her short story "*Harold's Search*" is included in the NCPA anthology: *More Birds of a Feather.*

Barbara lives in Northern California where she is working on her next books. Other writing projects include poetry and short stories. She is a member of Northern California Publishers and Authors, the Elk Grove Writers Group and the Elk Grove Writers Guild. She can be reached at barbara_barrett@sbcglobal.net.

STRAIGHT OUT OF JANE EYRE

M.L. HAMILTON

When I was growing up, my parents took the family on a vacation at least once a year. These vacations weren't luxurious adventures, flying off to hidden locales in First Class. Usually they were destination vacations where we went to a rustic cabin and stayed in a spot for a week. In fact, the more rustic, the better, according to my parents. They've always had a love for eating in any greasy spoon, damn the botulism, or staying in a run-down mobile home off the beaten track where you had to drive down a dirt road. Who needs emergency services anyway?

When I became an adult with my own children, we continued these adventures with my parents. However, I was a little more adamant that the locations had to be not only safer, but less remote than before. However, once in a while, they got the better of me, and the three boys and I wound up in some sketchy locations despite my protests.

One such location was a motel in Victoria, British Columbia on Vancouver Island. I'd been told Victoria was a beautiful city, but that wasn't the part of Victoria my parents were interested in. We wound up in a scary motel in the "bad" part of Victoria where there was dog poop in a corner of the room and the windows did not lock or even close. My parents had a room on the opposite side of the motel, and you could only reach it by walking along the second-floor balcony to the back half, which overlooked an alley that I felt sure was the murder capital of British Columbia.

During the evening, a group of bikers pulled in, set up lawn chairs outside my motel room and started smoking pot. Since I couldn't close the windows, the pot smoke wafted into our room all night because I was too terrified to ask them to move just a few feet down the balcony. I really didn't want to end up in a dumpster outside my parents' room, making orphans of my children.

Another vacation was to Coos Bay, Oregon. I was promised a house on the ocean (my favorite destination) with a view of a lighthouse. The house was massive. It had to be well over 4,000 square feet with several rooms like a catacomb down a long hallway. The house had originally been one building, but someone had added on wings to either side that we did not have access to. On the left was an apartment, which we fervently hoped was empty and to the right, a second story flat where a light shone out at night but we never saw a person inside.

One of the bedrooms was filled with mattresses. When I say mattresses, I mean it looked like a mattress warehouse. I think we counted a total of 25 arranged on their upper ends propped around the room. Of course, that room was off-limits to my young children because I feared they'd start a domino effect and send 25 mattresses down onto their toddler brother.

The kitchen was massive and had floor to ceiling cabinets. In fact, there were so many cabinets, we figured every appliance known to man had to be inside. Not the case. There was exactly one knife, one strainer, and a few paper plates. We wound up getting takeout the entire time we stayed there. Of course, my father promptly named the knife *Norman Bates*, which did nothing for my anxiety.

Behind the kitchen was a secret passage that led to the second story. This story had a bedroom with a wall of beds that overlooked the ocean, a secondary kitchen that was better stocked than the one downstairs, and a living room with an old-fashioned record player and a half-bathroom. The adults decided the now-dubbed *Anne Frank* room would be our location for the duration. Each night we slept huddled together on the wall of beds and woke to the sound of the lighthouse foghorn in the morning.

I had envisioned sitting outside a lot, staring at the ocean during our stay, but when I found the first sinkhole in the backyard lawn, I banned the kids from setting foot outside the house. I took to hanging out in the window seat upstairs, watching the pelicans drop into the ocean as I had done so many times during my childhood in San Francisco.

We lasted three out of five nights in that house before I couldn't take the constant fear of being stabbed in my sleep anymore. The weird light shining from the flat to our right had my writer's mind in overdrive. It was too Jane Eyre for me and I imagined Rochester's wife, Bertha, coming to burn the house down.

While that experience was an adventure, I decided from that point on I would handle our vacation plans and choose the accommodations. Still, when I think of all the crazy places my parents have taken me, I have to admit they may have gone a long way toward fueling my creative spirit and, in all honesty, may have made for more than a few murder plots.

 In 2010, ML Hamilton made her first New Year's resolution – to get serious about her writing. That same year she found a publisher, Wild Wolf Publications, in England and became a traditionally published author. After five years with Wild Wolf, she decided to venture out on her own into the exciting world of self-publishing. Since that time, she's published 55 novels, written an award-winning screenplay and sold more than 267,000 eBooks.

A full-time school teacher and mother of three grown sons, ML carves out time to write in the evenings, weekends and during breaks. Her most popular series, the Peyton Brooks Mysteries, is set in her hometown of San Francisco. The Peyton Brooks Mysteries have been in the top 100 on Amazon for over a year and have reached number 2 in the U.S. and number 1 in the United Kingdom, Australia and Canada in the Mystery Anthology category.

AN IRISH WOG
A.K. BUCKROTH

Although a "wog" denotes a negative, racial connotation in Australia, Britain, Ireland, and Scotland, this story projects quite the opposite. For good reason, I changed this adjective into a verb. To me it means "walking and running = wogging or a wog-run" for walking intermittently with running.

"Running?" you ask. Yes indeed, running.

Because of my sense of goodwill toward fundraising for worthy causes, a brochure from the American Diabetes Association (ADA) caught my interest. I had made life-changing commitments by walking numerous miles through different city streets in different states over numerous years, doing coast-to-coast fundraising for a cure of several different human diseases. However, this organization had something big on its desk to offer money-raising runners and walkers, diabetics and non-diabetics.

Through a mailed, open invitation, interested peers gathered for a tri-monthly ADA meeting in a plush, downtown Los Angeles hotel conference room to discuss, learn, and hear about positive advancements in the care and treatment of this disease with lunch included. I was in.

During this meeting, a special announcement attracted my attention. "This year we will sponsor a marathon in Ireland to raise research money," a speaker bellowed to the audience of at least 30 interested individuals. This meeting began the organizing of the ADA's first participation in a 26.2-mile run, walk, skip, jump, rubber-on-hardtop-or-concrete marathon. "Eager participants in this 'Friendly Marathon' in Dublin, Ireland should sign up immediately," she stated.

How exciting!

Dublin, Ireland? Never having been there, I became

so intrigued that I signed up on the spot. I paid the registration fee. Oh, what had I done?! Was I serious? Could I do this? Sure, I could. I sensed this wonderful opportunity would be personally empowering.

"For those interested," the speaker continued, "you'll find more information packets on the back tables. Please help yourselves."

Before she stopped talking, I approached that back table and gathered multiple explanatory brochures, flyers, business cards and whatever information I could carry.

Thus, began my personal training. I had participated in 5k and 10k fundraising walks for Cancer, Heart Disease, Alzheimer's, Multiple Sclerosis, Alopecia, Leukemia, etc. Now, I began pounding the pavement for diabetes. Training started in February and lasted through September. With California sunshine on my back, my prepping began after work each day with a two-mile walk, which extended a little longer each time. I looked forward to this routine. I grew stronger, leaner. I felt good in this new body!

Having received more of the required registration forms, an ADA administrator contacted me by phone with an invitation to another luncheon to be held in Santa Monica, California.

"...My name is Barbara Ann, and I'd like to welcome you to the marathon fundraising efforts with the ADA. So far, thirteen people have signed up for sure. Have you ever participated in a marathon?"

"No, I haven't and I have a lot of questions."

"Good, good," she responded. "Save them for the luncheon in two weeks. I'm hoping all thirteen of you will have many of the same concerns. I'll cover them all then. Are you excited?"

"Yes, I sure am," I blurted, "along with all the others."

"Good. I'll let you go for now. See you in a couple weeks! Bye."

She sounded friendly enough. My questions would just have to wait.

The main purpose of the Santa Monica plan was for

registrants to meet each other. Anxious, I happily drove the hour to get there. After a meatball and spaghetti lunch with a green leaf salad and iced tea, Barbara Ann encouraged each of the thirteen of us to not only get our passports in order, but to invest in good running shoes, foot tape for toes and upper foot bones, and a water bottle carrier. We were each given a white t-shirt emblazoned with the words "TEAM DIABETES" in red, along with a red tank top reading the same in white letters, and a navy-blue canvas duffle bag embroidered with the phrase "American Diabetes Association" in bright red. The plan was for all of us to meet at the Santa Monica Pier each Saturday to learn how to stretch properly, breathe properly and increase our mileage as a team.

At a Sports Authority retailer, I purchased a belted-waist water bottle holder, safety sunglasses to avoid dust and insects in my eyes, feet-wrapping tape, appropriate, high-soled, supportive sneakers, and white cotton socks. The sunny Southern California coast became my initial practice wog. I called my routine "wogging" for walking intermittently with running.

Trekking 17.5 miles beginning in Wilmington, California on the concrete sidewalk toward the shores of the Pacific Ocean in 3.5 hours, I passed through Harbor City, Lomita, Torrance, Redondo Beach, Hermosa Beach, all the way to Manhattan Beach. Although I wanted to go even further to Venice Beach, I did not, knowing I still had to turn around eventually and go home. With this trek confidently under my cap, I knew I was ready. At the age of 43, I had relearned how to take care of myself to participate in this goal, seeking a worldwide cure for the pandemic of diabetes.

On two separate occasions, different individuals blocked my pathway, causing me to veer into the street. "Wait, wait a minute, pretty lady," a grungy-looking, middle aged man said. "I want to talk to you. I see you running by every day."

Politely stopping, I kept a yard's length between us. Panting slightly, sipping my water, I quickly asked "What?

What is it?"

"Can I have some of your water? Or is that vodka?" he chuckled out loud, bending backwards in his foolish delight. "You're gorgeous. What's your name?"

A bit frightened by this confrontation, I didn't reply but hurriedly resumed my pace, veering back onto the sidewalk. I started thinking about people becoming a safety hazard. *Gosh, I hope he isn't waiting for me on my way back*. He wasn't, thank goodness.

The second time, in Lomita, a straggly, unkempt middle-aged woman blocked my path waving her arms to stop me. "Jesus Christ!" I yelled. "Get out of my way!" And I kept going. She hollered something at my back about wanting some food and liking my sneakers. *Oh my Gosh! I thought. I'm going to get clubbed over the head for my shoes!* Due to these confrontations, I changed my direction – forward and back – never seeing either of those characters again. Whew!

During the second Santa Monica meet-up, two of my younger teammates beat my time. I was appalled! Heck, a few of my teammates even ran up and down 27 concrete steps during these practices. I was jealous yet did not bust my butt to kill myself. I wanted to enjoy this experience.

Over the following seven months, I raised the required $3,000 plus, including the $672 roundtrip flight cost. My ego became inflated once again, and I was un-shy to ask for monetary donations from the restaurants I had passed daily. Employees and managers of numerous public establishments had seen, and wondered about me. One seafood restaurant gave me a check for $50; another Bar & Grill gave me a check for the same. Other checks were made out to the ADA. Onward bound!

On and on, my pleas for help for a cure of diabetes brought monetary success. Family, friends, neighbors, acquaintances of friends, medical doctors, etc. – I asked almost everyone I met or came in contact with. Blessings and good wishes poured in along with cash and personal checks! I was going to be part of the cure for this baffling disease. I knew it in my heart and soul!

DESTINATION: THE WORLD VOLUME ONE

Sure, not everyone believed in my hopes and dreams for a cure of diabetes, but I remained upbeat, positive, and pressed forward.

Scheduled for October 30th, this "Friendly Marathon" brought me a delightful, anticipatory planned flight to the other side of the world. My excitement overflowed throughout this entire participation and my having made such a *huge* commitment.

Taking a pre-planned two-week, paid vacation from work, I left Los Angeles International Airport (LAX) on October 25th for the 12-hour flight to Dublin International Airport (DUB), and arrived on October 26th. During the flight, I witnessed the awesome time-change in the sky, from very dark to a bright dawn in the same five seconds. Amazing! My spirit was aflutter with this experience. This endeavor was meant to be, I knew it.

Upon landing, the scent of rain filled the air, immediately invigorating and awakening my senses to the surroundings. Not having reviewed weather reports before leaving California, I thought I had all I needed. This early-bird arrival allowed me to get to my Dublin city hotel with plenty of time to get settled in and become familiar with my surroundings: restaurants, shops, theatre, etcetera. I was psyched and ready for my first marathon in an unfamiliar and strange country.

The following day, leaving the comfort of the Jury's Royal Hotel room, I wandered its lobby collecting various pamphlets of sights to see as a tourist. Despite reading the colorful and delightful variations of many different brochures with interesting venues, I knew I was here for one thing – the marathon. I was already living a dream just being here, without the enticement of touristy ventures. I was glad to have brought my old faithful hooded, winter butt-covering coat since the weather was unusually bitter-cold and rainy.

The country was experiencing "the worst storm in fifty years." Having to purchase a knit cap big enough to cover my ears for warmth, along with woolen gloves in the hotel's gift shop, I carefully bounded through the surrounding neighborhood within walking distance of the hotel. I wrapped my sock-covered feet in plastic bags for extra warmth, and resilience in my sturdy rubber boots. Numerous people walked the streets in long wool coats, covering their heads and faces with scarves and hats, for protection from the non-stop cold wind and heavy rains.

Grey hues in the sky matched the light grey and brown cobblestone streets and walkways. Cobblestones. I was used to seeing such a thing in movies, but coming up close and personal with having to walk on them became mandatory. They were unavoidable yet delightfully different at the same time, although a bit cumbersome to walk upon.

The hotel restaurant's numerous hot meals whetted my appetite: Irish Stew with lamb or beef, vegetables and potatoes; bacon and cabbage with a side of brown bread; something called a "rasher" and something else called a "Blaa." Prime rib with mashed potatoes, brown gravy and green beans – sounded tasty, safe and familiar – a leafy salad was available as well. Mm. Something called a "Colcannon" that consists of a bowl of potatoes mashed with milk, butter, scallions and kale; another available item called a "Carvery" would take too long to explain. The warm, freshly home-made lamb stew was a great choice on my first visit on this cold and wet weather day.

I realized it was October 28th, meaning I had actually lost a day due to jet-lag. I wondered about the other ADA team member marathon participants, hoping to meet with them. I sighted only one team member from the Santa Monica runs who stayed in the same hotel. Come to find out, others were in different hotels scattered around Dublin, not to arrive until later.

6:00AM, October 30th, marathon day, I taxied with two other marathoners to our designated starting point. Although the rain calmed to a drizzle, during this exciting set-up and meet-'n-greet, plastic trash bags were offered as body covers to the racers for wet gear protection with racing numbers safety-pinned to the fronts and backs.

I was ready!

Many times, during this long, Ireland walk-run, I

purposely slowed down to admire Ireland's beauty: ancestral, ivy draped stone buildings, wildly rushing streams, and the tremendous amount of bars as we wogged out of the city. Separated by speed, in no hurry and often left behind, I wogged alone. Realizing this, I decided to become a tourist after six hours, when I accomplished the 20-mile mark and a sharp, right knee pain gave me reason to stop.

That's it, I thought. *I fulfilled my promises to myself, the diabetics of the world and the ADA.* Climbing aboard a readied and pre-planned ambulance for a return ride to the hotel, I certainly was not the only one to stop early. We were each wet from the inside out due to the rain and sweat, so the warmth of the ambulance was most welcoming.

Once showered, comfortable, and full of some delicious Colcannon, I began to plan for the rest of my stay. The following day, I stiffly walked to Dublin's nearby rail tour/bus office for a meandering, half-day trip into the Wicklow Mountains, the ancient and monastic home of St. Kevin, along coastal scenery, and into Glendalough and The Vale of Clara. Due to the continuous heavy rains with flooding in areas, the tour bus carefully slowed down, causing the tourist company's scheduled events to change. I didn't care. I felt safe, happy, warm. For 24Ł, this experience could not be passed up.

Heading back to Dublin, the tour bus coasted through Cork, Limerick (home of author Frank McCourt), and through the cities of Cashel, Cahir and Clonmel. We passed miles and miles and acres and acres of bright green, healthy grasslands nourishing goats, cows, sheep, lambs, lambs and more lambs. Hmm, I couldn't help but wonder if the delicious lamb stew I had the day before had come from this beautiful pasture.

The early morning of November 1st found me on a tour bus to the historic city of Kilkenny. I greatly enjoyed a different yet delightfully delicious stew in the "Witch's House" Restaurant/Pub before crossing the street to a jewelry store. Yes, a delicate pair of emerald earrings came into my possession. Continuing along the east coast, the tour continued to the Waterford Crystal Factory, which is spectacular. I learned the ingredients in making lead crystal wares are a certain type of sand, potash, and red-lead. Most interesting — and expensive — but I sent home a beautiful, lead-crystal, cut-glass whiskey decanter along with a decorative vase of the same design.

On November 2nd, I made the tough decision to wander the streets of Dublin alone. After checking my expense account from the former purchases, I was good to go. Walking through the continuous rain along with numerous other people, I felt comfortable blending right in and happily found a gift shop where I purchased an Ireland shaped magnet to add to my prodigious refrigerator magnet-collection. I roamed the outer and inner grounds of Trinity College, and continued to the beatific Christ Church Cathedral near the Dublin Castle. Tired and cold, I hopped onto a convenient city bus back to Jury's Court. Buses were available every 15 minutes.

The next day, November 3rd, I purchased another bus ticket at 7 AM for a day trip to a place called The Burren, known for its scenic landscapes; on to The Cliffs of Moher, that included breakfast; then to Galway Bay, with a lunch stop at a seafood pub. There was enough time to enjoy a pint of Guinness beer while befriending another passenger with small talk of home. Back at the Jury's Hotel after 10 PM, exhaustion put me to bed fully clothed.

By now I was out of clean clothes, so I found the hotel's laundry useful. Purchasing 'slots' at the information desk, I was directed to the laundry area, ready to use the machines, and bought vending machine laundry detergent. Never having done this in my own country, I chalked this up to another experience. This time also allowed me to relax and rest my knee by using a hotel towel full of machine ice on my knee. That helped.

Finally, the rain stopped on November 5th. Hallelujah! This day, another point of interest offered Italian Gardens, Tower Valley, Japanese Gardens, Winged Horses, Triton Lake, a Pet Cemetery, Dolphin Pond, Walled Gardens, and

Bamberg Gate — all in one place. The history of these grounds begins in the 1840s, taking "one hundred men twelve years to complete." I did not view all these areas because my intermittent knee pain caused me to rest on the tour bus. No matter. Bus driver Owen and I befriended each other for the duration. His thin frame topped off with fluffy white, thick curly hair, remained seated in the driver's seat as he fondly spoke of growing up on the island. His light blue eyes sparkled through his stories. I intently listened to his smooth Irish brogue.

After a restful, peaceful sleep, November 6th greeted me with light grey rains as opposed to the former days of torrential downpours. My spirit remained heightened for the day's plans: a train ride past The Giant's Causeway, through the Glens of Antrim, and on to viewing the Wild Atlantic Coast but not for long. The downpours returned. This trip had to be halted due to a fallen tree blocking the train tracks. Another passenger invited me to play dominoes, and we pleasantly passed the time. Stuck on that train for I can't remember how many hours, I fell asleep at one point after being told that the food ran out. Oh well. I remained happy to be where I was — in Ireland.

Finally, another train pulled, or slowly dragged, the original passenger train all the way back to Connolly Station in Dublin. Gosh I had never experienced that kind of rescue before.

The whole trip was definitely something to write home about. I truly cannot state which was my favorite site or favorite experience. It was all good. Would I wog it again? Yes indeed!

A.K.Buckroth is a member of the Northern California Publishers and Authors (NCPA) organization. Once obtaining a Master's Degree in Organizational Management, she gained the empowerment and knowledge to write her first book. The Sacramento Suburban Writers Club and the California Writers Club guided – and critiqued – her efforts. *My Diabetic Soul – An Autobiography* © 2010 (Revised 2018) brought her numerous awards. She is responsible for three other books: *Me and My Dog Named Money...a child's story of diabetes* (Revised © 2019), *Me & My Money Too Book Two* (Revised © 2019), and *Kisses for Cash...T1D meets T2D Book Three* © 2016 which received an NCPA award. The Gold Country Writers established stimulation and encouraged motivation with the last three books. Available online and Audio.com, check www.mydiabeticsoul.com or #buckroth.

THE FALL BEFORE THE FLIGHT
BOB IRELAN

Falling out of a moving car at the tender age of two and then, nearly 40 years later, flying supersonically, New York to London and back, are among the stories that come to mind when reflecting on a long life punctuated by travel.

I'm not sure what, if anything, I remember about dropping to the pavement of Colesville Road in Silver Spring, Maryland 80 years ago. I expect my "memory" is drawn from hearing my parents tell and re-tell the story over the years.

Back then (1939), Sunday afternoon drives were a family treat, with the destination often being any place that served ice cream in cones. We had a black 1937 Pontiac four-door sedan, the brand most readily differentiated by its Chief Pontiac hood ornament and chrome stripes extending down the center of the hood and resuming on the trunk lid. Like other American-made four-door sedans of that era, its outside back door handles were located forward, next to the outside front door handles.

I was seated in back, on the passenger side. My aunt was in the middle and my five-year-old brother was on the other side of her. Having an adult seated between two active boys normally produced a more enjoyable ride for the adults. Dad was driving, Mom sat next to him.

Children fidget. I was no exception. This time, my fidgeting apparently caused a strap on my sporty sun suit to become entangled with the interior door handle. The door unlatched and, with a whooshing sound, swung open, dropping me on the edge of the road.

Good news: the cars behind ours avoided me. No small wonder because we apparently had been moving along at about 25 or 30 miles an hour. I'm told I screamed bloody murder even though I escaped with nothing more than a few bumps and scratches. Lucky boy.

Skip forward a half-dozen years and we buy our first new car. It's another Pontiac, this one dark blue and, for good reason, a two-door. There would be no more surprise ejections from the back seat.

With World War II's end, gas was no longer rationed, so that factor, combined with having a new car, ushered in our family driving vacations each summer.

My parents' aim was to see as much of the countryside as possible and to do it in a week, two at the most. This was before there was an interstate highway system, so we used undivided highways like U.S. Routes 1 and 40 and multiple state roads. Destination stays of several days or a week were rejected in favor of lengthy drives separated mostly by overnight lodging in cabins. That's right, cabins—not motels, which I don't recall seeing back then.

My brother and I would start pointing out cabins along the way in the late afternoon. However, Dad almost always seemed to want to log another 20 miles. That 20, sometimes became 40, and 40 sometimes 60, until we'd finally checked into a modest abode well after dark.

To keep my brother and me occupied and interested during these lengthy drives, my father would reward whichever of us was the first to identify a white horse. The competition was intense because the reward was a nickel a horse.

Mom kept a running tally and became the arbiter as to whether a particular horse was more white, than grey. When we tired of looking for white horses, the contest could switch to less-common brands of cars, like maybe a Packard or DeSoto. And for pure amusement, there were always those wonderful Burma Shave signs, each with its own corny verse.

Every summer trip was different. One year it would be Canada (Montreal and Quebec), another it might be Wisconsin or Florida. Looking back, I enjoyed each of them, but New York State was special. Lake George was magnificent (breaking tradition, we stayed two nights there).

My favorite was Ausable Chasm ("The Grand Canyon of the Adirondacks"), not because of its geological grandeur but because it had a gift store full of Native American souvenirs. Whatever the trip, I was always on the lookout for headdresses, wallets, tribal booklets, figurines, toy birch bark canoes, you name it, while my brother, most of the time, scanned each side of the road for any reptile farm signage. Our patient, loving parents understood these were mandatory stops.

Years later, as I proceeded through a stimulating corporate career, business travel carried me to a number of distant locations. Places like:

— India, where enough free time was found to ride atop an elephant in the heart of downtown New Delhi and travel by car to Agra to take in the architectural majesty of the Taj Mahal and nearby fort.

— Ghana, where, in the course of directing a documentary video, I survived the throat-burning experience of drinking home-brewed Schnapps in a remote tribal village.

— Greece, where an exciting new archeological dig that would uncover an entire coliseum was just getting started at Nemea.

— The Philippines, where a scheduled meeting at the Presidential Palace in Manila turned instead into a several-hour helicopter tour of typhoon-stricken villages across multiple islands.

— Japan, for a ship launching at Hiroshima and an opportunity to visit a museum devoted to showing the devastating, war-ending effects of the atomic bomb attacks on that city and Nagasaki.

There were business reasons for each of these trips but, clearly, there also was time for personal exploration and discovery. Some of the trips were aboard corporate aircraft, some commercial. But all were at a time when airports were less crowded than they are today, security was minimal, in-flight food was appetizing, and getting to and fro was mostly pleasurable. In addition, there was the now-lost sense of freedom and privacy because no one could contact you while you were in the air.

Unique among these experiences were two mid-1970s flights aboard a British Airways Concorde supersonic aircraft. My boss needed to be in London for a hastily-called meeting of several hours and be back in the U.S. for another meeting the next day. The only way to attend both meetings was to book passage on the Concorde. Because I usually accompanied him wherever he went, I was about to become a passenger on this magnificent marvel of air travel.

To say I was excited is an understatement. I had a natural fascination with aircraft, and, as a journalist some years before, had written a couple of magazine articles about a revolutionary and highly controversial military plane, the F-111. I had followed closely the development of the Concorde. It was in a class of its own. Developed by a British/French consortium, its pointed nose drooped down for landing and raised up for flight. Massive Delta-shaped wings helped maximize lift for takeoff and accentuated its dart-like appearance. It was long and slender, with two seats on each side of a narrow aisle. Nose-to-tail, it measured 202 feet, and its interior width was only 8 feet 7 inches. Depending on the cabin configuration, capacity was 92 to 120 passengers.

Ah, but was it ever fast. Cruising speed was Mach 2.02, or about 1,340 miles per hour—more than twice the speed of other commercial jet aircraft. I remember watching with wonder and excitement an on-board monitor as we crossed the Atlantic. The numbers on it moved ever closer to and then raced through the speed of sound. The sonic boom this kind of speed created precluded supersonic flight over land.

Both the JFK/Heathrow and Heathrow/JFK flights I was on took approximately three and a half hours. As if that feat wasn't enough, the Captain announced our landing into a foggy Heathrow had been "hands off." (I was glad he hadn't mentioned that prior to the landing.) The record time for that route, I read later, was two hours, fifty-two minutes, fifty-nine seconds.

Only 20 Concordes were ever built, and the last of them was retired in 2003. They never achieved commercial success, but the technology they stimulated and the "ride" they provided were incredible

I still have a souvenir deck of playing cards from one of the Concorde flights, having given the other to a collector friend; the slipper socks and pouch disappeared long ago. But the twice-in-a-lifetime experience remains fresh.

Who could have imagined the little boy who fell out of a car on a Sunday afternoon drive in Silver Spring, Maryland would, over time, see a big chunk of the world and—wonder of wonders—fly faster than the speed of sound across the Atlantic?

Bob Irelan's commitment to writing began in earnest when he majored in journalism at the University of Maryland, and grew steadily from there.

Following 10 years of newspaper and magazine reporting and editing, including stints at The Wall Street Journal and Nation's Business magazine in Washington, DC, Bob spent 32 years in public relations for a Fortune 500 family of companies. As a corporate officer, he directed the companies' internal and external communications for the last 12 of those years.

In retirement, he taught public relations courses for two years at University of the Pacific and five years at University of California, Davis, Extension.

Bob authored the novel, *Angel's Truth – One teenager's quest for justice*, which took second place in Fiction at NCPA's 25th Book Awards in 2019.

Bob lives in Rancho Murieta, California, with his cat, Jocko, who he wrote about in NCPA's *Birds of a Feather* Anthology.

BONNIE GOES A-ROAMING

BONNIE COLEMAN

It was the spring of the year. The snow had melted. The maple trees were arching their leafy canopies over the streets. The black squirrels were letting their little ones out of the nest. The old brick houses would be beautiful with the coming of the grass. This could only mean one thing: another cousin was getting married.

We were now in the realm of first cousins once removed, but the pull of Family was still strong in the Force. The child of my cousin is my cousin and I must return to the nest to attest to the joining, assist in the preparations and rejoice in the nuptials. And, of course, bring or forward a gift.

This, fortunately, was a local wedding, meaning we weren't meeting up in St. Bart's or Hawaii. We were simply packing for the probable season: late winter, early spring, spring, early summer, etc., or all of the above. It also meant booking passage for a 3,000-mile trip with the fewest, shortest layover(s), and putting one's passport in order. Easy-peasy.

Two little hitches in our get-alongs are that every shirt-tail relative in one's hemisphere must be consulted on, if they are going, when they are going (and coming back), and if they might change their minds if we all adjusted our plans on both ends to accommodate them. This can be both time-consuming and confusing. Plans change in a heartbeat whenever a new player joins the safari. The only immutable rules relate to the conveyers.

In the case of US/ Canada, this is pretty well confined to who's flying us and who is picking us up. Toronto (pronounced "*Tronno*") is about an hour from our final destination, Peterborough, Ontario. However, it is considered taboo to not offer rides to and from the airports to the destination, and back by one's self, or through a surrogate, usually a child of any driving age. It is also rude to refuse these rides, no matter the time one spends waiting at the gate for one's flight. Eventually these rites of passage are proffered, negotiated, ironed out, and resolved so everyone can book and buy tickets. In this instance, my mother and I would be traveling with my cousin.

Her husband travels for work, and she often accompanies him, so we assumed we would benefit enough from her experience to get us through the confusions that inevitably arise in the commute.

There are two absolutes in regards to traveling. First, you will probably have to visit an airport and second, all airports larger than your living room are under construction all of the time. I add that "probably" caveat because I did visit one in Missouri, a sort of Barbie-sized airport, that did not appear to be under construction. It had two small rooms, one for coming and one for going, and it did not appear to be in the midst of renovation; it also did not appear to be in use most hours of most days.

On the other hand, I have never been in any other airport that was not under construction. Travel to Ontario requires a trip through Minneapolis-St. Paul, Minnesota, which will usually include a fierce electrical storm, Chicago O'Hare, Illinois, which will include a strike, a cancellation, or a speed-walk from one terminal to another, or Denver Colorado International which will be enjoying a blizzard. Take your pick. We picked Chicago O'Hare. It sticks in my mind like anemone spikes stick in the sole of one's feet. We packed light, meaning giant purses and carry-ons. My cousin wore white plus every jewel she owned. I wore something black that looked like I may be called on to overhaul the engines. My mother looked like she was going grocery shopping.

My cousin carried her purse, a carry-on, and a smart, white rain jacket. I carried my purse, my mother's purse, my carry-on and my mother's carry-on, and two raincoats - - my mother having just come down with debilitating carpal tennis elbow or a rotator cuff in her shoulder, or maybe it was "spilcas" in her "connecticazoid" (see Mike Meyers in old SNL repeats). I just remember she was suddenly unable to carry more than a tissue.

So, thus prepared, we began our trek to the gate. This was in the days before 360-degree wheels, so the two carry-ons were veering around me wildly in separate random tangents. Signs steered us to a "temporary" detour, the likes of which I had never seen and hope never to see again. We were to hustle to a lower level on a stairway that looked like the servants' backstairs at Downton Abbey, go OUTSIDE, walk across the tarmac and up another twisting stair to the new, temporary gate. What fun! The stairs were narrower than the two carry-ons and me, so I had to drag one and push the other, raincoats and purses flailing about me at will. It was like being in the eye of my own personal hurricane.

After what seemed like all day, I waddled to the next gate and met my mother and my cousin who looked perfect, if somewhat impatient. We finally boarded and I stowed my mom and our gear. My cousin stood looking doe-eyed and helpless until some Lancelot rescued her, her goods and chattel, and we were off.

Eventually we arrived in Toronto, met our designated driver-cousin and drove through the gorgeous countryside that connects Toronto and Peterborough.

We re-met the family, exchanged hugs, and were dispatched to our assigned relations for maintenance and upkeep. The wedding went off with no more than the usual hitches and glitches that make each event unique, and caused us to laugh at later. We all dispersed with the usual promises to keep in closer touch in the future and went back to our normal lives.

Our departure from Toronto Pearson International Airport was basically the same travel-story in reverse, minus the indoor/outdoor stairways. Looking back, it would have been easier to overhaul the engines.

In hopes that those of you, who are experienced travelers, recognize this truth and be amused, and those of you who are new will be forearmed and not feel paranoid, I offer this and remain your humble servant....

Bonnie Coleman was born in Canada, in a log cabin.

The log cabin is a lie; it was a house. Her father grew up in a 2-story log house – much more romantic.

They emigrated to Castro Valley, then finally to Sacramento. Bonnie went to San Francisco to seek her fortune and then to Sacramento. She hop-scotched around county departments until retirement, which lasted about a year, then abandoned it to care for her mother, her mother's antics, events, and requirements.

Now, two years later Bonnie is devising a new plan. While working, she wrote for various entities, but only managed one paid article for *Sacramento Magazine* for which she was inordinately proud.

When she learned of NCPA, Bonnie decided to bravely go where she never thought she would, and is happy she did.

CASTLES IN THE AIR

BETTY STALEY

"Look at all those brochures for graduate school in Europe – Vienna, Prague, wow! I would love to go," I said dreamily.

"What are you doing, Betty, looking at places in Europe? Poor girls don't travel."

I heard those words and my stomach sank. Would I never travel? Would I always be stuck in the Bronx? I wanted to see the world. The words kept echoing in my head,

"Poor girls don't travel."

*   *   *

"Grandma, how many countries have you been to?"

"I don't know Charlie, let's count them."

"Have you ever been to Australia and New Zealand, Grandma?"

"No, Charlie, maybe one day you and I will go together."

"Grandma, tell me again about the most exciting trip, the one with the castle."

"All right, here goes. Are you ready?"

"It was 1959 and Grandpa Franklin and I were living in England where we were doing our Waldorf teacher training. We were only twenty-one years old. I was so happy because even though people told me I wouldn't travel because I was poor, I proved them wrong.

"We received full scholarships for Waldorf teacher training and we had saved enough money from our wedding to buy a car during our winter holiday break. In those days, 1959, the car only cost $1,000. You can't imagine how excited we were to pick up our little turquoise

Renault in France and start driving to Holland and Germany."

"Tell about the castle! Tell about the castle!" six-year-old Charlie said impatiently.

"It was a cold wintry December day, and we had been driving all day and were very tired. We were looking for signs to the youth hostel, in German, *Jugendherberge*, so we could have a good night's sleep.

"Finally, we saw a sign with an arrow pointing up. We parked the car because you couldn't drive to a hostel. Hostels were really for people traveling by train or hiking from place to place. We started walking and walking. It was dark and cold and steep, but we kept walking.

"I pulled my brown wool winter coat tight around my body to keep the wind out. We kept walking up and up and up. You know, Charlie, I have asthma sometimes, so I began to wheeze and we had to slow down. We could see the forms of tall trees around us, casting long shadows by the light of the slivery moon. 'Franklin, do you think this is the right way? I haven't seen another sign,' I asked.

"After what seemed like an hour, we saw up ahead the outline of a castle. I had never seen a castle before. 'Franklin, what is this? Where are we? I feel like we are inside a fairy tale.'

"'Just keep walking, Betty, we're getting closer. I don't know what we'll find. This is eerie, but don't worry.'

"We clung to each other as we took small steps, not sure what was next.

"We came to a moat, then crossed a rickety bridge into a long tunnel. An electric bulb hung from the ceiling, and bats were flying around. We could hear a dog barking in the distance. 'I'm scared. I don't like the feel of this. When does this tunnel end?' I snuggled close to him.

"We walked and walked further. Luckily, it was level so I didn't have trouble breathing. When we came to the end of the tunnel we looked out over a large field, and castle walls, all around us. In the distance, we saw light in one room. Everything else was dark. We walked carefully, until we came to a large wooden door with an iron handle and knocker. Grandpa Franklin rapped the knocker on the door over and over until we could hear the shuffling of footsteps.

"An old man carefully opened the door and looked at us questioningly.

"'What are you doing here? The castle is *geschlossen* in December.'

"'*Geschlossen*. Doesn't that mean closed?' I asked very quietly to Grandpa Franklin. 'We walked all this way in the cold and dark, and it's closed?'

"'Ja,' the old man replied. 'In summer, people come up here by *sesselbahn*. No one walks up the mountain. But come in and warm yourselves by the fire.'

"Relieved, we walked into the large living room with soft seats in front of a large fireplace. The heat felt wonderful, and the old man brought us hot tea. He looked at us for a long time. Then he said, 'Come with me.' And we walked through one hall after another, past closed doors, until we came to just the right one. 'You stay here,' he said to me. He continued on with Grandpa to show him where the bathroom was. When Grandpa Franklin returned, we walked past dozens of doors until we came to a huge bathroom where we brushed our teeth and got ready for the night. When we closed the door of our room, it squeaked. It probably hadn't been oiled in hundreds of years. We wondered if we would be able to open it in the morning.

"Grandpa Franklin and I looked at this small room with stone walls. There were three double bunk beds with piles of blankets at the foot of each one. There were icicles on the small window which had no glass, and the wind was blowing in. I was shaking. We put on all the clothes we had with us, our winter coats, our warm boots, our hats and gloves, and took the blankets from all the beds and piled them on top of us. We snuggled together to get warm and settled down to sleep.

"When we woke in the morning, light was shining through the window onto our bed. We got up, stretched our legs, and folded the blankets. We plodded through the halls to the living room where the fireplace was still blazing.

The old man came out to greet us. He told us that we were in a fort called *Ehrenbreitstein*, almost 2,000 years old. The fortress had held the relic of the holy tunic, a robe that legend said was worn by Jesus Christ before his death on the cross. 'That is not here anymore,' he said. 'Now, in the summer, this hostel is filled with young people who take the tram up from the bottom of the mountain. They dance and sing and have a wonderful time. There are 1100 rooms. You are the only ones who have walked up.'

"We glanced back at the tall stone walls and towers as we walked together to the end of the large field and looked down on two rivers which met together below us. 'This is the *Deutsche Ecke*. The two rivers are the Rhine and the Mosel. Well, young people, I will leave you now. Be careful walking down. The path is very steep. *Auf wiedersehen*.'

"Grandpa Franklin and I walked through the tunnel, across the moat, and carefully made our way down the mountain. It was much easier this time, but we were giggling with excitement with each step we took. When we finally saw our little car just where we had left it, we got in and started the engine."

*   *   *

"Yes," I said, "poor girls don't travel." And that was just the beginning.

I smile as I think about that day when I heard those words. In the sixty years since then, I have become a serious traveler. In some cases, I've led groups of high school students to Egypt, Israel, Greece, and Western Europe. I've led adults and students twice to Russia and Central Asia. I've done research in Kenya, Tanzania, and Morocco for my book on Africa. I've done a month's lecture tour in Japan organized by my Japanese college students. I've taken tours to China and Tibet, Vietnam, Cambodia, and Thailand, and to Guatemala, Honduras, and El Salvador. I've lived in England and eastern Europe, done research in Spain, visited friends in Mexico and Latvia. And I've visited Dubai and India.

So, poor girls don't travel. But travel makes poor girls rich with memories and experiences.

Betty Staley has been an educator with the Waldorf educational approach for over fifty years as a high school history and English teacher, and director of teacher education programs. She is an international lecturer and consultant, having worked with parents in many countries, as well as having led teenagers and adults on study trips to the former Soviet Union, Egypt, Israel, Greece, and western Europe.

Betty, the mother of three adult children and grandmother of six, lives in Fair Oaks, California. She is an author of eight books on child and adolescent development, high school curriculum, and adult psychology. Her most recently published book is *Tending the Spark, Lighting the Future for Middle School Students*.

WILMA

LOY HOLDER

Cancun, Mexico seemed magical with its silky, white sand, and warm, turquoise Caribbean Sea, but, soon, Jim and I wanted to explore. We signed up to tour Chichen Itza and the pyramid the next day.

There was a chill in the air as we boarded the bus. Dark clouds blocked the sun. During the ride, it poured. When we arrived, we stood under a palm tree to watch the torrential rain cascade down the pyramid. It was obvious we couldn't climb the 91 steps to the top. For us it would remain a treacherous waterfall.

Later, to soothe our disappointment, we treated ourselves to a sumptuous steak and lobster dinner at the hotel. Halfway through our meal, we overheard a man at the next table ask the waiter, "What do you know about a hurricane heading this way?"

The waiter shook his head. *"No lo sé, señor,"* then handed the dinner guest his change and disappeared.

Jim's eyes followed him. "That waiter couldn't get away fast enough."

I swallowed the last bite of my lobster and said, "Let's go to the room and check the news."

We took the elevator to the fifth floor, and Jim turned on the television while I got ready for bed. A half-hour later the news came on. The weather man said, "We are tracking the hurricane heading towards the Yucatan Peninsula. It's slow moving and probably won't make landfall." That was Wednesday.

By 6:00PM Thursday evening, we were in our room on edge and waiting for a call from the front desk. Would we be sleeping in our hotel bed that night, or in a downtown shelter?

The call came about 7:30PM. I answered and Jim

61

picked up the extension in the bedroom. The desk clerk said, "Mrs. Holder, we are sorry. Our management tried to convince the Mexican Government that this hotel was built to hurricane code, but they insisted that all guests within the hotel zone be evacuated. If we don't, the military will. Do you follow me so far?"

I swallowed and cleared my throat. "Yes, I understand, but I'm not happy. So, now what?" I could hear Jim's heavy breathing on the other line.

The clerk said, "I know this must be unsettling, and you need to hurry. Bring a small carry-on, a pillow and blanket each. Leave your belongings in the room, passport and valuables in the safe and come to the lobby within a half-hour. There will be busses to take you to the shelter. God bless." Then the clerk hung up.

I stared at the phone in disbelief, my heart doing the Watusi inside my chest. I felt Jim's hands, gentle on my shoulders, turn me to face him. His blue eyes steady. "We'll be fine. Just a little adventure. Let's pack and get going."

The crowded bus smelled of human sweat. The air sticky, as we huddled on hard, narrow seats. Children fussed. An old woman cried, and Jim sat stoic and still. I held his hand, and looked out the window as we jostled and swerved through rain-swept streets. The wind tossed trash can lids around like leaves.

The bus pulled beside another, unloading passengers. It was surreal – so many people filing into a small, geodesic dome through double glass doors.

We were told to follow them into the shelter. The horizontal rain stung my face and soaked my T-shirt as I shuffled along. Inside, two ceiling fans barely stirred the thick, steamy air. No cots for sleeping, just the red, adobe tile floor.

Jim saw folding chairs stacked along one wall. He grabbed two, while I staked out some floor space with our blankets and pillows. We stored our carry-ons under the chairs, and sat on the seats watching with concern as people just kept coming.

Soon, the shelter was a sea of over two-hundred people on blankets. The hotel staff stood at the entrance diverting late-comers to other shelters. Ours was full.

I noticed large letters painted above the stage at one end of the room, *Bienvenidos Sindicato de Taxistas Andres Q. Roo.* There were stairs to the stage on either side. Curious, I walked over to one of the staff. "What does that say over the stage?"

His badge said his name was Juan. He smiled and spoke perfect English. "It says, Welcome, Taxi Drivers Union Andres Q. Roo. This building is a taxi-driver union meeting hall. Q. Roo is short for the Mexican state of Quintana Roo. Does that help?"

I smiled back. "Yes. Thank you. Are you going to be staying here with us?"

"Yes, we all are, for the care of our guests." Another person had a question. I walked away, impressed that the hotel staff would be here with us, not their own families.

Before I went back to the blanket, I checked out the bathrooms. I went into the one marked "*Damas*" and discovered there were five stalls, but no running water. You scooped up a pail of water from the barrel near the stalls, and took it in with you to flush. Yikes! No toilet seats and no toilet paper. Oh well. I can deal with this for twenty-four hours.

When I got back to my blanket, Jim was already sleeping. How was that possible with a hard floor unfriendly to sore joints? I finally found a comfortable position, and lay there watching and listening.

Children whimpered and their mothers comforted them. Nearby, a woman in a wheelchair moaned as though in pain. The man with her, husband maybe, searched through a bag, found a bottle, and handed it to her with a bottle of water. Soon she was quiet. All I had to complain about was a sore rotator cuff and a little uncertainty.

Friday morning, I woke in total darkness, and the ceiling fans were not moving. I looked at Jim. "No electricity?"

Jim rolled over on his side and whispered, "Yeah, it

went out an hour ago. Go back to sleep."

I ruffled his hair and gave him a kiss. "I need the restroom. I'll be back." I stood and glanced at my cell. It was 5:00AM and my legs felt like lead. As I eased off the blanket, the wind howled through the trees outside.

I stepped carefully around the blankets to the women's bathroom. When I got there, men were inside and I had to wait. When they came out, Juan was frowning. "Sorry, *Señora*. We just refilled the barrel with rain-water, and don't use the end stall. The toilet's stopped up."

Faint light filtered through the windows as I eased my way to the barrel. When I finished in the stall, I used a bottle of water sitting on the counter and the communal soap bar to wash my hands, then returned to my blanket.

About 8:00AM, the hotel staff passed out tiny boxes of cereal and milk. That was breakfast. Some asked for more, but the answer was "No, not enough for seconds." My concern over food went up a notch. The good news? There was plenty of bottled water and my Verizon service worked.

After breakfast, I called home, and visited with other hotel guests. At 1:00PM the hotel staff provided half a ham sandwich and an apple, then announced Hurricane Wilma was coming tonight. With that update, the tension in the room was palpable.

An older man asked, "Will the roof hold?"

The woman in the wheel-chair asked, "What about those high windows?"

The manager stood and put up his hand. "Don't worry. The staff and I will do everything we can to keep you safe during this hurricane." Then he hurried off the stage without another word. I figured he didn't have answers.

As daylight slipped into dusk, Juan and two other staff handed out tiny portions of beans, and Spam® to each person. An angry man in the back yelled, "I'm gonna have to go hungry, so my wife and kid can eat."

Juan got on the stage. "Stores are closed, food trucks got hijacked, and the streets are flooded so we can't go back to the hotel for food. Please know we're working on it." Juan looked frustrated as he left the stage.

Some continued to grumble. Jim and I weren't that hungry as we turned our thoughts to the hurricane.

Soon it grew dark in the hall, and people got quiet. Jim and I were lying on our blankets. He rolled onto his side to look at me, his handsome face tight. "I love you, and I'm so sorry I got us into this. Please know that."

I took his hand. "Honey, we picked this vacation together." I gave him the best smile I could muster. "I love you too. Let's get some rest." Jim fell asleep right away, and I lay there repeating the Lord's prayer to myself.

I was just starting to relax when Wilma arrived. At first, a constant, low rumble became a tumultuous vibration with a high, continuous, piercing shriek, then a monstrous ball of energy slammed against the walls, tore at the roof, and shattered the high windows, sending lethal glass shards flying through the air.

Juan yelled, "Listen, please. If any more windows break out, we will have to put the women, children, and elderly into the women's restroom for safety."

What? Crammed in that smelly bathroom to stand on a wet floor with a hundred other women? No, that couldn't be good. An hour later, I breathed again. Thank God, no one was hurt by the glass, and the rest of the windows held. Then suddenly, Wilma grew still and I wondered why.

I watched a sliver of light grow brighter as people stood and whispered amongst themselves. It was now Saturday morning, and breakfast was a tiny slice of cantaloupe and two apple wedges. We ate slow to make it last and I studied my husband. His ankles were swollen, his eyes bloodshot. His blood pressure was up. I knew, and I worried.

An update came later that morning from the hotel manager. "Hello guests. We are now in the eye of the hurricane. That means the other half will be here this evening. And the latest on the food situation is that the trucks got stuck in the rain near Merida, and we don't know when they'll get here. The good news is that we're hopeful we can get you back to the hotel tomorrow."

Again, the manager left after his announcement, with no questions answered. A group of angry, young, male guests set out to find food. They weren't gone long, and when they returned, they told everyone that the area grocery stores were either closed or destroyed, and the flooded streets had turned into an alligator-filled lagoon.

Jim and I spent the day outside in the air, so heavy with warm moisture, it was like a sauna. Naked palm trees stood in the parking lot, their fronds stripped and strewn on the gravel with other debris. A chain-link fence surrounded the hall and the parking lot.

Jim and another man were talking and I was restless. I went for a stroll along the perimeter of the fence and met another woman about my age. We looked across the street at the destruction of Mexican homes and shops, the roofs gone, and adobe walls crumbled. Sharon shook her head, "Well, at least we have a home and life to go back to."

I agreed.

I wasn't surprised there was no lunch and by 4:30PM, the wind and rain returned. We went inside to our blankets. Jim worked on his word-search puzzles, and I wrote in my journal.

At dusk, dinner was a small piece of banana bread with a teaspoon of cream cheese on top, and a bottle of water. Both of us were weak and exhausted, from lack of food and sleep. We held hands, and lay on the blanket to wait for Wilma's second act.

We both dozed off, until I was jarred awake by clatter and a low, rhythmic rumble that continued while Jim slept. I lay there wide awake and looked at my phone. It flashed, "low battery" but gave me the time. 2:40AM. Then the tempo of Wilma's last dance became a slow waltz and lulled me into a sweet dream.

Sunday came quietly. No breakfast, and children cried for food. A diabetic man went into ketoacidosis. A doctor, and fellow hotel guest, yelled loud enough for everyone to hear. "This man needs insulin now!! Does anyone have some to spare?"

Two guests each gave the diabetic a syringe.

The building reeked of human waste and body odor. Only two flushable toilets in each restroom, no soap, and no way to shower. And there was mildew growing on the floor and walls, from the water that had blown in. Although sanitary conditions were bad, the good news was the hurricane was gone. Everyone was hopeful we would go back to our hotel today.

About 10:00AM, a member of corporate management got on the stage. He paused until he had everyone's attention, then said, "I'm so sorry folks. I don't have good news. The streets are flooded, and we don't know if we can get food to this shelter today. Communication lines are down, so we can't talk to our hotel, the airport, or the food trucks. I urge you to think about going to Merida. We will get back to you later regarding bus arrival and transport."

The corporate guy rushed out the door, leaving all of us stunned. We'd been told to leave our passports, plane tickets and valuables locked up in the safe. Our clothing was filthy trash. Some of us went to Juan and asked him to pass on our concerns for the Merida idea, and he did. Most of us calmed down, clinging to the hope that our own hotel management would get us out of here.

By 3:00PM, we were convinced Merida was a dead issue and suddenly, we heard the sound of large motors. Trucks? Yes, it was the Mexican Federales in huge military vehicles with supplies. An officer emerged from the cab and talked to Juan.

Within five minutes, all of the hotel guests, including Jim and I, formed a human chain from the two trucks into the hall. We unloaded hundreds of sealed bags of food, drink and new, white T-shirts. Unloading took two hours and it was an incredible effort of people selflessly working together.

Once the unloading was done, the Federal Officer in charge announced through Juan's translation, "This facility will be a distribution center for the other Cancun shelters. Your hotel will be given further instructions."

When the Federales left, we each got a food bag and a clean shirt. We put on the shirts and I called it "dressing for dinner." Next, we inventoried our bags. Dinner would be a can of Tuny, which is a small can of peas, carrots, and tuna, some Spam® and a cookie. My stomach was hurting, so that was enough for me.

While we were eating, Juan gave us another update. He'd actually talked to the hotel and we'd have to stay here another night, but we would be leaving tomorrow morning for sure.

Then, he had a warning for us. "We now have food and drink here, so we are in danger of the locals attempting to break in and steal our food, or worse. I recommend that you meet as a group and choose volunteers to walk the perimeter."

Since Jim was a cop, he volunteered for the 10:00PM to 1:00AM shift. An hour after he left, people started running for the restroom. Fairly soon it became clear there was a bug making everyone sick, including me. With the last trip to the restroom, I lost my last pair of underwear.

Jim came back at 1:00AM and knelt beside me, his face a mix of exhaustion and sadness. "It was tense out there. People hungry, and some tried to climb over the fence. I wanted to give them food, but instead we had to turn them away. I'm sick inside." He stretched out on the blanket, and a tear moistened his cheek. I told him I loved him and kissed him on the forehead, and he closed his eyes.

Later, a nurse came to my blanket and kneeled over me. Concern showed on her face. She felt my forehead and said, "You have a fever like everyone else. I feel so helpless. I don't have any medicine to hand out. Just keep sipping the Gatorade in your food bag, and eat the crackers." She patted me, then went on to the next person two blankets away.

Her voice woke Jim and he heard every word she said. The rest of the night he hovered, coaxing me to drink and eat. I didn't know I could love him more, but I did.

Monday morning the bus came. On the ride back to the hotel, signs, telephone poles, and street lights were toppled like fallen soldiers. The Mexican store owners were sweeping water and picking up trash from their store fronts, smiling and talking with each other.

Closer to the hotel zone, splintered boats were washed up on land and dead alligators floated belly up in the standing water. But the bus plowed through the flooded streets, and soon we were parked safely in front of the hotel.

The front of the building looked fine even though the plants and palms were pummeled to the ground. Later in our room, Jim gave me a hug. "Honey, we survived a hurricane. And it really was an adventure of a lifetime."

Loy Holder lives in Elk Grove, California and had always wanted to write. After retiring as an Information Technology Project Manager, she joined the Senior Center of Elk Grove Writing Group, and started writing.

In late 2018, Loy published a novel, *Dancing Up the Ladder*, for sale on Amazon. She is currently working on a new novel, *Cat and Mouse.*

When she first started writing, Loy saw a need for an easily accessible, and affordable, Writers Conference. So, she put together a team of people who liked the idea, and in October, 2018, Loy and her team produced the first Elk Grove Writers Conference.

Her team is now the Elk Grove Writer's Guild, Inc. - a public non-profit dedicated to helping writers, and providing another Writers Conference in October, 2021. You can contact Loy Holder at loyholder77@gmail.com.

SECURITY CHECKPOINT

DENISE LEE BRANCO

Who knew traveling to an out-of-state cat writers conference could start out as the cat's meow and end with a Halloween scary cat image personified? Houston, we have a *purr*oblem.

It was June of 2018 and my first Cat Writers Association (CWA) conference as a brand-new *Professional Member*. I traveled to Houston, Texas where the conference was being held, to gain industry-specific knowledge and meet new people not only in the cat writing community, but within the pet industry as a whole. As a cat mom of three, this feline-focused conference was guaranteed to be the highlight of my summer!

I had an opportunity to chat with the keynote speaker, Dr. Becker, after his presentation. Do you remember him? For many years, he was the veterinary expert on Good Morning America, fondly known as "America's Veterinarian." Since then he founded Fear Free Pets, where they take the "pet" out of "petrified".

It was a wonderful honor having a few minutes between sessions to chat with him. Dr. Becker is so down-to-earth and kind. I shared my revelation about something he said during his presentation, and that I had finally found someone who understood my pet parent anxiety completely. Dr. Becker cited the three reasons pet owners dread taking their pets for veterinary care: 1) Stress on the pet, 2) Cost, and 3) Stress on the owner. Check, check, and double check on number three.

The CWA conference was held in the same hotel as the Regional Cat Show. My new cat writer friends and I were allowed access to the show on Saturday afternoon since writers are technically journalists and some of my peers were reporting on the event. Never before have I seen so many gorgeous felines in one location. Several breeds participated in the show and were of a multitude of colors, hair lengths and sizes.

The super fun part about attending a pet conference is that you get to bring home all kinds of swag for your fur kids—treats, wet/dry food, and lots and lots of toys. I've noticed that as soon as you get back home, unzip your luggage, reveal its overflowing contents, and offer forgiveness for being gone, they quickly forget you've been away.

I had packed clothes and toiletries in my checked luggage and put all the swag cat food in my carry-on luggage to keep it cool and unharmed. When reaching any airport security checkpoint, I always remove all jewelry and shed as much clothing as legally possible before stepping through the metal detector so as not to risk rivets or metal adornment setting off any bells and whistles. My "system" proved successful once again, and my body made it through the scanner with flying colors

As I made my way over to the conveyor belt to pick up my personal possessions, it seemed odd that my carry-on, which I had placed first, wasn't in front of the two plastic bins which contained my purse, jewelry, and a light jacket. I looked back and noticed my carry-on was set to the side of the TSA agent. The conversation began in my head. *Hmm. That has never happened. My bag is about to be searched? Great. I'm getting in trouble for trying to smuggle cat food across state lines! Wonderful. Girls (my felines), see what I go through for you?!*

While I unlocked my luggage for the TSA agent, I told her that I had just attended a cat writers conference and confessed to its contents. As she opened the top flap, I started preparing for what I'd say next if this *travel paws* went drastically wrong. Okay, so, if I ask her, "Will you give all this cat food to local animal rescue shelters?" she'll go easy on me, right? She wouldn't arrest a nice person who helps homeless animals, right? The judge would surely throw out the case, right?

Turns out, the TSA agent was super nice,

completely professional and thankfully non-judgmental toward the cat lady standing in wait. She said I wasn't the first person who has taken pet food through the security checkpoint. I watched her squeeze a three-pound bag of dry cat food and meticulously sort through each cat food can and pouch. She zipped up my bag and said I was free to board my plane. I thanked her and rolled away with all my *feline contraband* in tow.

The William P. Hobby airport incident in Houston still comes to mind every time I pass through an airport security checkpoint. Maybe, just maybe, a scantily clad writer nervously observing a uniformed security official inspecting, squeezing, and touching every cat food bag, can and pouch in her luggage, will raise your spirits the next time you're in an airport and fate finds you, too, in a *travel paws.*

 Denise Lee Branco is an award-winning author and inspirational speaker, who continues to believe, dream, and overcome so those who meet her recognize the possibilities within themselves. Denise's first book, *Horse at the Corner Post: Our Divine Journey*, won a silver medal in the <u>Living Now Book Awards</u>.

Denise is a member of the Cat Writers Association, California Writers Club-Sacramento, Christian Indie Publishing Association, Independent Book Publishers Association, Inspire Christian Writers, and Northern California Publishers and Authors. She has been a contributor to multiple anthologies.

Denise is currently working on her next book *The Ride to Purpose: Finding Freedom on the Trail of Life.* She lives in the foothills of Northern California and loves biking on nature trails, any foods with melted cheese, and spoiling her three rescues.

Visit <u>www.DeniseInspiresYou.com</u> to learn more.

I CAN NEVER BE SWISS

ANITA KANDO

As a frequent visitor to Switzerland, the country never ceases to delight and impress me, and it is about as perfect a country as a country can be.

I've been very fortunate to be a guest of the Bienz family, my husband's cousins in Solothurn, a gorgeous little town between Basel and Zurich, where Hans and Esther Bienz will spoil you for all time.

They live in a charming three story rock-solid home with beautiful nature photography throughout, a garden that looks out over the *Jungfrau* and the *Eiger*, a winding stairway made of the most beautiful wood, and a state of the art kitchen where Esther (the best cook in our extended family – and the competition is quite fierce for that title) produces the most amazing Swiss dishes.

They have enticed us with unparalleled Swiss fondue and introduced us to the fun of sharing *raclette* at the kitchen table with the whole family. The air is crisp, cool; it's often sunny, and one sleeps like a baby in their upstairs, chalet-styled, wooden-ceiling bedroom with duvets and huge pillows that make it difficult to ever get out of bed.

We have made many journeys and side trips within Switzerland, and it is impossible for me to say which one has been more delightful. Just when you think it can't get any more stunningly gorgeous, Switzerland will find a way to show you it can. We took a train through the countryside to Appenzell. The entire ride there was like a travelogue with side visits to Schaffhausen and St. Gallen where we visited one of the world's most impressive libraries (we actually saw Napoleon's correspondence there).

We took this amazing little train that wound nearly vertically up a mountainside toward Appenzell. My husband and I looked at each other, laughing that at every turn the landscape just got more and more impossibly beautiful. Unreal, we thought. When we reached this Brigadoon of a town, we were convinced it could not possibly be real. Swiss architecture is always beautiful, and the people of Appenzell really outdid themselves when they decorated their buildings. Our hotel was a beautiful shade of red with a hanging medieval sign stating the name of the inn. There was a riot of brightly colored flowers in the window boxes. The inside proved to be equally amazing with everything made of beautiful wood. As we walked down the street, we realized all the houses were just as beautiful, or more beautiful than our hotel. I so admire the pride the Swiss take in creating such delightful, well-loved buildings.

The next morning, after another super-healthy Swiss breakfast like the ones served all over the country, we took a bus ride up the mountain to see Mt. Säntis. Hans and Esther made sure we had a front row seat next to the huge windows of the enormous bus while they took seats further behind.

Mt. Säntis is a formidable mountain, and there had been an unseasonably early snow-storm overnight, so it was covered with snow. We lined up for the gondola to go up the mountain, and at this point I was reminded again there was a whole different dimension to Swiss mountains. Yes, we have mountains in California, we have trams and ski lifts—I've ridden them up and skied down for decades. But the sheer vertical climb of this tram was something else, and I was getting nervous.

We arrived on top (yay, we were still alive!). The view was stunning—high white-topped mountains in every direction as far as the eye could see. We ambulated through a little museum, and the rest of my party disappeared for a few minutes while I looked at mountain goats perched precariously on the very edge of the mountain.

A few minutes later, Hans invited me to walk over to the restaurant. He turned to me as we were about to go out the door, and said, "But you might not want to do this."

Strange statement, I thought. Well, he was certainly right. The moment we went out the door, blizzard-like wind and snow hit my face. I was dressed in a light jacket, wearing my new athletic shoes.

No problem, I thought. But, as we ventured on a little further, I saw a semi-circular grated metal path suspended in the air with crevices stretching thousands of feet below. I walked timidly forward, only to realize the soles of my shoes were filled with ice and had become very slippery.

Then I looked to my right as best I could through the blowing snow, and saw this small metal bridge had only one thin guardrail with plenty of room to slide right under it. What was worse, a person could not hold onto the guardrail because there were foot-long icicles formed sideways—horizontally!—due to the fierce winds.

Okay, that's it, I'm going to slide right under the guardrail and end up as an archeological find thousands of years from now. I'll perish of a heart attack long before I hit the bottom of the crevice to become Homo Turisticus Americanus, eons from now, I thought.

Somehow, I stepped and slid onward with my purse (in which my passport and medications were stored) swinging precariously over the guardrail. Finally, I made it to the door. Thank God! I was in another of those gorgeous wood-paneled Swiss restaurants, and I was alive. I plopped down at the table out of breath and shaking. I saw a large bottle of Appenzeller Schnapps, and wished I could down the whole thing right there to stop shaking. I let out a sigh, "Okay, that's it, I've failed, I can never be Swiss."

We all had a good laugh over that, but it's true – I'm not rugged enough to navigate this terrain the way our cousins do. This formidable mountain's name should not be Mt. Säntis—*Spiritus Sanctus Mortis* is more fitting!

Esther took my arm and told me she would guide me back over the horrifying metal bridge. "Oh my God, is that the only way out? Surely you don't mean to tell me I have to do this again?" I was laughing and frowning at the same time.

Yep, no other way out. We walked side by side, and I was thinking this time we might not be so lucky and we'll both slide right under the guardrail. I was more than a little embarrassed that I was being guided like an infant, but I was also very grateful for Esther's Swiss expertise in navigating the dreaded path.

Ah, we were done! Back on earth! Then we took the sheer tram downward (a whole new definition of vertical drop!) and stepped out on flat ground.

Esther turned to me and said, "We thought it best not to tell you that last week, just a few miles away, a tram broke down and they had to rescue everyone via helicopter, suspended over thousands of feet, by ropes."

I was more than a little relieved they did not tell me this before we went up. I pictured myself in a nightmare like the Sylvester Stallone movie's *Cliffhanger*.

We settled down at the ground-level restaurant, sipping our delicious Swiss barley soup, watching amazing Swiss snow dogs that look like large balls of snow with legs and heads. Even the dogs are hardier here. What a gorgeous day as the clouds parted and the bright blue sky re-appeared.

Okay, it's true, I can never be Swiss. I'm not qualified. But part of my heart remains there. What a country! I hope to return, and I'll never quit trying to be Swiss.

Anita Kando is a medical editor for the UCD Medical Center and other hospitals, in the specialties of ophthalmology, orthopedics, neonatal ICU, urology, family practice and surgical procedures. She holds a B. A. in Sociology from Sac State and went to graduate school at Penn State.

Anita was born in San Francisco and grew up in many parts of the US, as she is an Air Force brat. She has traveled all over the world, including Australia, Canada, Mexico and seventeen European countries, several of which she visits annually.

Besides Switzerland, her favorite destination is Rome, a city which she knows through and through, and whose history she has thoroughly researched.

She has published chapters in textbooks ("*Different Approaches in Family Sociology*," in *Sexual Behavior and Family Life in Transition*, Elsevier, New York: 1978), and written travel articles, including *Falling in Love with The Eternal City*, (*European-American Life Blog, 2014*).

GOD BLESS SOUTHWEST
AN LA THANKSGIVING
BARBARA KLIDE

Part I
A schoolgirl friend of mine went on to become Director of Creative Arts for a major Hollywood movie studio. After being out of touch for far too long, Karen called to invite me to travel down from my home in Sacramento to LA for Thanksgiving, saying, "We'll go bar crawling. I'll introduce you to tons of fabulous movie stars. I know them all." We were both unattached and I couldn't refuse.

I booked a Southwest Airlines flight to Los Angeles and, on the day of travel, I left for the airport in a driving rain. I knew it would be a rough flight as there were reports of storms creating havoc up and down the coast. The good news was that Southwest's Boeing 737 series of planes were safe and reliable, their flight attendants often joked with abandon, and the total flight duration was only 59 minutes wheels up to wheels down. This couldn't be too bad.

It's always fortunate for the passengers if there's a "Johnny Carson" on the crew to entertain the passengers, and on this flight, it was the captain himself speaking into his mic, "We've been cleared for departure and whether you like it or not, this Boeing is going!"

It wasn't long before our plane *was* going. It was rocking and rolling and just as it seemed to level off, we were jarred some more as thunder cracked and lightning flashed. As for the in-flight beverage service, there was none. With all the turbulence, the captain never bothered turning off the fasten seat belt sign even when we reached our travelling altitude, which abruptly adjusted when the plane dropped some 20 feet.

The usually jovial Southwest cabin crew maintained a cool, calm demeanor in spite of the weather, but then they were buckled into their own seats much of the time. We never got to hear about the saffron and buttercup yellow oxygen masks designed by Gucci and Martha Stewart that would drop down in the event of a decompression, nor was anyone going to burst into song, point out the floor disco lights, or warn us about being naughty in the potties as they had done on other flights.

The only unconcerned traveler was my neighbor in window seat 8A. I don't know what he was made of, but he was fearlessly staring out into the dark stormy clouds, happy and smiling like he was on some sort of Disneyland ride. All the while, he was, well, he was humming.

The requisite crying baby was only two rows away with ear piercing shrieks that never let up—poor thing probably couldn't clear its little ears. Adding to the mix was the gag-worthy stench of someone's hamburger which gave me the dry heaves. Taking smelly food on board a plane should be a federal crime, as if you'd lit up a cigarette in the bathroom.

Anxiety spreading like a virus compelled the flight attendants to take action. Gripping a couple of passenger seatbacks, one of the crew told us we were going to have a contest–a word game. I'm good with words–a regular Scrabble aficionado. Maybe not the best, but I can still give someone a run for their money. Besides, having a competitive nature with a dash of obsession, I was "in". Truth be told, I was grateful for the diversion from an almost certain demise where my life, or more likely all the shoes I'd ever owned, would flash before my eyes.

Desperate, I gave the crew member my undivided attention as she laid out one simple rule: "Make as many words as you can out of *Thanksgiving*," at which point her cohort literally bounced down the aisle handing out paper and golf pencils. This was old-school early 1990s when the Smartphone was still in diapers and the iPhone was a mere twinkle in Steve Jobs' eye.

By the time I had scribbled down about 100 words, Disney guy turned to me and, raising his voice above the din, asked, "Do you know what the odds of being in a plane crash are versus a car accident?"

"Um, no I do not," I answered, focusing back on the game and ever so pleased with myself that I had come up with "haggis" and "tahini". Then I hit a snag wondering if "tsking", "skiving", or "visaing" were real or if I was now just making stuff up.

He prattled on. "We have a much better chance of perishing behind the wheel of a car than on a plane."

Well, that made me feel so much better.

"And," he said, "it's odd that people are more afraid of planes than automobiles when the risk of a car accident is one in 7,000 while it's only one in more than two million for a plane crash."

While 8A was spewing fascinating information, he had a smile on his face, as I was quietly wondering about other statistics like, what are the chances a character like this would be on a particular flight and be seated next to me? He turned back to the clouds just as golf ball-sized hail began pummeling the plane. I detected a hint of a wince at the side of his mouth, but then he resumed his infernal humming. I clutched for the pearls I was not wearing.

Right about then a well-known TV news anchor, who coincidentally was sitting directly behind me, placed his hands around my headrest catching both sides of my hair. He clearly had a nail-biting "fear of flying". I exaggerate because he couldn't actually nail-bite while his giant, white-knuckled fingers had part of my person in a death grip. It was physically impossible for me to turn around and tell this woeful soul to let go, so I carefully, but painfully, tried pulling my head out of his hold until, finally giving up, I forcibly yanked his hands away. At this point I didn't care anymore. For a while, I didn't dare lean my head back lest he do it again. Eventually, I relaxed back into my seat, feeling a bit sheepish about my reaction and knowing he must have been mortified, but also safe thinking he would likely find something other than me or my headrest to grab next.

I wasn't sure how much more I would have to bear when I felt the unmistakable onset of menstrual cramps. I had no water for a pain pill and dared not swallow one dry, after recalling an unfortunate past experience. I thought about using the call button, but decided not to force a flight attendant to leave the safety of a buckled seat to deal with my private discomfort. The thought triggered a reminder that we had been deprived of hearing a popular one-liner from the crew: "You've got two buttons above your head; one turns the light on and don't expect the other to turn a flight attendant on." Don't cringe. When delivered properly it always elicits snorts and howls.

I was wrenched from my reverie by more waves of pain, but vowed to be stoic until the plane landed. Then 8A's warning rose up from my reptilian brain, which was already on high alert—what if we were that one in two million flights? Surrendering to my helplessness, I eased into the fear and pain beating back my scaly Id. That the hail had ceased helped.

It was getting harder for me to root out more

"Thanksgiving" words, but when I glanced around and saw that some of the other passengers had abandoned the game it oddly made me persevere more, managing to squeeze out two additional words: "gags" and "sh_t". That's Scrabble-legal, right?

Not a moment too soon, the pilot made his "descent" announcement and, yes, our seat backs were in their upright positions and our belts securely fastened, thank you very much, and our carry-on luggage was stowed as it should be because nobody had freakin' dared to leave their seats let alone to pee.

After hearing the captain one of the crew called out, "pencils down". With the contest over she asked, "Who has over 50 words?" and a lot of hands shot up. "More than 100?" A few shot down. "Over 250? Over 300?" I twisted around as much as I could with my hand still in the air to see how many diehards were left. I had just over 300 words. "Over 325?" I dropped my hand in defeat.

There was only one winner and it wasn't me. The prize was a measly bottle of wine, so I didn't feel so bad, but I thought there should have been second and third place winners as a pat on the back for all our hard work and the distress we endured. I would have at least liked to see my opponent and pay tribute to this hardcore word-god, but this individual understandably never got up for a victory lap.

When the plane's wheels finally touched down, the entire plane applauded loud and long and I knew I was not the only one with tears welling up. Together we withstood a dreadful flight and though it was not at all equivalent to surviving something truly horrific like a war, with everything being relative, we still wanted to offer our gratitude. After all, the crew triumphed in their jobs to safely transport us, their terrified passengers, in a flying, pressurized metal tube.

As the PA system crackled on for the last time, I noticed there was no levity in the captain's final announcement. In fact, he sounded relieved, welcoming us to LA, thanking us for flying Southwest Airlines and hoping we'd all have a great Thanksgiving.

While deplaning, I tried to hand my golf pencil back to one of the flight attendants who said with a wink, "Keep it as a treasured souvenir."

I deemed this sliver of humor a consolation prize which made me smile, though not enough to calm my quivering chin by the time I reached the captain with the first officer by his side. To them, the only words I managed to say were "Great job! Thank you," but it was enough.

Walking towards the gate, I saw the anchor man, who shall remain anonymous. I caught up with him and said, "Rough flight, huh?" We made eye contact with a split second of recognition—he the famous newscaster and I the person who literally suffered at his hands. He flashed a smile with gleaming Arctic-white teeth and then his eyes darted away. I didn't know if he was embarrassed or simply wanted to decompress from the ordeal without chatting with an adoring fan, or in this case, one who knew his secret. As we walked our separate ways, in my head, I forgave him.

As for the onboard game, I later looked up the word "Thanksgiving" and, for the record, it's worth 28 points in Scrabble and you can make up to 348 words out of it to be exact, four nine-letter words, 103 four-letter words, and 17 two-letter words with many more in between. And yes, etiquette aside, you can use *that* word.

I never did see 8A again. For all I knew he was somewhere back on the tarmac communing with ground control or perhaps other forces in the universe.

Part II

Karen was waiting for me at airport arrivals. The rain was still coming down, but no matter, it was good to see my dear friend. We then drove off to shop for our Thanksgiving dinner. The next day we cooked and ate like kings and queens with interesting Hollywood types she had invited from both the movie and TV industries. To top off the feast, I had whipped up a pumpkin pie from scratch, served with honey-sweetened vanilla ice cream from a local creamery.

By the end of the party when all the guests had gone, Karen and I got ready to hit the bars. There was one little thing we hadn't realized till then, that many of the celebrities might be out of town or at home with their families during the holiday. Regardless, the pouring rain had let up and we were dressed to kill. Back then I looked a little like Sussana Hoffs of The Bangles, and Karen was a striking strawberry blonde with superbly cut wild hair she didn't bother to tame.

We started out at a legendary Hollywood hangout near the Sunset Strip where Drew Barrymore and her pal Lara Flynn Boyle, who had not yet caught the eye of Jack Nicholson, were charmingly holding court like a pair of Scarlett O'Haras. Drew was still in her teens at the time and her mom was the bar's hostess. Karen introduced me to a handful of producers and directors, whom she knew, though no A-lister actors had arrived. Disappointed, we set out to the next bar and the same thing happened. We hit bar after bar hoping our luck would change. Both of us grew up in NYC and we would spot celebs every now and then in Manhattan, but here in LA, the expectation was to see a large concentration of fabulous stars.

We next stopped at a coffee shop to warm up and

then on to a restaurant bar, nearly empty, where we recognized Dabney Coleman, an extremely talented veteran actor from *Tootsie, 9 to 5, WarGames,* and other hit movies. He was having a splendid time at dinner with a gorgeous redhead to his left and a stunning chestnut brunette to his right. They were strategically seated in a large rounded booth with vintage, thick-quilted leather backs, designed to be seen – and they were. Dabney gave Karen and me an unabashed up and down once-over as if wondering if the grass was greener in our direction or perhaps if we might like to join his party.

With a decent Hollywood story to tell, we moseyed on while a drizzle morphed into a bone-chilling fog. We made it back to the first bar to rest our feet, have a final drink, and collect ourselves before going home with our tails between our legs. Karen pointed out a fresh batch of D-list celebrities had arrived while we were gone, adding only slightly more to a crowd that never really materialized. We made the best of the situation by doing a lot of catching up, and just when we decided to end the disappointing evening, the door flung open and who breezed in, nope, not Brad Pitt, not Sylvester Stallone, not any one of the movie heart-throbs we had hoped to see. It was Chachi. Yup, Scott Baio, the sitcom darling, *Charles in Charge*, that one.

No disrespect to Chachi, but we laughed all the way to the car and all the way to Karen's place. We got out of our wicked high heels, hung up our wet garb, and Karen poured a couple of glasses of wine, making a toast to an uneventful, good-weather flight the following day. With the clink of our glasses and a resounding, "amen", we drank up. While we did not see the fabulous Harrison Ford, Richard Gere, or Patrick Swayze as we would have liked, we did finish off a most satisfying and fabulous pumpkin pie with an extra dollop of ice cream.

And yes, indeed, the next day, after an exceedingly offbeat LA Thanksgiving, the skies were blue, the flight smooth, and an animated crew had me cracking up all the way home. God bless Southwest.

Barbara Klide was born in NYC. She is the author of the book trilogy, *Along Came Ryan...the Little Gosling King*, the true saga of a mated pair of elegant, sensitive and smart Canada geese and their offspring that nested three years in a row where she works. She donates book profits to various wildlife rescue groups.

Barbara graduated with an MBA from Golden Gate University, San Francisco, and a Certificate in Graphic Design from the University of California, Davis. She is Director of Marketing for Quest Technology Management, California and a member of NCPA. Her Canada goose compendium series has received much acclaim including from Dr. Lorin Lindner, PhD, *Wolves and Warriors*, as seen on Animal Planet and Bill Bianco, President, Audubon Society, Sacramento.

Barbara and her longtime partner reside in Fair Oaks, California where they rescue, foster, and adopt out cats. Visit Barbara at: Barbaraklide.com

ALL DOWNHILL FROM HERE

AMY ROGERS

f I asked you to describe summer weather in California, what would you say? As a Sacramento resident, summer for me means HOT and DRY. I accept as dogma that I won't see a drop of rain from June through August. True, at that time of year the coast can have heavy fog, and San Francisco can be terribly chilly. But in the Central Valley, it's always safe to plan a pool party unless the annual wildfires are belching smoke in your direction.

As I packed a duffle bag for our family summer vacation, I thought I had the weather all figured out.

I knelt on a rolled-up sleeping bag, using my entire body weight to squeeze as much air as possible out of the down filling. Satisfied that the bag was as small as I could make it, I stuffed it into the duffel along with the basics: T-shirts, camp sandals, plastic cup, towel, swimsuit, insect repellant, a paperback book. I didn't like the haphazard arrangement inside the floppy duffel, but a firm-sided suitcase wasn't an option. It wouldn't ride properly on the pack mule.

With a sympathetic thought for the mule, I reconsidered the book. But the outfitter had given clear weight limits, and I was well within mine. The book stayed.

Hubby, two tween kids and I loaded up the car and headed east over the Sierra Nevada. Our destination was a pack station outside of Bishop, California. We followed Highway 395 down the arid, scenic Owens Valley in the rain shadow of the mountains. Every minute brought us closer to Death Valley and the Mojave Desert, two of the hottest and driest places on earth, though we weren't going quite that far. The temperature outside was 94 degrees.

We were about to embark on an extraordinary

wilderness adventure of horse packing in the High Sierra. With the able assistance of a wrangler and a cook, our party would ride horses rather than hike the many miles to a remote campsite high in the mountains. We would fish for legendary California golden trout, swim in icy clear streams, sleep amid the sound of frogs, and not see another human being for days. Mules would carry our food and gear. The plan was perfect.

Hot sun and dry, swirling dust greeted us at the ranch where we met our steeds. Based on our weight and height, each of us was assigned a horse of appropriate size. Hubby towered over us, high in his saddle. The kids were glad they weren't riding mules, an affront to their dignity last time we "horse packed". (Mules, I am told, are steadier, stronger, and generally a more reliable mount for kids.)

Even though I wasn't climbing the thousands of vertical feet between us and the mountain pass we would cross, I knew the day would be physically vigorous. The trails are narrow, overhung with branches, sometimes scattered with rocks, and often steep. A rider must do more than just sit there. You must stay alert, hold on tight with your legs, and constantly adjust your weight, leaning forward or back so you don't fall off on a slope. In anticipation of the exertion, I wondered what I should wear.

Hey, I'm not stupid. Despite the heat at the pack station, I knew that shorts would be a disaster. Bare sweaty skin of a city girl rubbing against saddle leather for six hours equals a lot of pain. I also knew that the inner seam of a pair of jeans would chafe eventually. I chose leggings: close fit, no big seams, and not too hot.

I also knew that the temperature would drop as we climbed toward the summit. In my small saddlebag, I packed a fleece pullover and a waterproof outer jacket. Not that it mattered, because it doesn't rain in July. I made sure the kids did the same.

And so, we set off in sunshine and high spirits, like the cast of *Gilligan's Island*.

The horses walked steadily on the familiar route, lifting

us above the valley. The view was spectacular as each hour took us higher and higher, eventually crossing the tree line. We reached a plateau and turned away from the valley, traversing a "saddle" of the geographic kind between two peaks. Rock walls formed a tunnel.

Without the expansive, sunny panorama to hold my attention, I started to notice the gathering clouds.

We had reached the pass, over 10,000 feet above sea level. The route led along a wide, barren, boulder-strewn path. I noticed a patch of snow that had endured into July. The wind picked up and the sky grew gray. We paused to put on our extra garments, and I started to worry a little. The temperature had dropped significantly. Without full sunlight, the harsh, exposed zone had a menacing feel. Nothing blocked the wind. I was cold and I wanted to be among trees again.

About thirty minutes later, we reached the other side of the pass. I sighed with relief. The path sloped downward into the trees, and it was all downhill from here. The temperature would rise as we descended and in two hours we'd arrive at the campsite, build a fire, and kick back by a stream.

Then the rain began.

I zipped my jacket and tightened the drawstring on my hood. Long sleeves, Gore-Tex, Velcro—I was ready. Wasn't I?

Fat droplets soaked into my leggings. Uh-oh.

The sun was long gone. The rain came thicker. Soon my lower pants were soaked and funneling water into my (waterproof) boots. Socks heavy with wet. I tried to find the best angle to hold the horse's reins to minimize dripping into my sleeves. The horse plodded on, seemingly oblivious to the change of weather. We crossed the tree line but instead of getting warmer, I grew colder by the minute.

My thoughts were of my kids, of course. I tried to see how they were doing. In the heavy rain, spread out single file along the trail, I couldn't talk to them. Their heads were down, focused on riding. I was helpless. We had no more clothing to put on—our duffel bags had gone ahead with the mules. We were hours away from civilization, and the only available shelter was the tents that still lay an unknown distance ahead.

There are three times in my life when I've looked around me and concluded, my children are going to die and it will be my fault. Not coincidentally, the other two also involved travel and a failure to anticipate the power of nature.

The trail became a river, a temporary torrent flowing inches deep over the rocks. I realized my life depended on this horse, its sure-footed clomping through the water, and most of all its body heat. By now my pants were utterly soaked, and wetness was seeping up my torso and arms. I had lost sensation in my fingers and toes. But the huge, sturdy beast beneath me was comfortably warm from its exertion, blanket, and saddle. Enough of that heat radiated between my legs to keep me going.

When we finally arrived at camp, I was unable to use my hands. By some miracle, although the kids were disgruntled and uncomfortable, they were not as badly off as I was. They swiftly assembled their own tent, while I did what I could to assist hubby with the same task. One of the happiest moments of my life was removing my soaked garments and crawling into that dry little space. Hubby had to manage my buttons and snaps—my fingers wouldn't move.

As I huddled inside my sleeping bag and my body temperature returned to normal, I pictured the scene not many miles away as the crow flies, down in the Owens Valley. Hot. Dry. Sunny. A proper inland California summer.

But not the only kind.

Amy Rogers, MD, PhD, is a Harvard-educated scientist, professor, award-winning author, and critic who switched from teaching university biology classes to reviewing, writing, and publishing science-themed thriller fiction. Her novels *Reversion*, *The Han Agent*, and *Petroplague* use real science and medicine to create plausible, frightening scenarios in the style of Michael Crichton. Compelling characters and fictionalized science—not science fiction—make her books page-turners that seamlessly blend reality and imagination.

Amy lives in Northern California where she also runs ScienceThrillers.com and is treasurer for Northern CA Publishers and Authors. Her nonfiction articles about science and engineering behind the scenes of everyday life first appeared in the *Inside Arden* newspaper and are now collected in her book *Science in the Neighborhood*. During the pandemic crisis of 2020, she became a trusted source of accurate, accessible science information through her blog at AmyRogers.com. Visit her website to learn more.

Amy@AmyRogers.com

Facebook.com/ScienceThrillers

TRAVELING TO AMERICA
EMMA CLASBERRY

Why I chose to go to Chicago

At a 4-year teachers' training college in the 1960s in Nigeria, I learned more about America, especially Chicago, in geography class than I did about my country, Nigeria. The picture the teacher painted describing Chicago was so inviting that students wished they could go there and see how beautiful it was.

One of the students, EJA (full name abbreviated), who later became my spouse, was so interested in going to see Chicago that he wrote at the back of his chair: "CHICAGO." "If I have any opportunity to study abroad, I will go to Chicago," he envisioned.

After graduating from teachers' college, EJA worked as a primary school teacher for a year or so. He later went to university to get his Bachelor's degree. With that, he got a job in the government civil service and worked for some years.

In the late 1970s, the door to the envisaged opportunity to study overseas knocked. He took advantage of it. His first choice was America so as to come and see Chicago. He left to attend the University of Chicago.

By this time, we were already married and had five children.

Two years after EJA left for America, I was now ready to join him. It was a hard decision for me to make because I did not want to leave my children behind. But my mother encouraged me and promised to take care of them. And she did.

I began to prepare myself mentally to join my spouse. I bought domestic airline ticket to travel from Calabar to Lagos on the 7th of November. When I went to pick up the ticket, the date had been changed to 9th of November.

"Why?" I asked.

"If you travel on the 7th, you will have to spend a night in Britain because there will be no connecting flight to US on the same day after you arrive," the ticket agent explained.

I picked up my ticket.

Story-teller in the bus traveling to Calabar

I had to take a bus ride to get to Calabar where I would board the plane to Lagos. In that bus was a man who loved retelling funny riddles to entertain the audience.

One of his story-riddles was about a man, his wife and a cow crossing a river in a boat. Suddenly, the boat is about to sink. "Which of the two – his wife or his cow, should the man try to save from drowning?" the riddle teller asked us.

A few passengers said the man should save the cow because he could sell the cow to get money to marry another wife. They said they did not mean it, but were just teasing the listeners. "This answer is wrong and should never be put to practice," they warned.

Realistically, all of us said the man should try to save his wife because he could get another cow. We all agreed that human life is irreplaceable and more important than a thousand cows.

"What we learn from this riddle is that sometimes in life, we may face situations where we have to make hard choices, choose the worse out of the worst options available to us at a given moment," the man advised us.

Cultural clash at Lagos Airport

I arrived safely in Calabar on schedule. Two hours later, I boarded the plane and arrived in Lagos safely.

While I was waiting at Lagos airport to board the plane, a Yoruba man greeted an Ibibio man (both Nigerians), "*Ekuno-o*," a Yoruba greeting that means 'Well done'.

But to the Ibibio man, *Ekuno-o* sounded like an Ibibio word that means murmuring. So, he thought the greeter was accusing him of 'murmuring' against him. This misunderstanding led to a verbal fight.

"I have not said anything to you. When did I murmur against you?" the Ibibio man confronted the greeter, defending himself.

Before the greeter had any chance to defend himself, to tell him that he was not accusing him of murmuring, the Ibibio man had already lashed out at the greeter, "It is your mother who murmurs. Your father murmurs."

The verbal fight now escalated to a violent physical fight where the two men gave each other a black eye because the Ibibio man cursed the Yoruba man's parents. To the Ibibio man, the worst curse to a person is cursing one's parents, especially the mother. So, that cursing gave him more satisfaction than anything else he would have said or done to the greeter, in retaliation.

Some standers-by were laughing at the two. Others sympathized with them for misunderstanding each other.

Immediately, two airport security officers arrived at the scene to intervene. At that very moment, the departure of my flight was announced. So, I left and boarded the plane.

I flew out of Nigeria by British Airways on the 9th of November, stopped in Britain and arrived safely in New York on the following day.

Hindsight: When I looked back, I realized I travelled on my birthday. Was it a coincidence or by divine plan? Maybe, it was by the latter. At the time, I was unaware of it because I did not usually remember my birthday, let alone observe or celebrate it in any form. That was the norm then, even up till now, especially among older folks.

Almost scammed and kidnapped at New York Airport

In New York, I was almost defrauded by one Kenneth, if my spouse did not give me some traveling tips before I set out on the journey. "When you arrive in New York, be vigilant. If anyone offers to help you or give you a ride to some place, do not accept the offer," he cautioned.

Without these tips, Kenneth could have taken my travelers check, forced me into his taxicab and taken me to what he called 'hotel' and probably disposed of me.

I told Kenneth that I was boarding the plane to Chicago in the next couple of hours, and I did not need to spend a night in a 'hotel'. He still took my luggage, put it in the trunk of his taxicab, and attempted to force me into his cab in broad day light.

At that point, I screamed. My scream attracted the attention of a few people. Quickly, he left me alone and drove away.

I departed New York a few hours later and arrived safely in Chicago that same day. Ever since, I love that city, Chicago. I have lived there for over two decades until a few years ago when my daughter got married and had to relocate to join her husband in San Jose, California. A few years later, I relocated to California to live close to her. Where I live now, I love it.

Culture Shock

From the day I landed in America till today, I once in a while run into fellow immigrants who shared their experiences freely with me. I told them about some of mine too.

"Are men in America wearing lipstick?"

One of my friends said she asked this question when she landed in New York airport in winter. She was shocked to see some men and women using lip balm. A few days after arrival, she herself began to use it. "Yea, it is to wet the lips to prevent them from cracking as a result of extreme winter cold." She soon found out why.

"Does smoke come out of their noses?"

Another friend asked herself this question when she arrived in Illinois in the heart of winter, and saw smoke coming out of people's noses. "They are not even smoking," she wondered. Soon she found out why when her nose too began to send out smoke, "Yea, it is linked to winter cold and the body's reaction to it."

"Is America painted with white wash (white paint)?"

This same friend arrived in America in the heart of winter. "I learned about snow in school in Nigeria, but never saw it. When I saw trees and the ground covered with snow, I thought the trees and the ground were painted with white paint," she joked about it.

"Do Americans steal?"

He just came to America. A couple of months past, he went to Sears Department Store and bought some goods. He came out of the store and waited outside for his ride.

"Oh! I need T-shirt," he remembered. He left the goods he bought outside near the entrance to the store, went inside, bought T-shirt, and quickly came out.

By the time the young man came out from the store to wait for his ride, all the goods he left outside by the entrance to the store were gone. In desperation, he exclaimed, "Do people in America steal? Do Americans steal?"

The hot dog scenario

It was lunch time, in the 1980s. I was just a few weeks old in school and three months in Chicago. I and two other students went to the school cafeteria for lunch and to return to the next class within 30 minutes.

The two students asked me what I wanted to order for lunch. "I have no idea of what is available," I told them.

They offered to help me choose. "Do you want nachos?"

I said, "No" because I did not know what it was.

"What of fries?"

I shook my head indicating, 'No'.

"What of hamburger?" they pointed toward it.

I responded with a question, "What else do they have?"

"Hot dog, bagel...." one of them mentioned other entries as options.

I did not even let her finish listing available meal options for lunch at the cafeteria. I interrupted, "I don't eat dog meat. Some people in my country do. The meal is usually prepared as soup and is the spiciest of all soups."

I don't remember what I ended up ordering. I probably settled with hamburger, just to have a taste of what it was. The two students ordered hot dog.

I was curious to see what American hot dog meal looked like. I expected to see each of them with a bowl of hot pepper-spiced soup with pieces of dog meat in it.

But what I saw was near-oval-shaped bread, split open into two, although not detached from each other. They called it 'bun'. In between it was one small finger-shaped meat they called 'hot dog'. On it were tomato paste they called 'catsup', chopped onions and what they called 'relish'.

I then told the two students what I expected to see in their plates.

"Oh no! We don't eat dog in America," they defended their culture in a loud voice.

"Why is it then called hot dog?" I asked.

They did not tell me, either by omission or design. But I later found out why, some months after, during a casual conversation with some other fellow students.

"The hot dog in the bun is likened to how a male dog's genital shapes during erection," they explained.

What a name for a meal!

This episode served as a brief cultural education exchange seminar that focused on dishes and food preparations.

Individual culture shock experiences in America

usually provoke humor whenever we immigrants share them in our conversations. We usually laugh about them and make fun of ourselves.

Discrimination encounters:

I have experienced countless race-based discrimination encounters in school and outside school environments. Some are bare-faced. Others are subtle. I am sharing a few here.

I and my spouse once went to one black-owned clothing store in the south-side of Chicago in the early 1980s to buy winter clothing. The workers refused to sell anything to us.

Why?

"You sold us. What do you want here? Go back to Africa. Even if you pay us a million dollars, we will not sell anything to you," they said to us.

We called the police for help. The police said, "If the store owner does not want to sell their goods to you, we can not force them to do so." We had no choice but left.

Another experience was at workplace in a nursing home where I worked as a wait person, setting up the dining table, serving food, cleaning up tables and washing dishes after meals.

With my African work ethics, I worked hard and diligently. I refused to be an eye servant, as most of my American co-workers were, pretending to work hard when they heard and saw the supervisor coming.

"We don't work like that here. By the way, what do you want here in America? You sold us and now you are here to take our jobs," they said to me.

Based on similar previous confrontations, responding to such challenges was dangerous, and exposed me to high risk of constant harassment and possible abrupt elimination. So, I left them alone and acted a coward.

In the university, I had encounters with two instructors in my last quarter in graduate program. One decided to check my grades in other subjects I had taken with other instructors in the past in order to decide what grade he should give me for the course I took with him. He became the judge and the executor because my paper was too good to be written by me, and suspected someone else wrote it for me.

Another called me into his office and asked me why I never came to see him in his office to seek help on any related topic. I told him I understood everything he taught. So, I did not have need to come and see him.

"Where do you come from?" he asked me.

"Nigeria," I answered.

"Are there no universities in your country? By the way, who admitted you into this program? Why did you not study Sociology or History, instead of Urban Planning, which will make no sense in your country?" he also asked me.

The instructor's behavior was a surprise. All that I could do was cry. I reported to my academic advisor, who referred me to the chairman of board of directors in relevant academic department.

The instructor was disciplined by the Board. He was ordered to apologize to me verbally and in writing. He did. I still have that letter till today.

Thanks to other well-meaning instructors, especially my academic advisor, who helped me, a foreign student on F1 Visa, to get financial assistance as a research assistant throughout my Master's Program.

Academic Challenges and Strengths in Graduate School

I was usually nervous whenever I stood before the class to present a paper on a given topic. Consequently, I would be confused and unable to adequately articulate that what I knew I knew very well. At one instance, it was so bad that the instructor said to me, "Emma, I don't understand what you are saying. Are you talking of being embarrassed?"

Yes, I was.

Yes, the instructor was right. No one in the class understood me. Even I myself did not understand what I was saying.

But there was an aspect that I was good at. They saw in me the ability to express myself very well on paper. How did I know that?

Many of my term papers or writing assignments usually came back with good comments by the instructors, "I wish everybody were able to write as you do." "Emma, this is an excellent work." "Emma, I want to be part of your career planning. You write very good papers."

As a result, my papers usually circulated among instructors. Sometimes, I was able to track them down and get them back. At other times, they got lost because they went through so many instructors that at some point, I could not trace to locate which instructor had them last.

Those embarrassing and encouraging times were learning periods for me, and when I began to think, "Maybe, I can share my ideas better through writing than through verbal presentation before a group of people."

Many opportunities to share some aspects of my culture

In the 1990s, I presented "African songs and dance" to 5th grade students in one Chicago public school as part of the Joyce Foundation Project, "Bridging the Gap."

A student asked me, "Do you have real big monkeys?" Everyone in the room giggled.

I told him, "I never see a live monkey. So, I don't know."

Another student stuck out his hand and asked, "Do teachers spank students in Africa when the pupils talk back to the teacher?"

I answered, "Oh yea! Any student who dared to do that would be laid on a long table and given 24 strokes of the cane on his/her buttocks. When he/she gets up and can not walk properly, he would not try that again."

A few weeks after, I was given an award for

outstanding participation in that project.

At one university in Chicago, I presented a 4-hour seminar on "Dance: an effective tool for educating African children" to graduate students majoring in Arts and Education. It ended with all of us dancing African dance. The students wished they had more of such presentations to help them handle minority students in class. The following month, I was featured in the university's newsletter.

I want to travel by bus to Africa

A participant in African Dance Project, an after-school project operated by African Peoples Institute, a non-profit agency I founded (1980s to 2000s) to promote cultural awareness among youth, learned a lot about Africa. She and other participants planned to visit Africa to learn some of its languages.

After I explained to her that they would have to travel by air for about 16 hours, changing planes, to get to Africa, she shrugged her shoulders and said, "No, I don't like flying. I will go down there by bus."

That was a learning period for her.

Traveling in general is educative. One has the opportunity to see other cultures, compare and contrast various aspects of different cultures, discard the obnoxious, admire the admirable and enjoy what is enjoyable.

Emma Umana Clasberry has authored many books on African culture. Her works reflect some of the ideas birthed at a Chicago non-profit agency, African Peoples Institute she founded (1990s through 2000s), to promote cultural awareness and pride among youth and to aid them understand how knowledge of their ethnic culture or lack of it can impact their cultural identity, self-esteem and confidence, their education and career choices, and economic welfare and cultural pride of a people.

Emma has been a Subject of Biographical Record in Who's Who of American Women, 21st Edition, 1999/2000, for Significant Contribution to the Betterment of Contemporary Society.

She earned a B.A in Political Science and an M.A. in Urban Planning & Policy from University of Illinois at Chicago, and a Doctor of Education degree from California Coast University.

Other books by Emma: *Culture of Names in Africa...; African Culture Through Proverbs*; and more. Amazon; Xlibris.

A HAWAIIAN HONEYMOON ADVENTURE

CHARLENE JOHNSON

"I'm so glad we finally decided to take this trip," Dex said as he maneuvered the rental car through the parking lot at the Lihue Airport in Kauai.

"I am too," Felicity replied, sitting back in the passenger seat. "I know we couldn't go on our honeymoon sooner, but we needed to be home since my father was having heart surgery. My mother would have been a wreck if we hadn't been there with her. She and my father have never been apart for so long. Staying with her while he recuperated was the right thing to do."

Dex reached over and squeezed her hand. "Well, we're here now and I can't wait to explore the island. I've only been to the Hawaiian Islands once."

"When was that?"

"After I graduated from college. A few of my buddies and I flew to Honolulu for a week of fun in the sun."

"Did you have a good time?"

Dex chuckled. "Not really. I spent most of the trip keeping my friends out of trouble. Guys fresh out of college have no common sense. They got drunk every night and hit on any woman who got near them. I don't drink much alcohol, I never have. Being stone-cold sober and watching them make fools out of themselves was a little hard to take. I'm glad the bar owner was used to rowdy young drunks or I would have been bailing them out of jail."

"Don't worry. That won't happen on this trip. I promise not to get drunk and dance on the table."

He laughed wickedly. "Actually, I might enjoy watching that."

Felicity punched his arm playfully. "Not happening, sweetheart."

"Damn," he exclaimed. "A guy can dream."

Settled in their hotel room an hour later, Felicity opened the sightseeing guide she picked up in the lobby.

"What do you want to do today?" she asked. "It's still early."

"What are our options?"

"On this side of the island is the Kukui Grove Shopping Center."

Dex wrinkled his nose. "I hate malls."

Felicity laughed. "You're right. We can do that at home. There's the Hauola Place of Refuge, the Wailua Falls or one of many beaches. There are a lot of them to choose from."

"What else?"

She looked at the guide and smiled. "I have the perfect excursion. What about a Wailua River Boat Cruise? It goes to the Fern Grotto."

"What's the Fern Grotto?" he asked.

"It is a lava rock cave that has ferns growing upside down from the roof. It is said to be millions of years old. At one time, it was considered a sacred place for Hawaiian Royalty but now couples go there to get married. Tourists used to go inside the grotto but there was heavy flooding in 2006 that prevents entry into it anymore. It can only be viewed from the observation deck."

"The boat cruise sounds interesting. Let's do that and then go to dinner. Since we're so close to the Wailua River State Park, I thought we could do a midnight run."

Felicity nodded. "Sounds good, Dex."

*   *   *

The sound of a ukulele and the dulcet melody of a classic Hawaiian song filled the air as the river boat slid through the Wailua River past the lush tropical jungle. It was a living canvas of vine-covered Rainbow eucalyptus, towering palm trees, banana trees and thatch screw pines. Emerald green ferns, vibrant bougainvillea, and birds of paradise gave the land along the shore a burst of color. An artist couldn't have painted a more breathtaking landscape. If only a soundtrack came with it to capture the cheerful bird songs that floated through the tropic air.

"It's beautiful here." Felicity slipped her arm through Dex's as they watched a hula dancer dressed in a brightly colored muumuu undulate to the music.

"It is," Dex commented, letting the warm fragrant air fill his lungs.

"I love that most of this island is unspoiled and the Hawaiian people take so much pride in keeping it that way."

Dex nodded and leaned in to speak in her ear. "Their legends are as fascinating as the island is beautiful. Take the night marchers. It's said if you are out at night and hear drumbeats or the trumpeting of a conch shell, you must get out of sight. They are the spirits of ancient warriors who go back to the places where they fought fierce battles throughout time. Or the mischievous Menehunes who play tricks on unsuspecting tourists who venture too close to their tiny villages. Or the Goddess of Fire, Pele."

"I know about her," Felicity said. "She lives above Kilauea and when angered, she causes the volcano to erupt and display her displeasure. It appears she must be terribly angry because Kilauea has been active for years."

"Yes, it's true, but Pele's anger is also a legendary contradiction. Although she sometimes destroys towns and great expanses of land, the lava causes the island to expand and grow. Where there's destruction, there is also creation."

"Such an interesting place, Dex. The rainforest is going to be magical tonight," she whispered. "Are there foxes here?"

"I don't know but no one will see us in the dark." He put his arm around her.

She snuggled against him. "True. I can't wait to see the Fern Grotto. The photos of it were gorgeous."

Fifteen minutes later, Dex and Felicity stood at the green wood railing on the observation deck in front of the Fern Grotto. There was a sense of peace and rejuvenation that only Mother Nature could create.

"What a beautiful couple you are," a female voice said.

Dex and Felicity turned to see an older woman grinning at them. She had snow white hair pulled back in a ponytail and soft brown eyes. She was wearing a black muumuu decorated with red and yellow hibiscus and emerald foliage.

Felicity smiled. "Thank you."

"Is this your first time here?" the woman asked.

"Yes," Dex replied and put his arm around Felicity. "We're on our honeymoon."

The older woman extended her hand. "I'm Molly."

They each shook it. "I'm Dex and this is my beautiful wife, Felicity."

Molly pointed at the grotto. "I come here every year. My husband, John, and I came here thirty-nine years ago for our honeymoon and we came back here every year until he died ten years ago. I've kept up the tradition even though he's gone now."

"I'm sorry for your loss," Felicity said.

Molly waved her hand in the air. "Don't be. John and I had twenty-nine wonderful years together. We had two kids, a boy and a girl. They are both grown and have their own families. Every year they volunteer to come here with me, but I don't need them to. Whenever I'm standing here, I don't feel alone. John is here with me."

"I can feel the unique energy here," Dex agreed. "I'm sure he is with you, too."

Molly smiled. "I loved my husband very much but the first time we came here, I wanted to throttle him."

"What did he do?" Felicity asked.

"It was before the severe rainstorms forced the closure of the grotto to tourists. We were standing inside as the tour guide told us about the tradition. The musicians performed at the top of the platform leading to the stairs of the grotto as they still do. It was amazing back then because the music would sound as if it were being played inside. It was tradition for the couples inside the cave opening to hold hands and sing the *Hawaiian Wedding Song*. After the song ended, the couples were supposed to kiss. John decided he didn't want to do either. He was more interested in the ferns hanging from the grotto ceiling. I was so angry with him. I didn't talk to him on the boat all the way back."

"Why did he do that?" Felicity asked.

"My husband was never one who liked to display affection in front of strangers. He was a private man, but he realized he really screwed up. When we got back to the hotel, he told me he was going for a walk. He returned with a beautiful orchid bouquet and sang the *Hawaiian Wedding Song* to me while we were sitting on our lanai. I couldn't be mad at him after that and when we came back here every year, he always held my hand and kissed me when the song ended. In fact, he sang the loudest. He had a wonderful voice."

"I'll have to remember his makeup skills," Dex commented as he gave Felicity a sexy smile. "I might need them someday."

Felicity elbowed him playfully. "I can't wait to see that."

Before they got back on the boat, the small band performed the song made famous in a place filled with tradition and love. Dex held Felicity's hand, remembering Molly's story. And after the song ended, he kissed her tenderly.

* * *

"Molly's story was so romantic," Felicity said as they left the restaurant.

"Yes. As hard as it had to be for her to go to the Fern Grotto every year after her husband died, she did it anyway," Dex replied, opening the rental car door for her.

"It is her memories of their love that keeps her going. I admire that."

Dex got in beside her and leaned over to kiss her cheek. "I hope that's something we don't have to worry about for a very long time."

"Me, too."

The Wailua River State Park was not far from their hotel and they followed one of the trails on the edge of the property deep into the forest. They found the perfect place under a banyan tree's mass of low hanging branches and aerial roots to undress and tuck their clothes away in a duffle bag.

Dex shifted into his red fox and Felicity into her artic fox. The high-pitched chirping of crickets and the halting, staccato sound of katydids echoed along the forest floor. Those sounds merged with the flute-like song of the Apapane, the hostile cries of the Alala Hawaiian crow and the repetitive chirps of the Kaua'i Elepaio creating an animated symphony.

The tropical rainforest was different than the redwood forest near where Dex and Felicity lived. They padded carefully along as they adjusted to the humidity and tropical scents of flora and fauna that were unfamiliar to them. The full moon filtered through the tall trees, scattering long streams of light on the forest floor.

As they became more comfortable with their surroundings, the foxes chased each other playfully through the forest until they came to a stream and stopped to drink.

"Aloha," a small voice said in the darkness.

Dex lifted his head, his furred body on alert. He growled low in warning.

Curious, Felicity tilted her head sideways and tried to see where the voice was coming from.

"I'm sorry," the voice said on the other side of the stream. "I'm not used to seeing any of my kind here."

Sensing no menace, Dex moved cautiously forward, sniffing the air and scanning the area. "Who are you?" he asked.

A small, brownish-gold lizard appeared in a sliver of moonlight. "My name is Kalani."

Felicity came up behind Dex. "I'm Felicity and this is my mate, Dex."

"Do you live around here?" Dex asked.

"Yes. I live in a small cottage outside of Wailua Town. Where are you two from?"

"We recently moved to Seattle. We're here on our honeymoon."

The lizard moved closer. "Congratulations!"

"Thank you," Felicity said.

"I've never seen a fox, let alone two on the island before."

"I thought it would be okay since no one would see us in the dark," Dex answered.

"Until you ran into me," Kalani said teasingly. "But I'll never tell."

"What type of lizard are you?"

"To the Hawaiian people, I'm the mythical Mo'o but in reality, I'm a shapeshifter like you," she replied. "The legend says I can appear in many forms to protect the ponds, the streams and the waterfalls. There used to be many of us here but I'm the last of my kind."

"How long have you lived here?" Dex asked.

"I've been here since the creation of the island. I was one of its first inhabitants."

"You must be lonely," Felicity remarked.

"Not really. I love the rainforest and I live much of my time as a woman. If you've been staying at the hotel here, you may have seen me in the gift shop. I brought some of my jewelry to the shop this afternoon for Malia to sell on consignment for me."

"I did see you in the gift shop when I went in there today," Felicity exclaimed. "You were taking jewelry out of a wicker basket. They were beautiful creations. I was planning on going back into the shop and buying something for myself and a few pieces to take home for my mother and mother-in-law."

"I'll be in there in the morning. Please stop by and see me."

"I will."

"Where were you headed tonight?" Kalani asked.

"Nowhere in particular," Dex replied. "We just wanted to take a run and explore the forest. It's our first time in a rainforest together."

"Then let me take you to my favorite place," Kalani said. "I think you'll love it there."

"Sure," Dex responded, swishing his bushy red tail.

"I'm game," Felicity echoed.

"Follow me."

Dex and Felicity followed Kalani through the forest until they heard the roar of a waterfall. Before them was a spacious valley anchored by the waterfall on one side and forest covered mountains on the other. The moon was directly overhead, illuminating it. It was magical.

Kalani stopped and turned around to look at them. "I love coming here so that I can be in my favorite form – a dragon."

"You shift into a dragon?" Dex asked, intrigued. He never tried to shift into any animal that big. And never a dragon. He wasn't sure it was possible.

"Yes. It's part of the ancient legend, but I do it because it makes me feel free. Do you two want to try?"

"I don't know," Dex answered. "I didn't know dragons existed."

"True dragons have been gone for centuries. But a shapeshifter can shift into one."

Dex turned his furred head to gaze at Felicity. "Do you want to try?"

"Yes," Felicity exclaimed, pacing with excitement.

"I'll shift first since you've never seen a real one," Kalani suggested. "Then you can visualize yourself as a dragon and shift."

One minute, Kalani was a small lizard and within seconds was a huge golden dragon with a twenty foot wingspan.

Dex moved away from Felicity and Kalani, giving

his fox room to shift. He closed his eyes and concentrated on Kalani's form until he felt his body begin to change. When he opened his eyes, he was amazed to see he was a green dragon slightly larger than the golden one. He swished his long-scaled tail back and forth and flexed his massive wings.

Felicity's artic fox padded up to his large snout and sniffed. She rubbed her furred cheek affectionately along his scale covered jawline. Dex nudged her gently away and tucked his wings against his long body. He moved closer to the golden dragon, giving the arctic fox room to shift.

Felicity closed her eyes and visualized her dragon. Seconds later, she was a red dragon, slightly smaller than the others.

The golden dragon was the first to take flight, sweeping through the expanse of the valley before turning to the left toward the waterfall. Dex followed, flying low, just above the treetops, feeling the wind propel him forward. From his vantage point, the land below him looked small. He'd never experienced such a sense of freedom in any of his other forms. It was exhilarating.

One of Felicity's favorite forms was the great horned owl so she was used to flying. None of the times she'd spent flying as an owl compared to gliding through the tropical valley as a dragon. The power of her wings and the speed she was able to achieve was tremendous.

The trio of dragons made two more trips through the valley and past the waterfall before returning to the clearing and shifting back into their previous forms. Dex and Felicity followed Kalani back to the stream where they first met.

"Thank you, Kalani. What a wonderful experience," Dex told her.

"It really was," Felicity agreed. "Thank you."

"You're welcome. It's been so long since I was able to enjoy the company of other shapeshifters. Thank you for making this night special for me. Please come back before you leave. We'll do this again."

"We'd love to," Dex replied.

"What an eventful day," Felicity said as they walked down the trail towards the hotel. "I can't believe we met a living Hawaiian legend and she is just like us."

"I can't wait to tell my parents and my brothers about it," Dex added.

"I wish I could," Felicity said sadly. "It will always be a part of me I can never share with my parents or my brother."

Dex squeezed her hand gently. "Never say never. A day may come when you can tell them. Your parents love you and may be able to accept what you are. You must have faith."

"I hope so."

"I can't imagine what we can do tomorrow that will top tonight."

Felicity grinned. "You never know. These islands have many ancient legends. I would never have believed they were real but look how today turned out. Anything is possible."

Thinking of their wonderous adventure in the clearing with the Mo'o made Dex smile. "You may be right."

Charlene Johnson is a romance author from Sacramento, California. She published four books in her Paranormal Romance series - Circle of the Red Scorpion, one book in her Romantic Suspense series - Sterling Wood and a book in a multi-author series, Crimes of Passion. She also published three short stories and three poems.

Homecoming, Book 1 in her Sterling Wood series was named a Book Excellence Award finalist in the Romance category.

Books have been her passion since age nine. Being a daydreamer and an incurable romantic with a Cinderella complex, she started creating her own characters and storylines because she realized she had her own stories to tell.

Her quote - I've traveled the world, crossed galaxies, traveled through time and explored history on the pages of books.

Besides reading and writing, she also enjoys photography, travel, music, and Elvis.

Websites:
https://www.charlenejohnsonbooks.com
https://www.circleoftheredscorpion.com
https://www.sterlingwoodseries.com

Email: circleoftheredscorpion@gmail.com

THE CHICLET ADVENTURE

JACKIE ALCALDE MARR

Jo sat at the tiny table where a splash of brightly painted flowers spread across the plastic tablecloth. I heard her forearms peel off the flat flowers when she reached for the big box of Zucaritas. She poured the sugary flakes into her hand. Breakfast. It's funny how Tony the Tiger looks just the same in Mexico as he does in the US. She was smiling and silently swayed her head and shoulders in smooth rhythm. No doubt it was Sade that streamed from her Walkman headphones into her ears. If it had been Jimmy Buffet, she would have been bouncing and nodding.

Our entourage of eight consisted of my three cousins, two of their significant others, a good friend of theirs, me, and my dear friend, Melanie. This was my third trip to Puerto Vallarta and it felt like home away from home. Jo was our ambassador. She'd been to PV several times and had made a whole community of local friends for us to call our own as well. The place, the people, and our experiences consumed a huge space in my heart, and I couldn't wait to share it with my buddy, Mel.

It was a good idea to take a what-the-heck sojourn up to San Blas to see some Bay Area friends – they had transplanted themselves to the tiny town for solitude and the space to raise their Macaw birds. The Macaws had been spectacular, colorful and huge. But the cockroaches had been huge in their own right, and much less colorful. It was time to leave the rustic streets of San Blas for the much more civilized, though only slightly less rustic, streets of PV.

We all agreed we had to go. But the cramped bus trip to San Blas had taken most of the day, three times longer than we'd expected. We were not going through that again.

So, we felt pretty pleased with ourselves when we chartered a plane to take us from nearby Tepic back to PV. Our own plane—how decadent! It was a worthwhile trade-off to buy less souvenirs and have more coveted beach time beside the Pacific.

Suddenly, there were arrangements to be made. At 10:00PM we'd knocked on the plaster wall beside the striped curtain that hung in the doorway. Inside, the sounds of a humble home seeped out, the TV blaring some sort of chase scene, and the kids fighting over a favorite toy. A man emerged, and after a choppy conversation, I thought we had an agreement. I had studied Spanish for eleven years in school, but I still couldn't be sure of anything. Don't put me in charge of negotiating international peace agreements.

"Well?" my cousin Alan asked with patience.

"I think we've done it! But we'll have to be up early," I answered, bolstered by my cousin's confidence in my ability.

Sure enough, at 5:00AM the next morning, two cars arrived to pick us up. It felt a little risky. Here we were, a group of twenty-somethings piling into two cars with all our bags, and our "taxi drivers" chattering to each other. One of them had tennis shoes with no laces, and the toes of his right foot spilled out, caked with dirt. The other decided not to button his shirt that day. I think it used to be white in a prior life. I didn't have time to dwell on these thoughts because Jo was already in the back seat shouting to us, "C'mon! We don't want to be late for our charter!"

We jiggled along the dirt road, each of us secretly keeping a keen eye on the bumper of our companion taxi ahead of us. The thought did occur to me – what would I do if that car suddenly veered right and we veered left? *How did we live without cell phones in the eighties?*

But we finally arrived at the Tepic airport, a one-room structure with a squat flight tower attached. We were all starving, so we raided the tiny snack bar: Jo bought the Zucaritas, Alan bought a couple of packaged muffins, Karen contributed a big bag of corn chips, Mel bought three bananas, and I bought a sleeve of cookies and several little bags of peanuts. Three orange Fanta's and two Nescafe coffees rounded out our feast.

When our plane arrived, we grabbed our collection of bags and hauled ourselves out the front door. There it was. So, that's what a DC-3 looks like.

"Yeah, that's it," Alan said. "You know, they used these in World War II." And it looked it.

To me it looked like an aluminum can that had been smashed then puffed up again on a second thought. The blue and red stripe on its dingy grey body did help a bit, I must admit. Mel and I looked at each other, silently sharing the same thought, *Are we really going to get in that thing?*

Jo was already shaking hands with a man who had lowered the wobbly staircase. The rest of us climbed the stairs behind her, teetering with our bags, and continued up the inclined aisle. But no one was talking much.

Once inside, we felt a little better. The orange seats had a familiar, albeit 1960s, kind of swirling pattern. But they had been adorned with an extra brown cloth where your head should rest, if you could ever rest on this plane.

We soon settled into enjoying the adventure. We spread out among the twenty or thirty seats, happy with our smart decision to go ahead and splurge on our own chartered plane. There was no door separating the cabin from the cockpit, and neither of the two pilots were in the plane. So, Mel and I posed in the cockpit, all giggles. Then I played flight attendant, pointing with two fingers to the one exit, assuring passengers that there were no oxygen masks, and handing out my bags of peanuts with a smile. We'd be back on the beach in PV in no time.

Despite a little bit of white knuckles, the huge propellers seemed to work, and the plane did climb up and float noisily in the blue Mexican sky. The land below held patches of green crops sprinkled across a dry brown canvas. The dark mountains rose up on either side of us, and I tried to keep my imagination in check. We were fine. We were on one more adventure. This is what life is…

Then the mountains grew taller. Or was it that we

were losing altitude? Yes! The plane was definitely descending. We all seemed to realize it at the same time. Kevin spoke up first, "I bet they have to get below some choppy wind."

I swallowed, wanting to believe that a merchant marine might know about such things. But my palms grew moist as we continued lower among the mountains. Earlier that week we'd been stopped on the road by militia wielding machine guns. Thank goodness our local friend who was driving talked to them calmly, and we were waved ahead. But the experience had shown us how different our neighbor Mexico was. We weren't in Kansas, or California, anymore.

So, was it possible we'd fallen into something sinister? How much did they think we were worth? Sure, we'd chartered our own plane, but we were just normal, middle-class kids. Shoot, my parents would kill me for thinking this was a smart idea. They'd refuse to pay ransom money, just to teach me a lesson! I tried to calm myself. And I remembered the children selling Chiclets gum on the beach. I guess to them we were the super wealthy Americans – it's all relative. Mel looked at me from across the aisle, fear creeping up into her eyes.

"Go ask him what's happening, Jack," Alan shouted to me, nodding toward the open cockpit. I gathered my courage and picked my way, seat by seat, up the aisle to the cockpit. The pilots were moving dials and flipping switches. I kept it brief – after all, would they really tell me their diabolical plan? I knew I probably wouldn't understand their reply anyway. I never learned vocabulary like "ransom," "drug lords," or even "crash."

I leaned my head in and shouted above the roar of the engines, "*Que pasa? Donde vamos?*" The one in the striped shirt said something over his shoulder, then waved his hand as though I was a pesky fly. I could see the brown dirt getting closer through the cockpit window. I quickly ran back to my seat. Mel was searching for her seatbelt. So was everyone else. We were landing.

We touched down hard, and a cloud of dust rose and

swirled as the propellers spun us around in a semi-circle. Through the cloud I saw a small building. The one-room structure was clad with a terra cotta roof. A rod protruded up fifteen feet or so, and a large windsock flapped to the left. High-tech instrumentation.

There were two cars beside the building. One looked like a 1950 Chevy that had likely been passed down two generations. The other was some sort of pickup truck, mucky red and weathered. The few people who were standing outside the building started gathering their bags.

"I can't believe it." Karen turned to Kevin with a bit of a scowl.

Kevin laughed out loud, "So, I guess they decided to make a stop to pick up a few *amigos*."

"What?" Mel moved across the aisle and peered out the window. "You're kidding me. You'd think they would have told us."

"But it's our own chartered airplane! They can't just make a stop and pick up a few people. On our dime, no less!" The injustice of the situation was heating Karen up. She turned and headed from the rear of the plane up toward the cockpit. But before she could get past a couple of rows, the one door burst open and people started flooding into the cabin like ants on a sweet cake.

Men with straw cowboy hats and buttoned up short-sleeved shirts, and women with their hands full of bags filed down the aisle. One woman had a baby cradled in a sling that crossed her torso, the baby wailing with impatience. Children chattered to their siblings and yanked on their mothers' sleeves. Baskets of cackling chickens entered the cabin and little white feathers floated around the new passengers as they moved in and settled.

None of us had time to react. We couldn't even gather our bags that we'd so lavishly strewn across many seats. The new passengers had already moved them and made themselves comfortable on our plane. They kept coming. A seemingly endless stream of people came from that small structure like the scarves streaming from a magician's pocket.

A little boy plopped into the seat next to me, his stuffed backpack ruffling that extra brown cloth on the back of the seat and bumping against the back of his head

I reached out to help him wrangle out of it and handed it to him when he sat back. A big rip on the side was repaired with duct tape and a sticker of *Clifford, the Big Red Dog* covered the bag below the Jansport® logo. The boy clutched the bag and smiled up at me, "*Gracias, Señora!*" His sweet smile revealed a gummy gap where his two middle teeth had been. He was a cutie-pie, even if he did rest his dusty sandals on my travel bag.

We took off again, and I craned my neck around to catch a glimpse of my own group. Karen was sitting tight-lipped beside the woman with the baby. Alan was sitting next to a large man, the rim of his cowboy hat scraping Alan's ear. Jo was trying to make conversation with a woman with a long black braid. Jo pulled her own long blonde hair over to the side. They both laughed. I couldn't see anyone else from our group.

The smell in the cabin became thick as though we were tea bags steeping in a brew. It was the smell of dust and sweat, and I came to know the smell of chickens too. *Just stay calm. We'll be in PV soon.*

The little boy beside me unzipped his backpack and rummaged inside. His hand came out with a yellow box of Chiclets gum. It was a common business for these young entrepreneurs, selling tiny boxes of Chiclets for a quarter. He held the little box in the palm of his hand and offered it to me, his toothless grin wielded like a strategic sales weapon. Ah, but weeks on the beach had honed my skill at the thanks-but-no-thanks reply. "*Gracias, pero no lo quiero.*"

The boy smiled wider and poked the fingers of his outstretched hand into my arm. "*Chicle!*" he proclaimed, as though I didn't know what it was.

"*No, gracias,*" I smiled back patiently.

He suddenly reached into his pack and pulled out another box, this one green. He held it in his hand and shook it, sure that the rattle of the little squares of gum inside would entice me.

Instead, I asked for his name. "*Como te llamas*?"

"Manolito," he replied. He shook the two boxes again and held them out insistently. "*Tu quieres*?"

I held strong. I knew that once you reached for your money pouch, it began an endless bargain for you to buy more and more of his inventory. And that could really turn ugly. In this luxury-chartered plane, we were the caged chickens. But I melted a little when he said his name. It was my father's name, and I immediately heard my grandmother calling him to help her in the kitchen. "Manolito!"

Finally, we landed. The door flew open and the passengers quickly oozed down the aisle and down the stairs. I caught sight of Mel as she glanced back over her shoulder at me, swept up in the flood like a leaf in a fast river. Manolito joined the river without even flashing me a smile. I was a little hurt.

Our group pooled together on the tarmac, counting bags, relieved to breathe the fresh air. We laughed at the turn of events. "That was unreal!" Mel laughed with delight.

"I know. I guess 'chartered plane' just doesn't mean the same thing in Mexico as it does back home," said Karen.

Kevin threw his arm around her, "Oh, I think it does." His blue eyes twinkled a bit. And we all laughed, a wave of relief amplifying the merriment. We were not calling home for ransom money.

I turned to see Jo hugging the woman she had been sitting with, another new friend. And, I saw three crouched boys, huddled together, arranging the contents of their backpacks. Big bundles of Chiclets boxes were stacked on the pavement. Each bundle must have contained thirty of the little boxes sold on the beach.

One boy saw me approaching and put on his sales smile. But I called out, "Manolito!"

He stood up straight, reached down to pick up two of the little boxes he'd offered me earlier. "*Tu quieres, Señora*?"

"*No, gracias*," I replied. But before he could try again, I held out a twenty-dollar bill and pointed to one of the big bundles. "*Esto.*"

There was a moment of shock among the three little boys, but Manolito quickly checked his disbelief before the American could change her mind. I was paying almost three times its value. We both knew it.

"*Gracias, Señora*," he said, smiling genuinely as we made the exchange.

"*Gracias, Manolito*" I smiled back.

I returned to my group and passed out tiny boxes of well-deserved Chiclets. Jo was bobbing her head and smiling to a tune. "...fins to the left, fins to the right..." escaped her lips unconsciously. Jimmy Buffet. The beach was waiting, and so was another Mexican adventure.

Jackie loves wine, nourishing old friendships, all things Spain, and the lessons found in history. She is a lifelong learner and loves to pack her bag for adventure.

After a long corporate career as an organization development consultant, Jackie created Evolutions Consulting Group. As an independent consultant, trainer, and certified leadership/life coach, she helps individuals and groups achieve their goals while accentuating their core passions. She works with private, public, and non-profit organizations, as well as individuals who are creating fulfilling lives.

Jackie has been published in the Sacramento Business magazine and the Organization Development Journal. She also co-authored *Social Media At Work: How Networking Tools Propel Organizational Performance* (Jossey-Bass).

She's currently writing the story of her family's immigration from Spain to Hawaii and then California and a memoir for her young granddaughter. She lives in Folsom with her husband Jeff and their mischievous mutt, Quincy Noodlebutt.

TRAVEL MEANS FLYING

SHARON S DARROW

There's a quote that says the journey is the destination. It's true for me when the journey means flying. Doesn't matter where I'm going or how long I'll be there, the thrill comes from just being up in the air.

The presence of white-knuckle fliers on my first commercial flight was a revelation. People afraid of being off the ground? Sure, we were stuck in an overcrowded metal tube in seats built for short-legged, skinny children, but what was there to be scared of? I stared out the window at the ground below in awe, but the guy in front of me glanced out the window once and turned green. That's when I realized not everyone shared my utter fascination with all things that flew.

Flying in dreams was how I found peace in a hectic life. Soaring over trees, arms outstretched like wings, my long hair streaming behind me, was my favorite secret fantasy as a child. Even now, I think leaping into the air like Superman would be heaven, the epitome of freedom. If some amazing inventor comes up with something that would let mere mortals do that, I'd like to be first in line to test it. So far, I've tried many different types of flying, but none are as simple as dream flying.

Hot-air balloons are gorgeous from the ground, the brilliant colors and designs above a square woven basket floating majestically in the sky. The reality is a bit different. The view is spectacular as the ground passes by below the basket. And the basket is just that—a woven square big enough to carry several people but with no padding, seats, or other creature comforts, which means no soft landings.

You have plenty of time to enjoy the view while you stand and lean on the basket edge, but talking about the sights is difficult with the deafening noise of the blower just a few feet above your head. Looking up at the blower flames aimed at the mouth of the enormous bag is mind-boggling, especially when you realize the heated air trapped under the thin layer of balloon material is all that holds you aloft.

Once you come to terms with that idea, you might be a little stressed when the blower turns off. Not to worry, that just permits the air to cool a little, to slow your ascent. The pilot will turn it on and off as needed to keep you on track, but your heart might race the first couple of times until you're sure the flames will go back on when needed.

My only balloon flight was great, but I always wonder whether or not I would have the courage to do what my brother, Mike, did. He and his wife helped crew a racing balloon for a few years, and during some practice runs they'd go up to 3,000 feet and take turns bungee jumping out of the basket. My heart throbbed from equal parts fear and jealousy just looking at the pictures.

Riding in a two-person helicopter is a blast because there are no doors and a transparent bubble floor. You can lean out in the open air, just like when I was a kid holding my hand out the car window for the thrill of feeling the wind rush through my fingers.

The view is incredible with nothing below your feet but air and land far below. A friend of mine watched me take off, horrified, afraid I'd fall out the door. I couldn't believe she was terrified. After all, I was wearing a harness just like in a car, so what's the problem?

Going from balloons and helicopters to a glider takes you to a different world, an experience poles apart in almost every way. You recline into a narrow cockpit with your legs stretched out in front, with a clear plastic canopy over your head, then you are pulled skyward by a towrope attached to a small plane. Once you reach the desired altitude, the rope drops away and you're left in near perfect silence, only a soft hiss of air moving past the frame. No engine to keep you aloft, just long narrow wings and a silhouette that matches a bird in flight.

Your pilot searches the ground for signs that indicate a thermal updraft, then steers for the heated air column, where the glider circles around, letting the warm currents carry you higher and higher. When you've reached your peak, just steer the glider out of the updraft and start drifting down toward the ground. This is when the fun begins because you have to choose the next thermal and get in place before you're too low to climb. Just like a bird, except you can't flap your wings to climb or speed up, so you don't dare let your attention wander.

My glider pilot must have sensed I was up for some adventure. At the top of a thermal, he leaned back and asked if I'd like to play. When I said "sure", he tilted the glider so the right wing pointed to the ground, causing the glider to fall straight down where the wing was aimed.

That sideways dive was amazing, fast and silent, as we plummeted toward earth like a hawk plunging towards a mouse. At the lowest point he brought the wing back into a horizontal position and took us right up with another thermal. I loved it, so we did it again on the other side. The only disappointment that day was when he said our time was up and we had to land. I'd love to go up in a glider again, but this time I want to find a pilot to try some spins and rolls along with the dives.

Ultralights remind me of what the Wright brothers started out with. Just imagine blending a lawn chair with a seatbelt, snowmobile motor, lawnmower gas tank, long wing, propeller, wheels from a kid's wagon, struts to hold it all together, foot pedals, and movable rods for hand controls. That's it, you've built yourself an ultralight!

My husband arranged for an ultralight flight for my 50th birthday. I went up in a two-seater, which was about as noisy as the helicopter. No cockpit or windscreen, so you feel like a noisy bird flying through the air. Communication was through the headset. After we'd been in the air for a while, my pilot said he'd been told I'd like to learn to fly an ultralight. When I told him that was true, he crossed his arms and legs and said, "So, do it."

There were only four controls, one for each hand and foot. The hand controls were long rods that could be pushed forward or pulled back to control elevation and speed. The foot pedals controlled flight direction. It was so much fun, right up until I had to relinquish the controls so we could land. Exciting ending too, since one of the tires blew when we hit the tarmac.

Flying in an open cockpit biplane is quite an adventure. The beautiful craft I flew in had gleaming mahogany on the dashboard and edges of the cockpit, and brilliant red paint on a body dating back to the first World War. Before climbing into the plane, I had to don a brown leather bomber jacket, goggles, then a tight leather helmet that encased most of my head and neck. The lack of a cockpit or wind screen made them necessary protection for my eyes and against the frigid wind.

The pilot sat behind me, but explained we wouldn't be able to talk during the flight. He said if I liked what he was doing to rest my left hand on the edge of the cockpit and point my thumb up. If I wanted him to calm the ride down, just point the thumb down. I pointed my thumb up as soon as we took off, and kept it that way until we landed.

When we walked back to the hangar, a helicopter landed near us and a woman got out and headed our way. When she reached us, she introduced herself as the pilot's wife and started scolding him about the wild ride he'd given me. According to her, they never take someone up and do spiral dives down toward the ocean, wild turns and aerobatics that included everything except turning upside down. He defended himself and said that my thumb was always up, proof that I loved it. He was right, but I'm not sure I could've moved my thumb if I'd wanted to, since it was almost frozen from the numbing cold and our wild ride.

The biplane ride made me want more, so I signed on for a discovery flight at Executive Airport in Sacramento. For about $100 I got to experience what it was like to pilot a four-passenger Cessna 172. It felt so cool to walk next to an actual pilot out on the runway to that little plane—-and I do mean little.

The pilot started us out by having me go through the preflight checklist. Outside, we checked everything you can think of: tires, flaps, rivets, struts, gas, prop, and the pitot tube. Who's ever even heard of a pitot tube? (He never did tell me what the darned thing does.) Then we climbed in for the cabin preflight, where I was told to take the P.I.C. seat on the left. Wow, Pilot in Command, I was over the moon before we even turned on the engine. By the way, if you've ever needed encouragement to trim down, climbing and strapping yourself into those narrow seats is powerful motivation.

The magic moment came when we received permission from the tower to take off. The pilot controlled the throttle, but told me to watch our speed and pull back on the yoke when it hit eighty. I did, and up we went. What an incredible feeling of freedom and power. I was grinning so hard it felt like my face might split. The pilot took me through all the essential maneuvers of climbing, diving, turning, and flying straight. Believe it or not, flying straight and level is the hardest skill for new pilots.

After we'd practiced for some time, the pilot said, "We've covered all the basics, so would you like to try a stall?"

"Yes," I said, with no hesitation whatsoever. I was having a ball just being in the air, so was game for anything he might want to do. He told me to aim the nose up in a steep climb, but not to advance the throttle. Up we went, and in seconds the plane began vibrating. Not a little tremble either, but hard shuddering as if a giant was shaking the entire plane like a pair of dice at a craps table. Then a super loud alarm, the stall horn, started wailing. I'm still holding the yoke, shaking like mad and going deaf from the alarm, when the engine quit. The pilot told me not to touch the throttle, just nose the plane over in a steep dive. When I did, the engine fired back on like magic.

After we landed, I was so stoked I signed up for lessons. The Discovery flight was a great success because I discovered flying that little plane was the most fun I'd ever had. It was a dream come true, and throughout the lessons every minute in the air was incredible.

I tried sharing my excitement with my best friend, Ann. I described the stall with great enthusiasm and in intricate detail, but she kept cutting me off. Turns out she's terrified of small planes and refuses to ever set foot in one even if it's tied to the ground. To my great surprise many more people have reacted to my story with horror like Ann did, rather than excitement. I still believe flying in anything is the most fun I can imagine. There's absolutely nothing for anyone to fear from flying—landing, however, might be a different matter!

Sharon S Darrow is an entrepreneur, business owner, award winning author, public speaker, and an expert in caring for neonatal orphan kittens.

Her books, *Bottlekatz, A Complete Care Guide for Orphan Kittens,* and *Faces of Rescue, Cats, Kittens and Great Danes,* are about animal rescue. Sharon's two memoirs, *Hindsight to Insight, A Traditional to Metaphysical Memoir* and *Tom Flynn, Medium & Healer,* are inspirational, and her fifth non-fiction, *Navigating the Publishing Maze, Self-Publishing 101,* is a training manual about publishing.

Sharon also writes historical fiction. *She Survives*, and *Strive and Protect* are the first two books in the Laura's Dash series, inspired by her maternal grandmother.

Sharon firmly believes that life just gets better and richer, the longer you live. Her personal motto is "Find harmony within, then all things are possible."

FOLLOW THE TURTLE

ELLEN OSBORN

C arol walked through the vacant corridors of their beachfront hotel in Puerto Vallarta on her way to the swimming pool for a late-night swim. She needed a little time away from her husband after their disagreement in the bar earlier that evening. They hadn't been married long, and this was their first real vacation together—and their first real argument. Maybe the exhausting trip to get there had made them both short tempered.

What she needed was some physical activity, and a warm evening swim sounded just right. When Carol reached the pool, she found it closed for the night. No swimming after 10:00p.m.

The sound of surf lured her. Alone on the beach, walking along the water's edge, Carol impulsively decided if the pool was closed, she would go for a swim in the ocean. The water felt pleasantly cool to her bare toes and the slight breeze was warm. Perfect. She shed the beach towel she had wrapped around herself to cover her bathing suit, left the towel on the sand and splashed into the surf.

Unaccustomed to swimming in the ocean, Carol struggled past the small breakers until she was in water deep enough to begin swimming, getting her first taste of salt water. Undaunted, she squeezed her eyes shut against the salt sting and swam straight out into the ocean as strong as she could against the inbound current. She swam until the brain fog of one too many Margaritas began to clear.

She stopped to catch her breath and look around. A heaven full of stars was reflected in the gently rolling mirror of the water. The beauty of the summer night held her in its spell. Turning in the water she saw a line of distant lights, then turning the opposite way, she saw an identical line of lights. Carol was ready to return to the beach, find her husband, snuggle in his arms and make their silly argument go away. But which way was the hotel? Carol remembered the warning from their waiter at dinner about swimming in the ocean at night. What was it he had said? Something about fishing boats, "sardine stranglers" he had called them, anchoring off shore at night, with their lights looking just like the lights on the shore. If you swam the wrong way, you might not have the strength to correct your mistake. "*Cuidado*," he solemnly advised them. Be careful. Maybe she should have taken his warning seriously.

Panicking a little, she paddled in quick circles, trying to decide which way to go. Suddenly, the night seemed colder as the breeze chilled her arms. Carol became frightened of the deep black water that held her. She began imagining what might lurk in the darkness below. What hungry creatures were there waiting for an exhausted swimmer? Even the spangle of starlight on the restless water's surface now confused her.

At that moment she noticed a dark object in the water. At first Carol thought it was an old car tire, or some other piece of garbage, floating on the surface. As the object came closer, she realized it was a sea turtle. The turtle was swimming toward one of the lines of lights. Since she needed to choose a direction, she chose to follow the turtle, hoping it was headed for the beach to lay her eggs. As this odd couple, woman and turtle, proceeded, it became clear they were headed toward the beach: the turtle to lay her eggs, and Carol to reach the salvation of dry land. She was filled with relief to have her feet on solid ground.

Once out of the water and onto the sand, the turtle moved much more slowly, scrabbling her awkward way up the gentle slope of beach toward the high tide line. When the turtle reached the sea grass, she began preparing a nest for her eggs. Curious, Carol had followed the mother turtle and now stood quietly watching as eggs began to fill the nest. She gradually became aware of a man dressed in white, standing silently nearby. She recognized him as one of the "watchers" who guarded the beach and the hotel guests through the night.

Carol said to him, "I wasn't supposed to swim in the ocean at night, was I?"

He responded, "No, it is forbidden." His job was to protect the guests, not the turtles, so he walked away to patrol the beach. But he didn't order her back to the hotel.

Carol returned her attention to the turtle. The eggs were laid; the nest was covered and hidden from view. The mother turtle had completed her task and was ready to return to the ocean, where she was at home in the salty depths. No sooner had the turtle turned her back on her offspring, when one of the hotel cooks, still dressed in his chef's uniform, appeared on the beach. He dug out the nest, exposing the eggs, and gathered them into his toque. He turned to leave, carefully carrying his prize in his tall white hat.

When he passed by Carol, she asked him in her limited Spanish "*Huevos*?"

"*Sí*" the cook replied.

As she turned away from the plundered turtle nest, Carol saw the welcome sight of her husband walking down the empty beach. He stopped to retrieve her towel and wrapped her gently in it. Carol took one last look at the rapidly disappearing turtle, and felt sad she hadn't been able to protect the nest. She whispered, "Thanks old girl for saving me even if I couldn't save your children."

"I have been looking for you. Ready to go back to our room?" her husband asked, putting his arm around her, steadying the towel, their quarrel forgotten. "How about tomorrow we go snorkeling and you can see what lives below the surface of the ocean?"

"Um, ok" was Carol's halfhearted reply. She wasn't sure she was ready for that. Unless they could see some turtles.

Primarily a writer of nonfiction history, Ellen is the author of the recently released history of El Dorado County *A Lovely And Comfortable Heritage Lost*. She has also written historical articles for such periodicals as *Sierra Heritage, Around Here* and the *Overland Journal*. She has contributions in NCPA's three previous anthologies, *Our Dance With Words* and *Birds of a Feather vols. One and Two*. A member of the Placerville Shakespeare Club, she helped research and write the well-received original presentation "El Dorado's True Gold Notable Women's Stories" in 2013.

Ellen is a member of the El Dorado Writer's Guild and Northern California Publishers and Authors.

A fourth generation Californian, Ellen graduated from San Francisco State. After spending her work life in the Bay Area, she and her husband are now retired and live in Pollock Pines, CA. She can be reached at slyparkbooks@gmail.com.

THE ROAD FROM SANTIAGO
DOROTHY RICE

The way is wooded, a canopy of leafy green overhead. My teenage daughter walks ten paces ahead of me in shorts and tank top, blond-tipped ponytail cascading over her pack. I let the distance between us lengthen, frame her receding figure in my phone's lens, centered between the arc of the trees, the stone walls that flank the trail, pocked and worn, some placed a thousand years ago, or more.

We are pilgrims, *peregrinos,* though of a different sort than the devout who since the early middle ages have travelled the *Camino de Santiago*, the Way of Saint James. They converge on the cathedral in Galicia's capital city, in Spain's rugged north, to pay homage to one of Christ's twelve apostles, whose remains, according to legend, are buried there.

I press the button before my daughter disappears around a bend, one of several such photos I will take over our week of hiking this quiet trail, interrupted by the occasional fellow traveler.

"*Buen Camino,*" the earnest young man from Italy, the starry-eyed student from Germany, the Spanish boys on summer holiday, call out to us in passing, scallop shells, the symbol of Saint James, dangling from dusty packs.

"*Buen Camino,*" we say.

I haven't been in Spain in close to four decades, not since just after college when I lived in Madrid for a year, dreaming in Spanish, fancying myself an expatriate. It is my daughter's first time in Europe, a high school

137

graduation gift for her and, for me, a belated return.

We walk 15 miles a day, up hill and down, wending our way through towns with narrow cobbled streets and barking dogs, beginning in Santiago—where most end their journey—destined for Muxía, a fishing village on the Atlantic Ocean. We pause for fruit and bread from our packs, water, to pee behind a bush alongside the trail, one keeping watch for the other.

My daughter, the youngest of five and the last child at home, will leave for college in New York City at summer's end, far from our California home. I am content to trace her footsteps, with the occasional exclamation on this place, these hills and unexpected jungly dips, thick with ferns, with wild flowers still fresh in August—yellow, white and orange—rivers of cold, running water and always stones, tumbledown walls, fences, the concrete pillars that mark the way forward, blue and yellow ceramic tiles with the familiar scallop shell and an arrow. Just as the distance between markers and fellow hikers seems long and we begin to wonder if we might be lost, another bright shell appears around the bend.

We are not lost.

At the crest of a steep hill, my daughter pauses, scents the wind, raises her arms overhead, a brave silhouette against a massive foreign sky. I trudge onward, count my breaths, in, out, forehead and cheeks red with exertion, blood pumping near the surface. My feet and toes are numb. I am hungry, sticky and tired, and I have never felt better.

"It's paradise," she says, reaching for the horizon, emotion at the wavery corners of her mouth, in her eyes, aqua against golden brown.

Another valley lies below us, fields fanning out for miles. In the distance, a curl of blue rimmed with white, an approaching promise, the sea.

"It is," I say.

And it is. Despite the way my legs wobble when I sit then struggle to stand, despite the biting flies that leave a trail of angry red welts on her tanned arms and the mysterious hives that blossom on my right shin, hot to the touch, itchy as the devil.

In the hotel that night we photograph our swollen feet, my ravaged leg.

"I bet these leave scars," I say, and I almost hope they do, a fleshy merit badge.

The hotel staff, two slender, dark-haired girls who look enough alike to be sisters, serve us in the deserted dining room, confused when we explain, as we have each evening, that my daughter is vegan.

"No fish?" they ask.

"No," we say, shaking our heads.

"No milk? No cheese? No meat?"

"No, *nada de animal*."

"*Nada de animal*," they repeat, each syllable weighted.

We hear them in the kitchen, repeating it to the cook. We picture their expressions. Perhaps there are hand gestures. They return with platters of salad and cut melon, the pickled white asparagus and salty fried peppers we are served wherever we go, potatoes sizzling with olive oil. They set each dish down with a somber flourish then hover, waiting.

I smile and extend my hands, palms open.

"*Gracias a todos para acommodarnos*," I say, which, inside my head, translated into English—*thank you all for being so accommodating*—sounds too formal, yet these are the words that spring from my mouth. "Our thanks to everyone, to the cook . . ." I say, waving an inclusive hand towards the kitchen.

My daughter's eyes are wide. She knees me under the table.

The younger of the two servers smiles. Her cheeks dimple and flush. Both girls nod, satisfied I imagine, as they leave us to our meal.

When they are gone, my daughter exhales. She sputters. Her belly quakes with laughter.

"Oh my God, Mom," she says, hunched forward, lowering her voice. "*Gracias a todos*?" She spreads her hands, mimicking my grandiosity.

And we laugh as we stab chunks of melon, the palest green, sweet as honey, at that precise moment of ripe perfection. And I do feel a bit like royalty, returned to Spain, words I haven't uttered in years falling from my mouth, the white tablecloth covered with *nada de animal*, a feast for two weary pilgrims. We are far from home, my last child and I, yet in this moment all that matters is close at hand.

"*Gracias a todos*," I say, embracing the room, owning my inept gratitude.

In the morning we will walk another 15 miles. For now, we laugh and we eat.

Dorothy Rice is the author of *Gray Is the New Black: A Memoir of Self-Acceptance* (Otis Books, June 2019) and *The Reluctant Artist*, an art book/memoir (Shanti Arts, 2015).

After raising five children and retiring from a career managing environmental protection programs, Rice earned an MFA in Creative Writing at 60 from UC Riverside's low-residency program. She now works for 916 Ink, a youth literacy nonprofit, and co-directs Stories on Stage Sacramento, a literary performance series.

For more information visit dorothyriceauthor.com.

THE TRAIN TO TSINGTAO

CAROLYN RADMANOVICH

Little did I know what problems I would encounter because of my decision to take my enormous suitcase to China. We took the trip in 1995 to attend our son's wedding. Much thought and organization went into deciding what to pack, and what suitcases to bring. I decided I needed my big suitcase, whereas my husband, Richard, was content with a medium-sized one. My sister, Sharron, accompanied us. Instead of packing one suitcase for her shoes only, and one for her clothes, like she usually does, she cut back and also brought one big suitcase.

After a few days of sightseeing in Beijing and walking the Great Wall, we grabbed our bags and went to the Beijing Train Station at midnight. My son, Dan, ordered us to stay in a tight group. We followed his serpentine trail, leading us past families sleeping on newspapers and groups of people milling around the train station. He warned us to watch for pickpockets and to keep our suitcases close.

After Dan bought our tickets, he told me we were lucky he had been able to book the last soft sleeper room for my sister and me. I imagined a small private bedroom with twin beds and plenty of room for our suitcases. The rest of our party, Richard, Dan, his fiancée Anne, would get soft seats, similar to reclining airline seats.

Dan accompanied me and my sister to our separate train car, carried our suitcases up the stairs, and left to join the rest of his group.

A 5-foot-tall conductress dressed in her snappy dark blue blazer and matching hat followed us into the train car. Her eyes grew enormous when she looked at our gargantuan-sized suitcases. She put her hands on her hips and hollered at us in Chinese. We had no idea what she was saying, so we continued toward our room.

She dashed in front of us, blocking our way, and kept shouting and pointing at our suitcases. If I could take a guess at what she said, it was something like: "You aren't taking those aboard my train, not while I'm alive and breathing. Those are elephantine, colossal, humongous, and mammoth. They are titanic, and it'll take down the entire car." Of course, I'm sure that's a loose translation.

As I listened to her drone on and on, I visualized her kicking us off the train. The train would hurtle away, leaving us holding our large suitcases, tears in our eyes. Our family wouldn't know where we were. There we would be, not speaking a word of Chinese, except hello, thank you, and goodbye. I suppose our next plan of attack would be to sink onto a train station bench, if there wasn't someone sleeping on it, or sit on the newspaper-strewn floor and have a good cry.

My stomach performed Olympic flips as I pondered what we would do. If we hailed a cab, we wouldn't be able to tell the driver where we wanted to go, plus we had no hotel reservations in this busy city. Perhaps the cabby would feel sorry for us and take us home with him.

When the conductress was about to grab our suitcases and throw them off the train, a middle-aged Chinese man approached us. "May I help you ladies?" he asked in perfect English.

Sharron and I both said, "Yes, please." Relief filled my belly, and my jitters subsided.

The man spoke to the conductress in Chinese. She continued yelling as she watched this five-foot two man take the suitcases to our room and fling them onto the top bunks. He must have been a weight-lifter when he was young.

I gushed, "Thank you so much. You were so kind to help us."

When I had recovered my composure, I looked around. Our deluxe bunkroom had four bunks. We were bunking with two strange men, or should I say one, since the man who rescued us was no longer a stranger. *Oh*

Lord, what would my mother say about our sleeping arrangements?

We introduced ourselves to our savior, and he bowed. "Welcome to our bunk room. My name is Mr. Wang. I am a salesman, and I have often traveled to San Francisco to do business. Why are you traveling in China?"

"We're attending my son's wedding just outside Tsingtao. After the wedding, they plan on moving to California."

"California is a beautiful place." A smile crinkled Mr. Wang's face, and his eyes brightened. "The ocean is quite lovely there. I loved the streetcars in San Francisco."

The train was warming up when Dan stepped into our room. "I came to check on you. Looks as if you got settled all right."

I told him how we were almost tossed off the train by the fierce conductress, but Mr. Wang intervened and hauled our luggage up to our bunks. He looked at the top bunks, then at Mr. Wang. "I doubt if I could have lugged those things up there. Mr. Wang, you're a strong man. Thank you for helping my mother and aunt." The two men exchanged smiles and handshakes.

I took Dan's arm. "Please ask everyone to come visit us first thing in the morning, and we'll eat our breakfast together." He nodded, then left our train car for his adjoining one.

My sister and I climbed the ladder up to our bunks, laid on our sheets and put our feet on our burdensome suitcases. We fell asleep to the roaring of the engine and clicking of the tracks.

Early the next morning, I searched for the bathroom. At the end of the hall, I found a huge barrel containing hot water. Mr. Wang was there ahead of me and he opened the nozzle and poured hot water into his glass canning jar which contained dried tea leaves. He screwed on the lid and went back to our bunk room. He was set with his morning beverage, but I knew there was no chance I'd find coffee.

Next to the container of hot water was a door. Inside, I found the facilities, which consisted of a single hole in the floor, a small metal sink, but no paper towels or toilet paper. I squatted as best I could. Before I left, I looked into the hole and saw the tracks speeding by. Anything that fell into this hole would dump onto the tracks. No sewage to store. Nice and efficient.

When I got back to the room, Richard, Dan and Anne were visiting Sharron. Thank goodness our two roommates had departed, so we could monopolize the one small table in our room. We emptied out our stash of water bottles, candy, cookies and granola bars for our instant breakfast feast. As we ate, we watched the lush farmland and brick farmhouses whiz by through our window.

Richard climbed onto the top bunk and gazed at the ceiling as if he were in a trance.

"Did you have any breakfast?" I asked.

Richard scrunched his eyes. "No, and I don't intend to, nor will I drink any water. That way, I won't have to use the bathroom."

"But it's been at least eight hours since we left the train station," Sharron said. "You might have to wait two or three more hours."

He mumbled something unintelligible.

Sharron grimaced. "I think you must be an alien. A human can't go without drinking water or using a bathroom for a day."

"No problem," he said as he laid unmoving on the bed, his feet on top of the giant suitcase.

"Suit yourself," Sharron said and finished her cookie.

When the train made the Tsingtao Station, Dan and Richard helped us lower our immense suitcases from the top bunk, rolled them down the hallway, and dropped them one step at a time to the station floor. Dan led our group to Anne's relative's waiting cars that drove us to our hotel.

When we arrived, Richard rushed for the bathroom. While I waited for him to return, I opened my giant suitcase and removed the items I would need for the wedding: my shoes, the dress I was to wear to the wedding, the dress for the pre-wedding party, a bottle of wine, boxes of chocolates, camera, hairdryer, makeup, and the wedding presents. The suitcase looked almost empty.

The red firecracker wedding, which was unforgettable, took place the next day. Anne wore a red dress to the pre-wedding dinner, a traditional Western white wedding dress at the wedding, and a red, mandarin collar dress for the post-wedding party. She looked elegant and jubilant. My son wore a gray suit he bought the night before at a store that had opened after-hours just for him. He looked very sophisticated and so happy.

The tradition before the wedding was for the close family to meet at 9 AM. The couple would sit on the "happiness bed" and each ate 2 soft-boiled eggs and 2 peanuts, which guaranteed their fertility. After that ritual, we followed as Dan carried Anne from the house to the waiting car. Dozens of neighbors stood watching and cheering.

When we arrived at the wedding, there was a wooden stand which held exploding, fat, six-inch firecrackers. We made our way through the smoke into the karaoke restaurant. The mayor of the town was on the stage and motioned for the couple to join him. Television cameras zoomed in on the couple. The mayor spoke a few words, and then asked the couple to tell their "love story," which consisted of meeting on the campus of the University of Beijing where they were students. Then the mayor insisted Richard say a few words into the microphone. The televised wedding must have been one of the big events of the year, with a headline something like, "Local Girl Marries Rich Westerner." If they only knew. After the speeches, we danced to karaoke music, and I danced with Richard and then my son's new father-in-law, who was quite graceful on the dance floor.

When the wedding was over, the families went to the restaurant upstairs, and several of the mayor's Communist cohorts joined us in a gourmet dinner and in toasting the new couple. To our surprise, the mayor sang part of a Chinese opera, and everyone clapped.

Richard and Sharron decided it would be polite to do several Chinese toasts, and each time raised their glasses saying, "*ganbei.*" We considered the meaning of the word to be similar to "cheers." We noticed the Chinese politicians were drinking a lot, but thought nothing of it, until Dan told us later it meant "bottoms up."

When the platters arrived carrying an entire fish, head and tail included, Anne's aunt stood and insisted the two eldest of our group eat the fish eyes. Richard told Sharron she better eat the eye or it would be an insult. She cringed and swallowed the eye. I watched as Anne's father pretended to eat the eye, but spit it into his napkin.

After dinner we retired to our hotel room, and Anne's relatives joined us. I took the See's candies, wine, and nuts which I had removed from my suitcase earlier and placed them on the coffee table for our guests. Since we didn't speak Chinese, Anne or Dan translated our attempts at conversation. Richard taught the men to put their fist in the air and say, "Go Bears," for his favorite UC Berkeley football team, and they taught him to say it in Chinese.

Dan and Anne said it was time to go to their room, and Richard needed to accompany them to barricade the door. Anne's relatives were supposed to make a play at stealing the bride back.

Richard honored this tradition by standing in front of the door with his arms across his chest, and a frown on his face. Anne's brother and brothers-in-law pretended to harass and threaten Richard by running toward him. Richard would put his arms out and say, "Go away."

We all had a good laugh, then the families got past Richard and slipped into the bedroom to put candy on their bed. As many people as possible sat on the bed with Dan and Anne, laughing, talking, and eating candy. Eventually, we let the newlyweds have their peace.

Flying home, I vowed I would never take a huge suitcase on a trip again. After all I had been through, it wasn't worth it . . . except maybe for a wedding.

Fascinated by the wild west, Carolyn Radmanovich earned a history degree from San Jose State University. After a near drowning incident on the Russian River, she felt compelled to write her first book, *The Shape-Shifter's Wife*, about an anthropologist who time travels to the California gold rush of 1848 and meets a handsome Frenchman. *The Shape-Shifter's Wife* won the 2018 Independent Book Awards for Visionary Fiction. The sequel, *The Gypsy's Warning,* is Carolyn's current project. Her short stories, "Tex's Dream" and "Frenchie – A Love Story," were included in the NCPA anthologies, *Birds of a Feather* and *More Birds of a Feather.* She won second place for the 2019 Memoir Contest for her short story, "Prod," with The California Writers Club, and participates in a Critique Group with the EGWA. Carolyn lives in Lincoln, California with her husband and cat, Tex. Check out her website at www.CarolynRadmanovich.com.

IT HELPS TO SEE WHERE YOU'RE GOING

NORMA JEAN THORNTON

B y mutual agreement, I was driving the motorhome as we excitedly chatted about our trip to the annual November deer hunt at Lake of the Ozarks, plotting out the order we'd do everything this year while in Missouri.

Getting there a week or so early this time, we planned to first visit my mom's family in Arcola and Greenfield, do a bit of research at the Dade County Library in Arcola, stop by some of my dad's family in Willard, then on to Springfield for more genealogy.

After that first year we went on the Missouri hunt, we were constantly amazed our families and friends were so close to one another in the same state, and that we had to pass by all the towns for each on the way to and from the Lake.

Hubby's long-time high school buddy was to drive over from Rolla, they would go to Bass Pro while I was in the Springfield Library for the day, then we'd stop by to visit him and his wife on our way home from the hunt.

Once we got to the Lake and checked in, we'd rent a car and visit Hubby's aunt and uncle in Iberia, less than an hour away, and since we'd still be getting there early, we'd have time for a quick hour-and-a-half trip to the State Archives in Jefferson City the next day, for more genealogy research, and a stop at the Golden Corral for dinner.

But first, just at dusk this particular night, we were headed for a KOA Campground in Williams, Arizona, when suddenly the temperature took a major dive, huge flakes of snow abruptly started pelting like rain from the sky, and conditions immediately went into an almost total white-out, causing all the cars ahead of us, none of which had tire chains, to start spinning-out, slipping and sliding, losing traction on the icy roads going up the hill. Hubby, being the better navigator, always checked the KOA book when it was close to stopping-time for the night, to find the nearest Campground, so we knew we were getting close.

Following behind a big-rig was working out okay, but although he was pretty-much clearing the snow off the road for us, we were concerned about being behind him in this sudden snow, going up hills, of which several more might be ahead of us, but we knew it wasn't far to the campground.

Instead of going to the KOA on the righthand side as we had previously discussed, Hubby barely saw a snow-covered KOA sign pointing to the left, and thought it was the one we were supposed to go to, so quickly told me to get in the other lane and make a turn to the left, headed towards the Grand Canyon. It's a wonder he even saw the sign through the 4"-6" of snow by this time that covered all but parts of it. Fortunately, there were no cars in the fast-lane behind us, so I could make the sudden move.

Not only was the snow worse heading down into the canyon, but so was that road! It was a little two-laner, with not enough room to turn our 36' motorhome around anywhere, and I was anxious to get off it, ASAP!

I noticed a clear driveway that led to a gas station on the side of the hill to our left, but it was a sharp turn up a steep incline, and we barely made it. At least we got turned around and headed back to where we had turned off I-40 to go to the KOA we had initially planned on.

Looking at the map while sitting at the gas station, Hubby had found our original destination was at the next exit, which was only a mile or so further east on I-40. The KOA ahead of us on this horrible road was several miles, taking us deeper into the canyon, where snow was piling up fairly quickly. I visualized being stuck in that canyon for the rest of our trip, because there's no way we'd have been able to come out of there if it continued to snow like this. That road was already covered with snow.

By this time, it was dark, so VERY carefully, I pulled back onto I-40 and made our way to the far-right lane where we needed to be, in anticipation of turning off at the next exit. I made the turn at the exit, but instead of a road, we were immediately faced with nothing but a sea of 8"-10" of pure white, unadulterated snow covering the entire area as far as the eye could see; both sides and directly ahead. It was made even more eerie by shadows on the snow from the slowly-moving glow of our headlights.

For some distance, there was no sign of a road, but fortunately, there were soon cars parked along both sides in front of us, on this snowy path, so I very, very carefully, drove straight down the middle, hopefully straddling the white line, if there was one, by using those parked snow-capped cars as guides for where to go. Thankfully there was zero traffic, so I could follow the snow-covered car-dotted pathway most of the way towards the campground, which seemed to be 1,000 miles off the highway. Because we were barely moving, it felt like it took days to even get close.

Hubby saw an airport sign and freaked, thinking we had gone the wrong way, or too far, and suddenly yelled for me to *"Turn!...NOW!"*...I just stopped and looked at him, because I couldn't see anything and was quite sure neither could he, but he again insisted *"Turn around now!!! NOW!!!"*

Gingerly, and very hesitantly, with a grimace of anticipation, my shoulders hunched up to my ears, and tightly gripping the steering wheel with both hands, causing a very tense neck and back, I v.e.r.y .s.l.o.w.l.y inched forward, attempting to turn....WHUMP!!! The right front tire suddenly sunk down for what seemed like at least a foot, and we were stuck! Hubby kept saying to back up, but it wouldn't budge...the dual tires just dug in deeper. I finally refused to try anything else.

We had electricity, a cell phone (thank God for cell phones!), a TV, stove, refrigerator, food, a generator, heat, bathroom...even our two male cats, Demon and Beelzebub...plus everything else we'd have if we were in a house. The difference was, we were tilted on an angle, stuck in a hole sunk up to the bottom of the motorhome.

We sat parallel to, with a perfect view from our dining room window, the freeway we had fortunately just gotten off only a quarter of a mile away.

Jumping out in the snow that reached the bottom of the door, Hubby quickly checked to see "whatever", while I turned off the ignition, turned on the TV, got a pot of coffee going, and called AAA for assistance.

While on hold, we could hear the screeches and bangs, and see the lights shining in the air, of the several-vehicle pileup on the freeway, as one after another was crumpled by slipping, sliding cars, speeding, skidding trucks, and spinning-out big rigs. They were coming from behind and going in opposite directions, on both sides of the icy, yet spotty-snow-covered road and had nowhere else to go except to crash into each other.

Ironically, we were seeing and hearing the same thing on the local TV, as breaking news was reporting the storm being the worst they had experienced in years. It hit so suddenly and fiercely it took *everyone* off-guard. There were well-over 50 vehicles in that mess we had luckily just missed being involved in, and I swear we heard and saw each one as it occurred, on TV and real-time-stereo.

AAA told us it was chaotic out there, and would be several hours before they could get to us; we told them not to worry, we were fine where we were, and to take their time. We could see there were obviously others in more need of their service than we were. Even though we were stuck, it was nice, warm and comfy inside, a lot better than being on that freeway getting crashed into from all sides. We were all in one piece, basically enjoying ourselves at this point.

I was fixing dinner when the TV National news broke with weather, which meant everyone back home could see it, and knew we should be in the vicinity. We called one of the kids to let them know where we were, we were ok, and to pass it on to the rest, since we didn't want to stay that long on the phone. We were in the middle of dinner when the owner of the home we were stuck in front of came zipping down his snow-covered driveway in a dune buggy, carrying a thermos of hot coffee.

We invited him in for dessert, and our own coffee. He was a hunter and stayed for quite a while, totally intrigued by the motorhome with all its amenities. We chatted about a plethora of things, mostly hunting and the motorhome. He was still there when the tow truck arrived hours later. By the time they finally got us pulled out, there was a huge mudhole in their front lawn! I had hoped we were in a gully in front of his property, but no such luck.

We finally made it to KOA, less than a mile up the road from where we had been stuck, hooked up to electricity, and went to bed.

The following morning the sun was shining brightly, the snow had stopped and was melting, so we fixed breakfast, loved on the cats, grateful Apache, our little female kitty, was no longer with us, and watched TV as we waited around awhile to let the roads clear. On the way out, we went by the place where we had gotten stuck the night before. What a mess! Hubby tried to give the owner money to cover the damage that night, but he refused, so we sent him a check when we got home three weeks later with a bunch of wrapped deer meat in the freezer, lots of genealogy research, and a great story to tell.

Speaking of Apache and getting stuck in the snow, reminded me of that one year we had her with us on one of those annual Missouri-hunts. If she had been along on this one, no telling what else would have happened! So, on to part 2, since she was mentioned above with our two fur-boys.

Part 2: Apache, Ditzy-Kitty

Apache-Kitty wore a calico coat of multi-colored orange, white and black with a touch of light brown tossed in for effect. Her face, a patchwork of color with a bright spot of orange on one side and a vivid shiny square of black on the other - each surrounding its own eye - made her look exotic.

Her first New Years' Eve day, tiny five-month-old

Apache bit through an electric cord from a lamp, and we found her lying on the floor, breathing shallowly with dark marks on her little lips. A quick trip to the ER-vet became top priority over preparations for the party we were headed for that evening.

The emergency vet said everything was in working order, but it wasn't; her brain had been short-circuited, and Apache wound up a ditzy-kitty. Her sweet-loving ways soon became over-bearing and annoying. If she found us sitting, she'd immediately plop down in our lap, and cling like a leech; we could barely pry her off in order to get up. Those claws clung tightly!

She'd be walking, sitting or sleeping, and for no apparent reason, suddenly jump up and take off running, sometimes in circles. Apache began to sit on the window-sill and stare outside without moving, for hours.

Gorgeous dark long-haired spitfire tabby Beelzebub, one of her two feline-brothers, started chasing her whenever she was away from the window, and became her task-master, constantly sending Apache back to her window perch! More mellow Demon, our handsome dark long-haired male tabby, just watched from afar.

One November, we took all three cats on a combined extended vacation-genealogy-and-three-state-hunting trip in the motorhome. The boys were fine; they always stayed right where they were supposed to, but not Apache.

Salt Lake City was the first leg of that hunt, visiting another high school friend of Hubby's. We left the cats in the motorhome in the driveway, and Apache disappeared the whole time we were there. The morning we were leaving for the second hunt, in Montana, she crawled out from under the hood of the warm motorhome, while we were cutting and wrapping the deer in their garage. Those friends were prepared to keep her, if she hadn't shown up before we left. Fortunately for them, the smell of that raw deer meat as we were going back and forth, carrying packaged deer to put in the freezer in the motorhome, was too enticing for her to resist.

Since we left the heater on in there for the cats, most

likely the heat seeping through the thin walls gently helped warm wherever she was staying. Apache would curl up in any unlikely place inside the motorhome she could find. In Wyoming, she jumped on the stove while the gas burners were on, lightly singeing the pads on her feet. I doubt she even knew it, but we did; burning cat fur smells horrible! Thankfully, there were no lasting effects.

She was good in Montana, but hid in the bottom cupboards in South Dakota while we visited Mt. Rushmore. We were so close to Minnesota, we took a jog up there just to visit another state, and spent an extremely cold night at a motel in a little town, took the cats to our room and headed for the spa. After we went to bed, Demon began howling, and frantically scratching at the door! He wouldn't stop, no matter what we did. We opened the door and looked outside the room in case of a fire. Nothing, yet he still howled.

Demon eventually shut up and we went to sleep. We got up in the morning to find a cat missing, and deduced someone tried to get into the room while we were in the spa. Apache apparently ran out the door when it opened, and probably saved us from being ripped-off.

Was she at the door the night before, and Demon tried to tell us? We searched the hotel, then went outside, where we saw a trail of tiny kitty-tootsie-prints on top of the foot of fresh snow. I knocked on doors for two-blocks, looking for her, but she was nowhere to be found.

In the hopes Apache would somehow appear, *we told the hotel clerk we were going for gas and breakfast, and would be back in two hours,* in case she showed up. (Remember this. It's important to the story.) We stopped for gas, and, blinking back tears, I relayed what had happened to the female attendant who asked what was wrong.

She asked if we'd called the police, or the local radio station?

No, why should we!? We soon found out.

The clerk called the radio station and gave them all our information.

Less than two hours later we were back at the hotel; Apache had been found under another bed where the maid had sucked the cat's tail up in the vacuum cleaner. They said they tried to call us at home IN CALIFORNIA, but since we didn't answer (!?), they left a message. (Before cell phones.) Then they called the police! On a cat!

We called the *Chief of Police, who had picked Apache up from the hotel.* He said he'd taken her to the vet, who was now closed for lunch, but would re-open in an hour, and we could pick her up then. Raving about what a great kitty she was, he said she just sat in the front seat with him, like she belonged there. We tried to talk him into keeping her and he was almost willing, except the department had big dogs that didn't like cats.

Reclaiming Apache, we headed to Missouri to finish the final, third leg of our combo-visiting-genealogy-annual-hunting trip, where she promptly disappeared in the motorhome twice more, two days each, while we visited more family and friends. Because we weren't sure if she had somehow gotten out the door when we had company, we were afraid to leave, so we lost four days of visiting other family members, prior to the hunt.

During the three days Hubby hunted Missouri, I had time to search every inch of the motorhome for the cats' hiding places. I found three; two were not an issue, but the third could have been fatal! Apache had squeezed, until out of sight, inside the fairly long, and large, vent area from the dashboard-heater close to the floor on the passenger side. Had she gone further inside, she could have wound up in the engine area, or clear outside...while we were moving!

That might have been what she did in Utah, and actually used it as an entrance/ exit, but we weren't going to find out! I packed it full of washrags and dishtowels, so she couldn't get in there again.

On the way home, somewhere between Utah and Nevada, we saw what looked like Apache's face in the clouds, took a video with the camcorder, and forgot about it (until years later, while watching that video for the first time. There she was! Apache's face with almost the exact markings, superimposed in the clouds!)

Once home, I called my cousin who lived close by, and told her what happened. She said next time to leave Apache with them. We did, and they wound up so attached to her, they asked if they could keep her. Yes!

* * *

We got home to California six-weeks later to the *phone message from Minnesota:* they had "*...found your cat; Chief of Police took her...can pick her up at the police station.*"

Her baby sister called her Nonie, her great-granddaughter calls her GumGum.

Norma Jean Thornton, AKA Noniedoodles, a multiple County and State Fair award-winning baker, candy-maker and art-doodler, plus award-winning writing granny from Rio Linda, California, attempts to create her doodle-art, and dabbles with her writings at the computer, with unwanted help from her feisty cats.

lulu.com/spotlight/nonie
lulu.com/spotlight/TheGrannysWritings
noniedoodles@yahoo.com

*"Love Never Dies" in Harlequin's Inspirational Anthology, A Kiss Under the Mistletoe

*Nonie's Big Bottom Girls' Rio Linda Cookbooks (4)

*Nonie's "Stuff" Cookbooks (Candy &…Stuff; Cookies…&…Stuff; Soups &…Stuff)

*Nosie Rosie's Diaries: (True cat diaries, written by The Granny & The Windy)

(Years 1 & 2 of 15-years so far)

*Nonie's Cat Anthologies (Fun, not-so-fun, sometimes crazy short cat stories) 2 Volumes

*Nonie's Wet Kitty Kisses Anthologies (Mostly humorous Short Stories) 2 Volumes

*noniedoodles color books (artwork by Nonie's original doodles) Several Volumes

*Doodles the Dorky Dragon, in the Dorky Land of Noniedoodles

BAJA PEPSI

JUDITH VAUGHAN

1972

"We're running out of time," Jim said. We were
negotiating the plans for our first vacation
since our honeymoon in 1968. Throughout his
youth, Jim drove the Colorado mountain four-wheel-drive
roads to explore the ghost towns near Cripple Creek. For
years, he had wanted to drive down the Baja Peninsula's
four-wheel-drive road, the site of the Baja 1000 road race

Construction of a paved road had already reached
Mulege, a small resort town near the halfway point from La
Paz in the south. Mex 1 would be extended north to
Ensenada beginning in a few months. This year, 1972,
was his last chance, our last chance to follow the primitive
road south.

Jim was a law clerk in Albuquerque. I was a neurology
resident at the University of New Mexico Medical Center.
We had two precious weeks of time off. It didn't seem
enough for Jim's plan. I agreed to take this vacation under
two conditions: I didn't want to spend all of the time in the
Bronco and our daughter Betsy, who spent my workdays
with a babysitter, had to be a part of it. After a tumultuous
birth, I would not lose two weeks of her life.

Jim patiently persuaded me. My parents loved Mexico.
They could fly to Mulege with Betsy and share several
days amid our two weeks of vacation. He showed me the
itinerary. We, two young professionals, stretched to our
limits, would drive through the first night to cross the border
by the second morning. He'd divided the route into
segments, starting near Ensenada where the paved road
ended. We had only to travel a hundred miles a day along
the route. We would camp wherever we stopped in the wild

Sonoran Desert.

A hundred miles a day. Even if we averaged twenty-five miles as hour, we'd have plenty of time to camp and rest, and admire the desert flora and fauna. A piece of cake. Just four driving hours per day.

"We won't drive home on the unpaved road," he added. His fingers traced the road south. "After our stay at Mulege, we'll send your folks back to Guaymas with Betsy, and then drive south on the paved road to La Paz. We'll have a mini-cruise on the overnight ferry to Mazatlan, and then drive home on Mexico's mainland to Albuquerque through the port of entry at Douglas, Arizona."

A cruise. My eyes went misty. *On the Sea of Cortez.*

The day of departure, the driveway at our house on Guadalupe Court in Albuquerque's North Valley was strewn with gear. Our trip budget, such as it was, was shot. Every night Jim came home with stuff for the trip. Gas cans had to be new for safety. I wouldn't argue with that. A new compact tent, a large food chest steaming from dry ice ready for frozen meat competed for space with mechanics tools. A shelf projected from the back bumper for the red rectangular gas cans, spare tires, and Coleman fuel. Betsy's stroller would be tied on top.

For Betsy, my twelve-month-old baby, I packed disposable diapers, a new product. I took non-fat dry milk, easy to mix with boiled water for safety.

Our neighbor, Carol, a toddler clinging to her legs and a baby in her arms, found it hard to be supportive. "Mexico...the water...outlaws...*nonfat* milk? Betsy might get sick. Disposable diapers? Worthless!"

Maybe this plan was way overcomplicated. Betsy *could* get sick. Diarrhea in Mexico? Ugh! I remembered my reluctance before I agreed. Was it too late to back out? I had now consigned my most precious possession to the trip. The baby who had had such a perilous start in our lives.

The breech presentation last year was followed by a long silence in the delivery room while a blueish baby gathered the strength to breathe. When we her got her home, the phone was ringing. I was ordered to take her back to the hospital. She required treatment for jaundice. How had I missed her yellow skin? I knew jaundice. It was a common cause of cerebral palsy, a condition my specialty, neurology, treated. I was devastated, crushed with fear that she might have developmental delay or motor impairment. Amidst my tears, it seemed impossible to accept reassurance that the condition was now curable with light therapy.

My parents arrived and after Jim deflected their smart remarks and advice about the loaded Bronco, I strapped Betsy into their Lincoln Continental for the drive south to Guaymas, Mexico where they'd take the flight to Mulege.

Jim and I waved good-bye, squeezed into the Bronco and began our own drive.

Hypnotized by the hours of highway, well after dark, beyond the border crossing at Calexico, we found a cove along the Colorado River delta and set up camp, the desert already free of habitation. As Jim cooked the thawing sirloin, I heard a splash near the stone ledge bordering the water. The flashlight found a sea lion poking its head up, unconcerned by my presence. I felt joy banish my fatigue, a reward for finding the courage to take the trip.

I didn't get my wish for short car days. It took all day to go a hundred miles—every day. The road was the tracks of the last vehicle that had gone by, winding up, through and down the desert arroyos in a general southward direction, at first along the west coast, later more inland. Coyotes howled at our campsites. Pristine starlight washed the sky and picked out reflections from the eyes of unnamed wildlife. We passed few vehicles travelling in either direction.

We marveled at unique vegetation. Our favorite, the boojum tree, had a cactus-like trunk with leaves stuck on with almost no intervening branch. The trunks pointed ten feet skyward and arched like a crooked finger. We'd stop just to smile.

Jim and I savored celebratory bottles of Dos Equis in the cool, open air cantina. Just minutes before, five days after we left our home in Albuquerque, we had completed the drive down the old Baja California four-wheel-drive road from Ensenada south through the desert peninsula to the Mexican oasis town of Mulege.

A bray of laughter shattered the late morning calm of the near-empty bar. "I worried about that poor baby..." said the ruddy American, dressed in safari style khaki at the next table, "...when I saw the stroller tied to the back of your vehicle. I was right behind you as that four-wheeler bounced over the washboards."

We stared at the guy, our mouths and eyes wide open. He had to be talking to us.

I remembered a blue Scout behind us for the last few hours. Must have been this jerk, passing too fast and kicking up dust. Then stopping a mile later at a roadside hovel, Baja's version of a convenience store, where dodgy gas was sold from a fifty-five-gallon barrel and the spray-painted wall advertised Fanta soda and *llantas*, well-used tires.

"That Jeep was so dusty, I couldn't tell the paint color." He shook his head. "Loaded to the springs, was it?"

Jim's face reddened as he nursed his *cerveza*. "It's a Ford Bronco, not a Jeep..."

The guy took another swig. "Dirt brown, maybe?"

"The paint color...is...Hot Ginger Metallic," said Jim through his teeth.

The boor turned to me.

"How's the baby?" He put his hands on the bar. Drops of his spittle missed my face. He met my gaze like he really cared, but he never offered his hand.

I smiled. "Our baby has been spared." A shiver grabbed me. She was at the moment in a small plane over the Gulf of California, somewhere west of Guaymas.

"Thank God." His body slumped in feigned relief.

"She arrives today by plane in the loving arms of her grandparents," I said, wondering why I was giving the man the time of day, letting him besmirch my precious vacation.

I checked my watch. Jim stood up. "And we've been missing her."

"Yes," I said, "and we have to unload our Ginger Metallic Bronco before we pick her up at the airstrip."

Jim bought a six-pack to go. I mouthed, "Get me out of here."

My husband took my hand as we climbed into our vehicle. "I should have punched that guy in the nose," he said.

Jim drove our dusty overloaded Bronco from the cantina to the one-story hotel near the town plaza in Mulege. We unloaded our camping gear to clear the back seat, hosed off the stroller and wiped it down, before we headed to the airstrip.

Weakness flowed over me. Mother deplaned with Betsy in her arms from an impossibly small aircraft. My dad followed, carrying her newly invented baby bucket seat. How could I have thought it would keep her safe over the vast Gulf of California?

Jim was radiant with no hint of my relief. "It's your daddy!" Betsy did not leap into the outstretched arms of either parent. She looked at my father, then squirmed around to check her grandmother's face. Would it be okay to go with these filthy people she'd never seen, who were wearing ball caps?

That afternoon we went south along an endless choice of white sand beaches. Gentle waves broke a hundred feet from the shore. I sat in the shallow water with Betsy, and kept busy pulling sand and shells from her mouth. Granddaddy Beil read in a chair on the beach and Grandmother beach-combed for small shells. Jim messed with the Bronco.

We skipped the beach the next morning to allow Jim and my dad to fish from a chartered boat in Concepcion Bay a few miles south of town. Mother and I wheeled Betsy to the town market in the stroller along one of Mulege's few paved streets.

Bright cotton blouses and dresses, hand embroidered, caught our eye. The smallest was yellow, a sleeveless smock.

As Mother counted the pesos to buy it for her

granddaughter, the craftswoman picked up Betsy, my blue-eyed blonde, and stroked her head. "*La rubia, tan ojos azules,*" she said.

Betsy reached for the dress, comfortable in the arms of the Mexican woman clothed in the same lively colors.

"*¿Como se llama?*" she said.

"Betsy," I answered.

The woman cocked her head. "*¿Que?*"

"Her name. It's Betsy," said Mother, folding the dress into a paper bag stenciled with the market logo.

The woman still looked puzzled, but not enough to interrupt her play with the child.

"*La niña,*" I said. "*Se llama Betsy.*"

"*By ... Buh.*" Her face brightened. She tipped an imaginary soda bottle to her lips. "*¡Ah...Pepsi!*"

I smiled. "*Si, Pepsi.*"

The next day, as we drove the Bronco, overflowing with family, from the beach through town we heard, "*Pepsi, Pepsi*" from the front porches and the market. Jim slowed the Bronco, and I held Betsy up to give a finger-wave.

Too soon, Jim and I said good-bye to my parents and hugged our baby as they took her back to the plane. The smooth, newly paved highway to La Paz flew by. Its many hotels and restaurants contrasted the quiet of Mulege. How right Jim was to want this experience now.

We arrived at the dock of the ferry to mainland Mazatlan with enough money for the pricey vehicle ticket and the very reasonable passenger fare. After checking out the wooden deck chairs in the second-class lounge, we booked a *cabina* with bunk beds for the overnight voyage across the Sea of Cortez, the southern end of the Gulf of California. To top off our mini-cruise, we splurged for a local fresh fish dinner in the ferry's restaurant.

After a stunning sunset, we settled into the cozy bunks of the cabina. Too early the next morning, a demanding bell announced our imminent arrival in Mazatlan. As we offloaded, the ferry official measured the Bronco. "The cargo step," he said, "with the fuel cans and the buggy required a surcharge." Jim's hands spanned his hips. He frowned as he listened to the unexpected added fare. Uh-oh, the budget. We had a long drive through Mexico back to Albuquerque.

As we drove north along Mexico's west coast, we counted our pesos at every fuel stop.

"Look, Jim," I said, pointing out cheap oranges at a market nearby. "We can eat oranges all the way home, buy no more food, and use the rest of the money for gas."

"They're good," said Jim, juice dripping onto his tee-shirt, peelings fluttering to the ground. "That might just get us home. Our credit card was denied at the last Pemex. The cash is all we've got."

Jim held my hand as the vehicle rattled on. "I'm so glad we did this...and Betsy, well she's Pepsi now," he said.

"She was our little ambassador." I squeezed his hand back. "The children, the mothers—we were comfortable with each other. Before long, a blonde child won't be a novelty in Baja. It was a beautiful connection."

At the border crossing in Douglas, Arizona, our Bronco was stuffed, baby stroller now attached to the rear with the grimy gas cans We were dressed in the most informal of clothes—cut-off jeans, Mexican sandals. We were none too clean, and I'm pretty sure some carefully budgeted beer had passed our lips. The Border Patrol pulled us over to the parking spot for further inspection. It was 1972. They were looking for marijuana. The officer peered into the Bronco and moved dirty clothes and sand toys here and there. He wrinkled his nose at the smell of the beach and us. He rattled the stroller and checked its attached shopping pocket.

He stepped back. "Unload your vehicle," he ordered Jim.

Jim's eyes widened and his mouth dropped. He stammered. I watched my husband mull this over. Would he tell him he was a clerk in the Federal District Court? That the Bronco was loaded like a three-dimensional wooden puzzle?

Jim looked at the ground and the agent looked at his

blocky digital watch. 4:00.

It would take time, maybe an hour to unload. Jim might never get the reload right. What would we leave behind? A seven-hour drive to Albuquerque remained. We were exhausted.

And—we were soon to be hungry.

"Oh, okay," said the officer, throwing up his hands. "I'll pass you on the drug inspection, but I can't waive the agricultural. I have to confiscate the oranges."

Judy Vaughan grew up in Northern New Mexico engrossed in her father's horse breeding hobby. She left the family ranch for boarding school in Colorado, then attended Carleton College and the University of New Mexico School of Medicine. She has composed stories since childhood, and began to hone the craft of writing after forty years practicing neurology. She lives in Elk Grove, California, and writes with Elk Grove Writers and Artists.

Works in progress include her New Mexico memoir, *Strawberry Roan.* Her stories have placed in short story contests and have been published in NCPA Anthologies. Judy is a member of the California Writers Club, Northern California Publishers and Authors (NCPA), and the New Mexico Book Association.

Contact her at jfbvaughan@comcast.net.

THE EUROPEAN TOURAMA 1987

BARBARA YOUNG

"Hi. Y'all travelers at the hospital?"

"Yeah, I'm Angie. I speak *'y'all'* too, from Georgia; been here two weeks, in cardiac ICU."

"I'm Heather, just started in neonatal ICU. Buffalo's my home, where folks are still shoveling snow. But I'm in California, sitting by the pool in February."

"Carrie, from Waco, Texas. I start my contract on Monday in neuro ICU. May I join y'all?"

"Yeah, sun feels good," Heather invited.

"Texas was my first contract," Angie related. "Speaking of buffalo, I didn't see any. But instead of locking the IV, they buffalo-cap it."

Wrinkling her face at the odd use of the name of her hometown, Heather blurted, "That sounds nasty—like nothing I'd want near my IV. What's a buffalo cap?"

"The little rubber plug you put on the hub of the IV cannula to maintain it after discontinuing an infusion; it may be bigger is all. Ya know, everything's big in Texas!" Carrie's cheeky explanation showed pride in the colloquial medical slang and spirit of her home-state.

"How can it be the same job, but different method, perspective, or terminology at each hospital?" Angie asked.

Each agreed, saying aloud in good humor, "You say potayto, I say potahto."

"And y'all's favorite part of this contract?" Carrie asked.

"Days off!" Angie and Heather said nearly in unison.

"On mine, I take a road trip," added Heather.

Angie agreed, then challenged, "I want to go someplace different."

"Upstate New York—*camp-nursing—that's* different,"

Heather wagered.

"Travel-nursing's a splendid way to see America, but what about Europe? Let's go together after this contract—for fun," Angie invited the others into her vision.

"We're all done in three months," Carrie realized. "I need to make the money first."

Heather chimed in, "That'll be easy, there's plenty of overtime in the units."

"And we'll keep each other motivated," Angie confirmed.

"I'm in!"

"Me too!"

"We're going!"

The serendipitous travel-nurse-amigas shared a dream. They worked diligently to pre-pay their European Tourama vacation—twelve countries in forty days.

* * *

The full moon rose as the flight from San Francisco, via "Santa's Shortcut", took them over the uninhabited tundra of the arctic.

When they arrived in London, it was the next afternoon, local time. They settled in their room.

As travelers, it was second-nature to find their way around unfamiliar places and learn the customs. A few steps from the hotel, their adventure began.

"Toxi fir meh ladies?" a driver offered.

"Naow fenk ye, sir," Carrie attempted Londonese with her Texas drawl. "Weyr in Landon, 'tsgrate innit meh ameegaz?"

"Cabbies are friendly here. Back home, you must flag them down," Heather mused.

Looking up from the visitor's guide, Heather pointed to a brick wall with *To the Trains* stenciled in yellow letters, outlined in black. "The Tube! A subway like in New York."

"Let's walk. We're nurses and haven't been on our feet for hours," Carrie playfully suggested.

"Look, a Hard Rock Cafe. I'd like a salad after the styro-food served on the plane," Angie proposed.

"Always ready to eat," said Carrie.

"I'm feeling like I walked from California. Food and a bed are what I need," Heather admitted.

*   *   *

Mid-morning the next day Angie was still asleep. Carrie and Heather had left earlier to walk the city.

A helpful intruder, cleaning the room, was startled to find a person in the messy heap of bed linen.

"An upset stomach kept me awake all night," Angie shared with the petite lady.

"I'll wahm the kettl' then. Cuppa tay, that'll settl' yu," the self-appointed caregiver decided.

Sitting bedside, she told stories of her mum in a soothing bird-song voice, while Angie sipped the chamomile tea.

Angie relaxed. The words faded as she drifted into sleep.

The next morning, Angie awoke feeling energetic, no longer jet-lagged.

"Bland diet for me for a while," she announced, inspecting the basket of pastries, fruit, and cheeses delivered to their room. "Yum, Captain's Wafers! These buttery crackers were my favorite as a kid."

The other two amigas alerted when food became the topic.

"Europe's gonna be one huge smorgasbord," Carrie predicted as she reached for the pastries.

Heather raised her left hand to her forehead, "I see in my future lots of chocolate." She snapped out of the vision and explained, "Yesterday I began a new addictive relationship with malted milk balls. Much creamier than back home. 'Nothing pleases like Maltesers!' What's in that jar?"

"Nutella," Carrie read from the label, "a sweet hazelnut cocoa spread from Italy."

Heather squealed, "Chocolate for breakfast!"

*   *   *

During their several-day stay in London, the amigas bumped often into the language and customs of Britain.

"So a 'rubber' is an eraser," Heather mused.

"For use *after* you make a mistake rather than to prevent one," Angie giggled.

"And you don't wear a boot—it's the trunk of a car. I guess there aren't any cowboys here," reasoned Carrie.

Heather added, "And Brits consider Americans daft because we think we speak English and they say we speak American."

"Potayto, potahto," the three amigas mocked.

The morning arrived for them to join the bus tour. During the ride from London, Heather and Carrie chatted like magpies about the food they hoped to encounter. From the window, Angie snapped photos with her manual Nikon.

"The license plates are different," Angie thought aloud. *Long and skinny, generic black and white.*

As she looked, Carrie blurted, "It feels weird driving on the wrong side of the road!"

Gertrude, the tour guide, explained, "In Britain they drive in miles per hour on the left side of the road. On the mainland of Western Europe, we drive in kilometers per hour on the right."

* * *

It was breezy in the seaside parking lot where they waited to meet the ferry to Belgium. Whitecaps stood out against the murky water of the English Channel.

Wrapping in her sweater, Angie turned to watch the departing bus wind along the road toward a split in the cliffs, where it disappeared.

"These cliffs are *white!*"

Heather and Carrie spun around to see.

In three-part harmony, they giggled and sang, "There'll be bluebirds over the white cliffs of Dover."

The song echoed in their heads as they boarded, continuing until the hypnotizing hum of the engines took effect. Slouching and shifting for comfort in their seats, each prepared for an oncoming nap.

Angie watched the shipboard activities with bleary, sleep-filled eyes, uncertain whether she wanted to join, or doze.

A woman seated near the center of the lounge caught her attention. The woman's busy fingers danced in fanciful yet orchestrated movements, with colored string appearing from the lap of her white-aproned, solid blue dress.

Angie approached with respect and curiosity. A flow of melodic words burst from the woman. She explained in Flemish what Angie could see—she was tatting lace doilies. Newfound friends, they communicated using dramatic motions and mimes, smiles and laughter. As the ferry entered the Ostend Harbor, Angie traded American dollars for two delicate doilies, one pink, the other green.

*   *   *

The following morning, Carrie mumbled through a mouthful of thick pastry and cream, "I'm in Belgium eating a real Belgian waffle."

Later, the amigas walked to the historic Grand Palace, a medieval town-square with ornate seventeenth-century buildings.

"A street vendor selling Godiva chocolate!" Heather delighted.

Wandering the spindly cobbled alleys, the city's chocolatiers, bistros, galleries, and music engaged the amigas for the rest of the day.

Against the dim light of dusk the subdued warm glow from the street lamps highlighted their own whimsical metal scrolling, and the route toward the hotel.

Angie paused for a few photos. "Such a fairy-tale place. It seems, any minute Cinderella's horse-drawn carriage might scurry by, then we happen upon..."

"A statue of a cherub-boy peeing in a fountain!" Carrie snorted. "The Manneken Pis." She summarized the legend revealed on a plaque, "A monument of a father's love for his son who went missing. He vowed to create a statue of the boy doing whatever he was doing when found."

*   *   *

Thereafter, the bus left most every morning for another wondrous adventure or country.

"Look at the haystacks!"

Throughout Belgium and the Netherlands, Angie photographed the manicured green fields dotted with unique sculptures of the harvest.

In Amsterdam, Heather suggested, "Let's bike-tour today."

"I need the exercise," Carried agreed. "My clothes are getting snug, and I've only dined in three countries."

Colorful, funky houseboats lined the canals.

"California or bust." Heather read the hand-painted sign on the cluttered deck of one boat. "Take a photo, Angie."

Mounting her bike after visiting the Anne Frank Museum, Carrie reflected aloud, "More than two years in hiding..."

"Not able to go outside—unimaginable," Angie paraphrased Anne's words, "The best remedy is to go outside with nature, only then does one feel that all is as it should be."

Next the bus drove through the northern part of West Germany and up into Denmark. Then onto a ferry providing a short-cut return across the Baltic Sea.

While chatting about the highlights of Scandinavia, Carrie asked, "What do you think the mermaid in Copenhagen was thinking about?"

"She's sad," Heather said.

"Realizing she can never go back. To have her dream of becoming human, things had to change. Though no longer a mermaid *in* the sea, she'll always be *of* the sea." Angie philosophized. "This dream-come-true vacation may change us too."

"I'm changed already—I never want to work again," said Heather.

Carrie mused, "I already need larger clothes. Those

Danish pastries were amazing, but the fluffy light French ones are still to come—*after* the pasta in Italy."

Heather offered, "I have a chocolate-stuffed Danish, wanna share?"

* * *

In West Germany, the Autobahn was famed for having no speed limit. But the border patrol in East Germany restricted the bus full of Westerners to 20 kph less than the maximum posted speed on the motorway. There was no leeway on this because behind the Iron Curtain the authorities decide how the rules apply and enforce them rigorously.

Next, Aric, the driver, shared that they were assigned only two relief stops along the 170-mile route to Berlin. The first stop was a dilapidated structure with no facilities. The group voted to "hold on" until the next place.

"Ladies first, eh blokes?" suggested Aric as they disembarked at the second stop. "The building looks altogether, but boarded windows? I dunno."

"It's locked," an Aussie Tourama-mate confirmed. "Well, mates, we're about to get real familiar."

Heather remarked, "No bushes!"

Already finished squatting, Angie stood strategically and said, "A hidden benefit of a travel skirt—privacy. I'll block y'all from view."

Once under way, Heather read from the Europe AAA travel guide and broke the sleepy quiet on the bus.

"*Bagno*, that's Italian for toilet."

"It was easy in Britain, ya just asked politely for the *privy* or casually for the *loo*," Carrie commented.

"This says a *pissoir* is a public toilet in France, but it's a *toilette* in a restaurant or home."

Though the word "toilet" was common throughout Europe, the amigas found using a toilet was a unique cultural experience. Some bathrooms were "coed"; others were open-air, as in behind a wall along the street. The least technical required the most skill: a hole in the concrete floor at the Yugoslavia–Italy border. How to flush was also a challenge—using a pedal, lever, pump, or chain. Another matter was the quality of paper provided for the job.

No competition for Charmin, Angie thought as she unraveled a sheet of tree-bark-like paper from the dispenser in East Berlin.

Its abrasive quality matched the bristly experience of scrutiny at Checkpoint Charlie, the crumbling buildings and rubble that remained from WWII bombings, and the stiff, impersonal affect of the tour guide in the gray city behind the Wall.

* * *

Next, the Tourama brought them safely back into West Germany.

"Nuremberg is a quaint town, but it feels heavy here," Heather sensed.

"Its tragic history still looms in the landmarks and lore," Carrie validated.

After the Nazi occupation, it became the place where the Allies held trials for war crimes, and crimes against peace and humanity.

Back on the bus, Angie found a brown paper bag in her seat.

Maggie, a Tourama-mate on holiday from New Zealand, said, "I hope you enjoy. It's from the local market."

"How thoughtful!" said Angie, admiring the deep green peas and vivid orange carrots spiraled together inside the jar.

At tour-group meals Tourama-mates bid for Angie's meat portion in trade for potatoes, bread, and the seldom served vegetables or salad.

In the next moment, she opened the jar, drank the liquid and fingered the delightful bits into her mouth. She felt her body absorb the vitamins and nutrition.

"This makes Nuremberg delicious to remember."

* * *

Onward to Munich where the amigas walked from their hotel through Marienplatz square, as the musical two-level clock in the New Town Hall tower bellowed five chimes.

"We're in time to watch the *Glockenspiel.*" Heather looked at the others for consensus.

"Okay, it's only a few blocks from here to the *Hofbräuhaus.* I'm looking forward to some Bavarian brew," Carrie added.

Mimicking the life-sized figures in the festive performance within the clock tower, Angie twirled and enticed the other two to indulge her. "Weeee."

A short while later, they joined the merriment at the famous brewery pub—swaying with the crowd, lifting their liter mugs of beer, and howling in a blend of every language present, "One, two, drink up—cheers!"

"We'll share the beef and dumpling stew," Carrie requested from the waitress dressed in traditional Bavarian dirndl. "Then the cream cheese strudel and vanilla sauce."

"And German chocolate cake for me," added Heather.

Angie spoke up, "I'll have the vegetable pie. A scoop of vanilla ice cream with fruit sauce for dessert please."

The next day the bus toured through Austria. Heather and Carrie, haunted by the effects of too much Bavarian beer and German chocolate truffles, dozed all day. Their only experience of Austria was a continued restful sleep in a cozy motel in Graz, site of Liebenau, the former Nazi forced-labor camp.

As the bus journeyed the following morning into Yugoslavia to visit the caverns in Ljubljana, Angie recounted to her amigas the *Sound of Music* sights she had visited around Salzburg

"And I stood in the actual gazebo!"

* * *

Time quickened amidst the aliveness, merriment, and

wonder of Italy.

"*Mangia!*" Carrie encouraged.

The amigas feasted on insalata, antipasto, minestrone, primavera, and gelato across the country.

Gliding through the waterways, the gondolier's rich voice surrounded them as part of the history, tradition, and romance of Venice.

"Make a wish!" Heather prompted as they tossed coins into Trevi Fountain in Rome.

In Florence, Carrie ogled at the David statue. "Quite the anatomy specimen."

"Right, Carrie, nice arm veins," Heather teased.

In Switzerland, on the slow aerial-gondola to the ice cave on Mount Titlis, the amigas shared a creamy milk-chocolate bar from the shop in Lucerne. They floated over the pastured valley below. A musical blend of bleats and moos, with tinkles and clinks from collar-bells wafted upward.

Later, while meandering north through the countryside of France, Gertrude led the oom-pah chicken song and arm-flapping dance in the bus aisle.

A three-day Parisian spree followed the extravagant Palace of Versailles. The intricate city-view from Sacré-Cœur Basilica atop the highest point, and the opulence and sizzle of the Moulin Rouge were exciting contrasts to the slower pace ahead of exploring the lush, friendly, mystical Isle of Ireland on their own.

"It might be late tonight when we find a B&B," Carrie said as she wrapped the remaining pastries for the journey.

"*Au revoir Arc de Triomphe*, *Notre-Dame*, and *Louvre*," Angie reflected, gazing at the Seine.

"Thank you, Paris, City of Love. I found mine in wine!" added Heather.

* * *

Awakening the next morning in a farmhouse, Angie said, "Ah, fresh air!"

"Fresh-baked bread," Carrie corrected. "Perfect call to

breakfast."

At the table, Heather complimented the bread, "Sweet and light."

Angie added, "Fresh eggs—golden yolks!"

Host-mom poured cornflakes into each bowl and drizzled on milk from a white pitcher.

Each grinned, concealing what she was thinking:

Really, cornflakes? With all this homegrown, homemade food?

I've never liked cornflakes.

Just eat 'em, they're worse when soggy.

Crunch...Crunch...Crunch...

"So creamy-sweet—without sugar!" Carrie, delighted.

"Or chocolate," said Heather, amazed.

"It's the fresh milk," Angie said. "PO-TAH-TO!"

The amigas continued their left-lane tour in the Ring of Kerry—pubs, cows crossing the road, castle-ruins, vistas of a thousand shades of green, and the lightest misty-rains. They stayed in Cahir Castle, a beach house in Youghal, and kissed the Blarney stone before sleeping in their own beds in California.

* * *

Back by the pool, Heather said, "I joined a gym, but I still have chocolate left."

"This is my new, larger swimsuit," Carrie confided. "Working extra will help me slim for Hawaii in three months."

"My photos turned out great. I made a scrapbook," Angie shared. "But I recall most fondly the Royal British guard laughing at Carrie's antics, and the Italian man in Tivoli running across the street to give me flowers."

Heather added, "The store owner in Limerick who'd rather live in Orlando to be by Disney World and the guy who let me go up the Eiffel Tower even though I lost my ticket."

"Don't forget the friendly dogs that led our walk through the French countryside," Carrie smiled.

"People are the same. We like to relate, share, help,

dream, create, give, and receive. That isn't in the photos, it's in our hearts," Angie relayed in a sentimental tone.

Carrie teased, "Yeah, but one'll say potayto and another potahto."

Barbara Young enjoys travel, almost always on the road less traveled. She hopes her stories in this year's NCPA Anthologies stir wanderlust, warm hearts, open opportunities and build bridges. In 2018 she published an empowerment book for nurses, *The Heart that Rocks Health Care,* and in 2019 was included in both volumes of NCPA's Anthologies, *Birds of a Feather* and *More Birds of a Feather*. In addition, Barbara also creates poetry, children's stories, plus gift and coffee table books that feature her photography.

Learn more at www.byoungbooks.com

TRAVELING WITH MY BEST FRIEND IN SEOUL, KOREA

CHRISTINE "CHRISSI" L. VILLA

Do you and your best friend have a list of things you want to do together? My best friend, Diane, and I had one dream at the top of our bucket list—to travel together in one of the Asian countries. It seemed like a remote possibility since we lived oceans apart (I, in the US and she, in the Philippines), but in February 2019, our dream came to fruition when we bought two tickets for a four-day vacation to Seoul, Korea. I was going to the Philippines for a book event, and to visit my family, so we managed to book a flight departing from Manila.

As you read along, I'm not just going to try to amuse you with travel stories. Consumed by wanderlust, I not only learned so much about what to see and do in Seoul, Korea, particularly in Hongdae, but also picked up some travel guides, specifically on how to travel with a friend. So, buckle up and brace yourself for some practical tips and tricks which you might not be aware of, or have taken for granted.

Lesson #1 Do research before your trip.

Don't expect your friend to do the research for both of you. Before your flight, do not just Google the top fun things to do at your vacation destination, but first and foremost, find out how to reach your guesthouse or hotel from the airport. I thought I already had enough information from the internet as to which train to take and how many stops until we got there. I found out later, the information I got from the guesthouse's website, where we were supposed to stay, was not accurate. So always double check! Also, it seemed easy to know where to get our ride from the airport. I knew we just had to look for the airport train terminal, but finding it was difficult in a huge airport filled with non-English speaking Koreans. Have a map available for each place you are going, including where to get your first ride.

Lesson #2 It pays to be friendly and cautious at the same time.

On our fourth attempt, we found an English-speaking person to tell us how to purchase our train tickets. The next challenge was in making sure we took the right train. How do we know which one to take? Fortunately, an older, gregarious man in his 70s said "hello" to me and waved at us to follow him. He asked if I was a Filipino and said he would be happy to help. He was with a woman about his age so we thought we were safe. True enough, they were our guardian angels! He regaled us with his trips in the Philippines and before they got off the train, they reminded us to get off on the 16th stop. We believed him because he made more sense than the inaccurate directions we got online.

Lesson #3 You need more than comfortable shoes.

A pair of comfortable shoes is one of the must-haves for any traveler, especially when you are expecting long distance walking. Aside from knowing what to wear and what to pack for a short overseas trip, luggage should be carefully chosen. Ditch the old non-360 swivel luggage you used in your past vacations! I couldn't believe I was still plodding along with my two pieces of ancient luggage. These turned out impractical while we were on our trek to finding the airport train terminal, for getting on and off the train, and for slugging through the seemingly mile underground route to the exit escalator leading to the street of our guesthouse.

Lesson #4 Get a recommendation on where to stay.

One of the reasons we picked Seoul, Korea was because my niece highly recommended a guesthouse in Hongdae where she frequently visited. "Full of fun activities" and "youthful vibrance" were the words that attracted my attention. Owned by a sweet Korean woman and located in the heart of the bustling food and shopping areas, our fifth-floor room, with a spectacular view of the city, had a clean, wide bathroom, fully-equipped kitchen, eating area, and three-queen size beds. Our room was comfortably warm while it was freezing cold outside in the winter. We didn't even need the electric blanket the owner provided us.

Lesson #5 Anywhere you go, keep the guesthouse address with you.

On our first night, after a KFC dinner across from our guesthouse, we bravely ventured into the cool, hip neighborhood teeming with cafés, bars, restaurants, and shopping stalls. Since Hongdae is close to Hongik University, the streets are packed with strolling millennials in their black winter jackets.

The bright neon lights and delicious smell of street food propelled us farther and farther from our guesthouse until we were caught in the middle of a crowd of screaming fans, elbowing their way to see a celebrity who happened to stop by. I was in utter panic because I get claustrophobic in such crowds.

It didn't help when Diane pulled at me to weave our way into the crowd rather than skirt our way around it. I yanked my arm back and insisted we go the opposite way. To make a long story short, we realized we didn't know how to get back to the guesthouse. All that time, I was counting on her for directions.

Learn from my experience. Never depend on your traveling buddy to know where you are! I found out, that in all her Asian trips, she had always relied on her instincts for location. I am the complete opposite. I'm a traveler who always has an address written somewhere, a map in my hand, and a phone or iPad to navigate with. Thank God, I had the business card of Hongdae Guesthouse in my pocket, so we were able to get back before we were totally worn out.

Lesson #6 Know how to adjust with your travelling buddy.

I had known my best friend for almost 20 years, but we had never travelled together, had lived in two different countries for a long time, and had perhaps, grown older in different ways. I found out she needs to go to sleep at the same time, which is midnight or later, regardless of what she will be doing the next day. I am a night owl myself, but when I'm traveling and completely exhausted, I can go to sleep earlier as long as everything is so quiet you can actually hear a pin drop and not even a sliver of light is visible in the room. She prefers some light in the room so we agreed on leaving the bathroom light on, but I had to lie in my bed, tossing and turning with my eye mask on and ear plugs in until she was done rummaging through her luggage. Every night, there was always this swishing sound coming from plastic bags. I made a mental note to buy her some travel kits so she could noiselessly store her personal things.

The whole trip, we didn't totally adjust to each other's idiosyncrasies, so our differences escalated to one little argument. It was the ultimate test to whether we were perfect traveling partners. Whether we were or not was out of the question. We had to make the choice right then and there to make the most out of our vacation.

Lesson #7 Find out what you both like to do together.

On our first day, we both decided to explore the Trickeye Museum and the Ice Museum. Before we got there, we strolled narrow streets with stalls selling yummy-looking street food and eye-popping specialty stores. I went crazy going in and out of affordable jewelry, skin care product, and cell phone case stores. Diane followed me all around, but most of the time, left me in one of the stores to feast her eyes on some street food. She is more of a food lover than I am so she prodded me to experiment on some Korean specialties. I was leery at first because of sanitation concerns, but after a few minutes of inspection, I was convinced Korean street food was not only clean but very tasty as well. We enjoyed devouring sugar-coated strawberry sticks, egg buns, and *takoyaki* (octopus balls), the last of which became my favorite snack during our vacation.

The visit to Trickeye Museum was an out-of-this-world adventure where two-dimensional wall paintings are combined with AR (augmented reality) effect via their own Trickeye Camera app. We rode unicorns, swam between sharks, crawled on walls, levitated, shrank to teacup size. There were endless fun possibilities! The Ice Museum was also an unforgettable experience as we huddled together at -4C temperature and enjoyed the variety of ice sculptures.

Since we didn't visit Hongdae during March-November, we missed witnessing the city's most creative artists at work in the Hongdae Free Market. We only had the busker's street performers at night to entertain us. We enjoyed the K-pop dancers the most even if we were not die-hard K-pop lovers. I even went to the second floor of a nearby café to get a bird's eye view and picture of a group of guys dancing.

Lesson #8 Allow serendipity to intervene.

To my delight, when I drew the curtains open on our third day in Hongdae, I saw snow flurries for the first time. Although I lived close to Lake Tahoe and other snow-covered locations, I had never experienced snowfall. I was like a child eager to go out and play. Despite our eagerness to start our day, I could tell that deep-down Diane was worried about being outside in extreme cold. She had lived all her life in the Philippines and never experienced winter. Armed with layers of clothing and a beanie hat, she was still in desperate need of warmer gloves when we went outside. We were supposed to take a two-hour train ride out of the city to explore new scenic spots, but when we couldn't find the uniformed tourist guides in the streets to instruct us where to go, and she was shivering in the cold, we decided to stay close to home.

Though we stayed within our neighborhood, we found more things to do. While walking, as light snow fell on our beanie hats, we discovered The Gyeongui Line Forest Trail Park. There was nothing much to see since the ground was covered with snow and it was too early for street performances, but we took pictures of the view and some selfies. Before long, we came upon the Line Book Street, a unique urban "reading park" composed of train-shaped bookstores. On our way back to the guesthouse, our snow-soaked shoes led us to an unfamiliar back street where a charming Korean restaurant strongly appealed to our grumbling stomachs. It was cozy eatery! We feasted on a hearty lunch of warm noodle soup and Korean beef.

That night, we decided to do our own separate exploration of the city so we could spend time to do our own thing. We both were already familiar with the area so were confident enough to come back safely to the guesthouse, alone. I visited the Kakao Friends store to drool over adorable characters and asked some tourists to take pictures of me inside the store. I scoured the laneways for a cute cell phone case and ended up buying a violet one, with a bear glued to the edge. There were tons of skin care products for sale everywhere I turned so I was easily enticed to buy facial masks, lotions, and moisturizers from Etude and The Seam. I also bought some reasonably priced fashion earrings and ear cuffs. The last item on my shopping list was to find myself some contact lenses. It was incredible how cheap and varied the choices were. I had fun frolicking around with so many young people unwinding on a Friday night.

Surprisingly, Diane and I bumped into each other in front of one of the food carts. It was so hilarious when she told me she had gotten lost and couldn't find her way back to the main streets. We agreed to continue our shopping separately and to be back in our room by 10 pm. When we got home, we showed each other all our gorgeous finds. She found some coasters and refrigerator magnets at Daiso, a Japanese-owned store that sells products from $1-$2.

Lesson #9 Contact a friend who knows the place.

Fortunately, Diane's friend and schoolmate, Dolly, who lived for so many years close to Hongdae was kind enough to tour us around. Our first stop was the majestic Gyeongbokgung Palace, meaning "the greatly blessed palace," the oldest Grand Palace built during the Joseon Dynasty. Not only did we have the chance to witness the changing of the Royal Guard-ceremony, we were also able to take pictures in front of a serene pond, away from the madding crowd of tourists.

It was a lovely sight to see groups of young girls and couples romping around in their rented *hanbok*. I wanted to see myself in one of those Korean traditional attires and have pictures taken of me, but Diane wasn't keen on doing the same thing. We also didn't want to waste time when we had more places to see, such as the National Palace Museum of Korea, which housed relics from the palaces of Joseon Dynasty. After that, Dolly treated us to lunch. Each of us hungrily gobbled down a huge bowl of *Gomtang* (bone soup). It was the perfect soup to soothe our chilled bones.

Our next trip was to Insadong, where we did more souvenir shopping. While Diane and Dolly were on a hunt for traditional Korean snacks, I came across a refrigerator magnet with two Korean girls, that looked like Diane and me. It was something I couldn't live without!

Then, we took a bus and headed to view the N Seoul Tower. Even though it was a long and steep walk towards the top of the hill, it was worth it. Beside the N Seoul Tower, we saw countless locks of all colors hanging around the viewing deck and bridge. It was a romantic sight as dusk fell, and lovers fastened love locks on the fences to symbolize each other's everlasting love.

Our last stop was Myeongdong Shopping Street. Since this shopping area had bigger department stores, cosmetic shops, and fashion boutiques and our feet were tired from walking, we just sampled more street food. Even now, I can still remember the delicious taste of taiyaki (a cake with red bean paste filling).

At 6 pm, we hailed a cab and headed back to the guesthouse to say our "goodbyes" and "thank yous" to Dolly. I thought the night was over, but after a short rest in our room, we were lured back to the streets of Hongdae to do our last-minute shopping.

The night was still young in Hongdae! I bought a souvenir key chain doll and some more jewelry accessories for gifts. In one of the stationery stores, I found a couple of cute paper dolls. It reminded me so much of my childhood, I bought them for myself.

By 11 pm, Diane and I laid on our backs on one bed with our legs stretched up on the wall, our feet displaying the cute Korean socks we had been eying on the stalls, and finally bought. We took one final shot, a close-up picture of our socks covering our tired little feet.

We shopped till we dropped, but we were both happy and contented. And, like I said at the beginning, I learned a lot.

Lesson #10 It's never too late to apply what you've learned.

Earlier that night when we came home from Myeongdong, we went to see the owner of the guesthouse. We hugged and thanked her for her hospitality and made sure we had a cab the next morning to escort us back to the airport. We swore we were not going to go through the same transportation ordeal again!

Christine "Chrissi" L. Villa founded *Purple Cotton Candy Arts*, a small business that started out exploring her creativity in the field of arts and crafts and later expanded into publishing her children's picture books. She has published eleven children's book titles since 2014, two of which won first place in the Northern California Publishers and Authors (NCPA) Book Award Competitions in 2018 and 2019.

Recently, *Purple Cotton Candy Arts* started offering publishing services to other aspiring children's authors and publishers.

As a gifted poet, Villa's haiku and tanka have appeared in numerous online and print journals worldwide, she's garnered several awards, and has published her first poetry book, *The Bluebird's Cry*.

Chrissi is founding editor of *Frameless Sky*, the first haiku and tanka journal, available on DVD, and *Velvet Dusk Publishing*.

She is also the new editor of Ribbons, the official publication of Tanka Society of America.

SAILING TO PERU

LINDA VILLATORE

We cruised to Peru as the weather grew cold in California. My husband and I prefer the sea to being on land.

In a stiff November wind and on a small yacht, I've sailed the San Juan Islands. With the keel leaning over 30 degrees, the sea churning like a washing machine in the portholes below, I happily prepared hot meals. The year my dear father died I took a dive trip through the Similan Islands marine preserve off the coast of Thailand. As I grieved, I was healed by passing lazy days in crystal water, astounded by the iridescent life forms below. Fortified by the sea and the exquisitely spiced food prepared by our modest Thai chef, I was renewed.

Since childhood, and currently on my sixth passport, I've sought to become an invisible observer in nature. I will sit silently in comfort finding the wildest natural places I may ever reach. It pleases me to be there, as after a few moments the local creatures ignore me. I eavesdrop on them as they go on about their own lives. I hear the buzz of insects, the popping open of dry seed pods, and the hiss of the wind high across the pines. So, in this way, I find solace and an amiable kinship with the fellow creatures on our beautiful Earth.

As seniors now, we chose a more modest blend of luxury and exploration: a mid-sized cruise ship on a 22-day journey to Peru and back, roundtrip from San Diego.

Like a magic carpet ride, sailing on a large ship is effortless. For exercise, I'll walk around the decks, swim in the ship's pool, and explore the ocean along the way, by snorkeling whenever I can. To avoid overeating, we sample small tastings from the daily menu, finding appetizers to sample, and then create our daily menu.

Once selected, our meals can be delivered to the stateroom on self-heated trays. Each item is presented on fine china. Silverware is rolled in crisp linen. One of my favorite dishes is the Forest Mushroom Soup; a smooth blend of truffles, crème fraiche, and scallion churro.

Seated on the balcony, my husband and I enjoy our meal and the pleasure of the ocean view. In this way, tidbits of nightly flavors may be enjoyed without having to dress for dinner, or sit indoors and forsake the happiness of sunsets.

At night, while our ship courses through a glassy sea, I look up to greet the unfamiliar stars in the southern hemisphere. On the balcony, the breeze is so clean it has no smell. With the company of sea, air and sky, I am not lonely. I ease into a clear landscape of thought. The only sound is a soft swish as the ship glides through the water. Looking down, I see the great hull softly push waves to the side where they dissolve into an enigmatic sea.

As we had come by ship, we first saw the coastal sand dunes of Peru. This coastline is a harsh, bone-dry desert running the entire length of the country. The snow-capped Andes are but a shadowy blur beyond the grey dunes along the coast. A cold ocean current running north from Antarctica drives the wind and weather up along the continent here. That frigid upwelling keeps the fisheries rich, prevents rain, and forms constant grey clouds like a lid. It is an unforgiving land. Yet the Moche Empire thrived here long before the Inca or Spanish arrived to enslave them.

The morning we arrived in the northern coastal city of Trujillo, I planned to visit the ancient palace of Huaca de la Luna, the Shrine of the Moon. Located south of the current city of Trujillo, this region was home to the ancient Moche people. Their civilization had lasted almost one thousand years, from about 100 CE to 800 CE. Early in the morning, under level grey clouds, our Moche guide Maria was taking us to the temple of the moon

Maria was a direct descendant of the Moche, she told us. Her people were some of the original people to settle in

Peru. They were the first to farm, establish culture, and build temples to worship their many gods. The moon and sun were only two of their gods.

She was voluptuous but tiny, almost a woman in miniature, with dense black hair she pulled back with a hand loomed cotton band. She had driven all night from the mountains to meet our small tour group on time. Once joining us, she graciously led us for the next eight hours. For her it was a 24-hour day. The work meant that much to her.

Her people had worshiped the moon here in the temple. Men only; the women were forbidden to enter. To punish captives, or appease the weather and other gods, ritual sacrifices were carried out as evidenced by the fearsome images of the creator god Ayapec who was also called the *Decapitation God*.

People use what they have. The temple was made of sand with a few timbers here and there to support a low roof. The site was opened to tourists in 2011. Much of it is still buried in the sand. The friezes are nightmarish and surprisingly well-preserved. The original temple walls were hidden behind plain adobe walls, apparently added much later. Perhaps this may have been to preserve the original site from the invading Inca, whom the Moche fought ferociously for many years as they tried to avoid domination. Maria proudly explained that her people were fierce warriors, the last tribal culture to be assimilated into the Inca Empire. Only fifty years later, the Spanish conquered the Inca, enslaving the Moche people again.

Maria was tired. She worried this would show. Almost imperceptibly, she pushed herself as though it was a day-long ceremony, to engage each tourist's question, deliver her scripted lectures at each site, and gracefully field all incoming questions. She hid her fatigue like a master of camouflage in the jungle. She disappeared herself into the work. In each moment, we saw only the guide. While she clung to her branch, she achieved her private standard of hospitality as a Moche of Peru.

Each marauding group had enslaved her people. They

renamed the settlements, imposed a new god, and regulated the conquered innocents with a dismissive cruelty. With cookie-cutter precision the Spanish uniformly stamped down city squares throughout their domain. These squares always contained a church, government buildings and the cross. I was beginning to see history through Maria's eyes.

Maria resented the Spanish more than the Inca; all of them usurpers to her past and her future. Her anger's memory was strong. The stories of injustice and brutality had been retold with succeeding generations for 400 years. They were vivid. In her role as a guide, Maria hated showing us the colonial town square in Trujillo, but dutifully did her job.

This was where she dropped her disguise and showed herself to me.

There were hundreds of people in the square that day. It was noon. As we stepped down from the bus, a warm sun was melting the cool fog. I could make out a misty, veiled and moving blue sky above. In the center of the well-groomed square, surrounded by old Spanish buildings, stood a huge complex statue comprised of four large male figures, each facing away in four directions.

We slowed our pace together and walked side by side. My head tilted inward towards hers. I asked her to repeat, when I didn't fathom. After 400 hundred years of fighting, she told me, the Moche finally routed the Spanish, and her people were free. She lingered with me alone, as she described the strength of their rebellion. Each figure's contorted face and body captured one moment in their rise from pitiful slavery. When slavery is so clearly remembered, freedom is exalted.

Maybe it was because I listened carefully, for as I took this all in, we were approached by a man who hosted a local radio show. Perhaps seeing me leaning in to hear Maria, he asked permission to interview me, and politely asked for my impressions of Trujillo.

On the spot, I forced out a cliché I'm not proud of. I praised the beauty of the place, the people's industry and their sense of pride. It felt inadequate.

Of Italian ancestry, I know a great deal of the history of my own people, as well as my personal family heritage. But unlike Maria, my ancestors were the conquerors. The story is quite different from my perspective.

Is it too much to say that I was able to sail for pleasure in my later years, built on the accumulated wealth of generations, drawn down the centuries from the conquering ancient Romans? Is it true, that the unseen confidence of this cultural treasure benefits us, and underlies any individual striving and talent we may add?

Could it be that the lush landscapes and warm, accessible seas of Italy enriched the creative imagination of my people, more than the grey desert and cold skies did Maria's people? How much do landscape and weather effect human imagining? And how do we balance the uneven nature of human history, as we strive for a cohesive human future?

 Award-winning educator with over 30 years' experience in custom web based and classroom instructional design and training, Linda is an author of several acclaimed activity-based courses, has been published in multi-media, staffing and production magazines; and an award-winning dramatic actress and stage director, as well as a documentary television producer with high-level expertise in communication and media production.- She now specializes in executive coaching, strategic planning, facilitation, and project management.

Linda has taught in universities, community colleges, and the public and private sector for clients in over 40 industries. Awarded by the U. S. Army for educational counseling, she was nominated for the California *Governor's Award for Environmental Economic Leadership, Who's Who* in *American Colleges and Universities,* and played competition chess with Bobbie Fischer at the age of seven.

Education and certifications
Master of Fine Arts in Directing
BA Liberal Studies

Multimedia Project Management Certification Bay Area Video Coalition (BAVC)

http://lindavillatore.com/

THE ROAD AHEAD

SANDRA SIMMER

I tried to appear confident, but my head was pounding and my hands were damp with sweat. After months of feeling like butterflies were swirling in my stomach, the day had finally arrived. It was time for me to leave behind my extended family, my friends, and the place I had always called home. I was moving to Los Angeles, California—the land of "swimming pools and movie stars."

I had spent the previous night at one last marathon slumber party with my junior high girlfriends. We had overdosed on junk food and soda pop, then bunny hopped down my street at midnight. I was the center of attention as everyone speculated about my new life. My friends thought I was going on a glamourous adventure, but they had never been out of Montezuma County, Colorado.

I had been to L.A. a few years earlier when my older brother, Tom, graduated college. Visiting Disneyland and seeing the ocean for the first time had been exciting. However, I also remembered the countless miles of freeways that snaked through a sea of houses so close together they almost touched. The buildings flowed in every direction into the horizon, getting lost in the mist of yellow smog blanketing the L.A. basin. I was not sure I could live or even breathe in such a place.

My father lost his job that spring of 1969 and could not find work in our small town. When my parents left for California on Tom's promise of employment, I stayed behind with relatives to finish the eighth grade. Now it was summer and my mother, Ruth, had come to retrieve me. She had driven back to Colorado with my sister-in-law, Debbie, who wanted to visit relatives with her two young children. In the days before car seats to restrain children, and DVD players to entertain them, Debbie needed help traveling the 800 miles with toddlers in tow. After a week of vacation, they were ready to return to California. Having me along as an extra baby sitter was welcome assistance.

I blinked away tears as I loaded my few boxes of possessions into the large trunk of Tom's 1960 Ford Galaxie. Though the blue paint was faded, it was a sturdy looking vehicle sporting the big hood and long tail fins of the era. I had given away my childhood toys to younger cousins, but my precious portable record player and albums were tucked carefully next to my suitcases. I closed the trunk quietly and forced a smile on my face as I joined the group curbside

No one noticed my discomfort as they gathered around the car to see us off. After many hugs and kisses from tearful relatives, and promises to write from my friends, we set out for California. I waved goodbye to a chorus of "Good luck, Sandy", then quickly turned to face the road ahead. Debbie was behind the wheel, my mother sat up front with her, and the babies and I sprawled across the large bench-style back seat.

The adults had piled blankets on the seat to make it more comfortable for us. My niece, Susie, was almost one year old and my nephew, Eric, was going to be three in the fall. They were active children and excited to be on a road trip with their young aunt. They gave me no opportunity to reflect on my mixed emotions. My legs were soon bruised from entertaining them by holding their hands while they jumped up and down on my thighs. I sang every nursery song I could remember until finally they grew tired and settled down.

The old Ford did not have air conditioning. We headed south on highway 160 and, when we crossed the border into New Mexico, the temperature in the car started to get warm. To keep the morning sun from shining into the back seat, I stuffed my sweater into the top of the window and rolled up the glass to hold it in place. I rolled the window down on the other side to get a cross breeze going with the windows up front. It helped a little to get some fresh air but it grew hotter by the minute. The children whined at the heat and leaned their sticky little bodies against mine. Soon they were lulled into a fitful sleep by the steady roar of the V-8 engine and the rhythm of the tires on the highway.

Trapped into a frozen position by the gently dozing babes, I stared out the open window at the desert scenery flying past. We were driving through the Navajo Indian reservation so the occasional Indian Hogan appeared on the horizon, and a few thin scruffy sheep wandered into sight. There was mostly rocks and scrub brush to keep my attention.

When we passed the large rock-formation called Shiprock, I knew we were leaving the Four Corners region behind. Overhead was a bright blue sky with very few clouds, and lots of sunshine; lots and lots of sunshine. I was hot, bored and generally miserable. Too tired to focus on the soft conversation coming from the front of the car, I fell into a kind of highway hypnosis. I must have dozed off. Before I knew it, we were pulling into a small dilapidated truck stop and gas station.

"Time to stretch our legs and get something to drink," Debbie called out cheerfully. Her voice woke the children who started to whine again, but they eagerly followed her out of the car.

"Wait here with me until they come back." my mother said. "We need to pump the gas. Plus, we can't leave the car alone." Her quick look around alerted me to the other customers. Men in pickup trucks were scattered around the station. A few had Indian squaws and children from the reservation in the back of the truck bed. All were looking at us curiously.

Even though tourists often came through the area, not many women and children traveled alone. I nodded and stayed beside my mother until Debbie returned with her refreshed and wide-awake children. After our turn in the roadside restroom, everyone climbed back into the car to start our next leg of the journey,

"I got you and Eric a soda and here is a bottle of formula for the baby," said Debbie, as she passed back the items to me. Great, I thought, I hope the kids don't get car sick. I tended to feel queasy from motion sickness so I hoped the little ones had stronger stomachs. But they seemed to be fine. Eric entertained himself with his Hot Wheels cars and Susie seemed happy to pull my hair and pat my face while she drank her bottle.

After a while my mother turned and looked back over the car seat. "Thanks for your help with the children," she said. "I'll trade places with you at the next stop for gas, unless Debbie wants me to drive for a while." The smile on her face showed her appreciation for my silent assistance.

I held my breath until my sister-in-law replied that she was fine to keep driving. We had a long way to go yet, but a break from the back-seat playpen was much needed. I had a strong feeling Debbie had no intention of riding in the back when she had two capable baby sitters on board.

We climbed out of the desert and up into the mountains near Flagstaff, Arizona. The green pines were a nice visual relief from the dry desert landscape and the temperature was noticeably cooler.

"We should stop to get something to eat," suggested my mother.

"Oh," said Debbie, "let's just get some burgers and eat them on the road. I don't want to spend the money for meals in a café or take more time away from driving."

Sticking to a frugal budget was a way of life for Debbie and my brother. Tom was in his first year of teaching and Debbie worked as a part-time bookkeeper. My parents had always been very careful with money as well, but I was the last of five children living at home. Things like meals out were a little more common. But Debbie was the one in charge, so after another quick stop, we were on our way again with me riding shotgun this time.

The old Ford headed out across the Arizona desert. It was getting to be late afternoon. My mother was reading picture books to Susie and practicing colors and numbers with Eric. I looked out over the view again, this time through the big front window.

Saguaro cactus jutted out of the earth at every turn,

their large branches saluting us as we passed. Other interesting chaparral and plant life were visible from the road. Large puffy clouds filled the sky. The view was much more engaging and I was beginning to enjoy the ride. I was pointing out to Debbie the beautiful rainbow that had appeared as we rounded a big curve, when it happened.

"Wham!" a loud bang sounded as the car shook violently and the entire windshield went black. We all shrieked at the loud noise. "What happened? Can you see?" I shouted at Debbie. I looked over to see her hunched down over the steering wheel trying to peer through a crack of glass at the bottom of the windshield.

"The hood of the car has flown up over the windshield," she replied. "Stick your head out the window and see if I can pull over." Debbie slowed the car while trying to stay on the pavement. "I don't want to get stuck in a ravine." I quickly rolled down my passenger side window and leaned out so I could see the road ahead.

"You're okay," I said. "The road is flat here and it looks level just ahead. Pull over to the side when I say stop." The car was creeping along at 5 miles an hour now. The back-seat passengers were silent after their first yelp of surprise. Even babies seem to know when to be quiet in dangerous situations.

"Okay, stop!" I yelled back into the car. "You can pull over here." I had spent most of my childhood living on a farm and had experience with all kinds of weather and roadway conditions. This dirt looked solid and level. We would not get stuck if we stopped here.

Once we came to a complete stop, Debbie shakily turned off the engine and took a few deep breaths. "Is everyone all right?" she asked, as she glanced into the backseat. My mother gave a quick nod of affirmation, while the children sat still looking at us with large round eyes. Debbie and I got out of the car to assess the damage. The hood of the Ford was bent straight back over the windshield. It was hanging by a couple of broken bolts on either side.

"What do we do now?" I asked.

Debbie looked at me, then back at the car. "I guess we have to take it off the car," she said. She was only in her early twenties but was also raised on a farm. People don't panic when equipment breaks down. You just fix it and move on. I felt dazed by the incident, but Debbie was cool headed.

"Ruth, please keep the children in the car while Sandy and I get the hood off," Debbie called into the vehicle.

We got on either side of the hood and started to wiggle it side to side trying to break it free from the remaining bolts. Suddenly a pickup truck pulled up behind us. There had been little traffic on the remote highway but now we had company.

"Need any help, ma'am?" drawled a middle-aged man in a cowboy hat and boots. He was by himself and looked decent enough, so Debbie engaged him in conversation. It happened that he had a bag of tools in his truck and was able to knock the bolts loose with a big heavy wrench. The three of us lifted the hood off the car and set it on the side of the road.

"Looks like you have to leave the hood here," said the man. "It's too bent up to put back on the car even if you had the right bolts. How far are you plannin' to go? Do you want me to follow you for a while?"

Debbie gave me a quick look and lied. She told the stranger we were visiting our folks just up the road and needed to get going as they were expecting us for dinner. We thanked him, and he waited until we were all loaded up and the car started before driving off. Debbie pulled back onto the highway and slowly followed the truck until it sped out of sight.

I did not ask her why she had lied to the man. Country girls learn to watch their backs. Friends and neighbors are close, but you can never be too sure about strangers. *I'm moving to a place that is an ocean of strangers,* I realized. Would I sink or swim in my new environment?

The roar of the engine was even louder without a hood to muffle the sound. Now that the adults seemed less tense, the children felt free to start whining again in earnest. My morning headache returned with a vengeance. To give Debbie a break, my mother suggested she drive for a while. But Debbie wanted to continue on in case there was another problem with the car. They say not to tempt Karma with your fears because they might happen.

We had not been driving for 30 minutes when the highway seemed to get even bumpier. The back-rear passenger side seemed to be the roughest and a thumping sound started to come from that direction.

Debbie decided to stop when we saw signs for a turnoff to a small town up ahead. She pulled into a roadside gas station with a small garage attached to the side. It was staffed by a couple of well-worn mechanics. Their hands were stained by car oil and their skin weathered by years spent in the desert sun. They first wanted to know about the hood, but lost interest when told we had left it behind. Then Debbie mentioned the bumpy rear tire and their eyes lit up.

Before we knew it, the car was up on a rack. The rear tire was declared beyond repair and in fact the whole set of tires was ready to blow at any minute. Fortunately for us they had a set of new tires that would fit this car just fine.

Debbie was no pushover, but after what had just happened, she did not want to tempt fate again. She found a pay phone and called my brother collect to tell him about all the car trouble. I could hear him yelling at her through the phone complaining that he just bought new tires at Sears at half the price. But then Debbie pointed out the tires were in L.A. and we were not. He reluctantly agreed to buy the set of tires at the inflated desert outpost price, and Debbie told the mechanics to mount them on the car.

The faded old Ford with the missing hood was all dressed up in a shiny new set of tires. I felt like we would safely get to L.A. now. I wondered at how Debbie had kept from yelling back at my brother. Didn't he want his family home safe? He was lucky he didn't have to drive to the middle of Arizona to pick up a blubbering bundle of females.

To keep the kids entertained during the tire fiasco,

Mom had been feeding them toasted cheese sandwiches in a nearby café. She thought we should stop to rest for the night in Williams, Arizona, but Debbie did not want to spend money on a motel. She just wanted to get home and get this trip behind her. She insisted we all get back in the car and keep going. I was placed in the back to baby sit again.

The sun slipped into the horizon and the car grew dark. The toddlers snuggled down to sleep. I could have slept too, but my thoughts raced through my head. My optimistic sendoff had been worn away by the setbacks we had experienced.

What did I know about living among strangers? Who could I trust? How would I make new friends? Would my country-based survival skills be of any use in the big city? I knew how to take care of myself in familiar situations, but everything was going to be new to me. Suddenly the reality of how my life would change became clear, and I was afraid.

As we got closer to Los Angeles, the towns became bigger and the highways wider. When we arrived in San Bernardino, the lights were so bright the night disappeared into day. Though still early morning, I could clearly see my surroundings. The tires started to thump again, but Debbie said the freeway was bumpy because so many large trucks traveled on it every day.

We traveled through the endless miles of buildings so close to the freeway it seemed we would be crushed. Lights flowed in every direction like we had landed in a milky way of stars each one as bright as the desert sun. I was an astronaut, who had traveled across the universe in the span of a day, to settle down in some unknown world never to be the same again.

Sandra Simmer is a first-generation college graduate who grew up in a remote rural area of Colorado, rich with family and community traditions. As an adolescent, she made the difficult transition to Los Angeles during the counterculture hippie era. San Diego was her home for many years while raising a family and working full time in human service industries.

Recently relocated to the San Francisco Bay Area, Sandra has followed her love of the written word to write about her colorful life; both real and imagined. She is an active participant in the Pinole Library Writer's Group and the Albany Senior Center "*Memoiristas*". She credits much of her growth as a writer to the encouragement and critical feedback of her fellow classmates and muses.

Sandra can be found on LinkedIn and contacted at sandpiper99@hotmail.com.

IT STARTED WITH AGRITURISM

L.D. MARKHAM

Traveling in Southern Italy a few years back, my husband and I had just left the UNESCO site of Matera (just north of the instep of the boot) for a small, largely unknown town on the opposite coast. Since we were on vacation, we took the scenic route. Rolling green hills guarded by ancient castles and fortresses soon gave way to jagged mountain ranges. As the day grew late, a dark foreboding sky settled over us—we were in for a downpour.

After two wrong turns, we opted for the main highway to meet check-in time at our agriturismo—a bed and breakfast on a working farm in Paestum, Italy. I have loved everything I've ever seen in Italy, but had never heard of this place.

My husband had researched and discovered Greek ruins there. The majority of our trip was coordinated by an experienced and reputable tour company specializing in Italy; however, Paestum was a location this group had not previously scouted. Interested in the agriturismo experience, while still at home we found a location online. The photos were quaint and met my expectations for comfort, budget, and a morning meal (European breakfast of breads, cheese, and meats).

Although excited to book a room online, I was also skeptical of what I was seeing. Foreign country. English a second language. Booking long distance: Too many possibilities for things to go wrong. I decided to channel my inner explorer. After all, it would only be a couple of nights.

Leaving the freeway for the route to our accommodations, the landscape changed to farmland. Rain had created large puddles everywhere, but we found Azienda Agrituristica Seliano. Weather-worn stucco entry pillars signaled our turn. The pathway was muddy and lined by weeds. At first sight of the farm, a chill ran down my spine. With the dark skies and eerie building, I fully expected some slasher to spring forth. Had I seen too many thrillers?

The first building we passed was a dilapidated, reddish-rose and mottled-grey masonry manor. Its features were reminiscent of money and grandeur in an earlier time.

The second building was newer, yet still an aged, grand earth-tone stucco. We parked our rental for a closer look. The place seemed empty and we weren't sure where to check in, nor did we see other cars. My anxiety grew. Was the location correct? Did I screw up the reservation?

Walking around the building, we found workers in back near the pool area, who showed us where to park, and contacted someone to assist us with registration. We hadn't seen the guest-housing building on our initial approach. The guest quarters appeared to be a converted barn. I loved the romance of the stucco wearing away on the wall, exposing the red brick underneath. Potted plants and cacti lined the walls leading to the entryway. Deep green ivy clung to one side of the house. The building wasn't some trendy replica; it had history. Each of the windows on the second floor had a curved wrought-iron Juliette balcony.

The cook showed us to our room after introducing us to the resident host and storyteller, Nicholai. With only my basic travel Italian, and the cook's total lack of English, our body language was our only communication.

Our room had deep-brown wooden-pole beams, an antique headboard and furnishings, with shutters at the window. It was a long, spacious room with a fully tiled bathroom in a royal blue and white print similar to a Delft design. Antique knickknacks were sprinkled throughout our room and the building.

My husband noticed a series of black and white photos of American soldiers from World War II. We met the people in the room next to us and learned they were from Iowa. Yay someone to talk with.

Earlier, Nicholai had invited us to dinner. We hadn't realized it was an option, and considering the thunderstorms outside, took him up on it. Walking through the main building was a museum experience; more antiques, historical oil paintings, and ornamental Japanese silk robes were displayed on walls.

By eight o'clock sharp, we were all seated at an enormous round wooden table. Our dinner party consisted of Nicholai, our new neighbors, a couple from France, and a family of three from Germany, Heike, Heinrich, and Heidi. The dinner was a five-course epicurean marvel.

We each started with a small plate of light and fresh buffalo mozzarella, progressed to a fried potato appetizer with prosciutto plus a mini lasagna, followed by a small plate of corkscrew pasta drizzled with olive oil, parmesan, and basil, then the entrée of water buffalo, raised at their ranch, and roasted pumpkin, ending with a dessert of layered sponge cake. Of course, there was homemade Limoncello.

The mozzarella was better than anything I've ever tasted, and my first encounter with tender, surprisingly sweet water buffalo, was delightful. The house chianti was poured liberally throughout the meal. How do the Italians do that so well? The Limoncello recipe was sweet and lemony with a mere suggestion of alcohol. The final *pezzo de resistenza to this foodgasm* was the nightcap of espresso.

The conversations throughout the evening were pleasant and lively. Several questions from the French couple related to American politics, and the German family had more questions about America. Nicholai spoke Italian, German, French, and English and shared varied stories of his travels throughout Europe, and his friendship with Baronnessa Cecilia Bellelli, who turned her husband's family estate into this agriturismo.

I'm sure Nicholai was an actor in another life; he certainly knew how to entertain and engage an audience. He spoke with such confidence you could be certain he'd traveled often and experienced much throughout his life.

The next morning, we met our new friends for breakfast. The German family invited us to join them for a tour of the owner's water buffalo ranch, led of course by Nicholai. We learned the Bellelli family owned both properties, and the family matron, Cecilia, ran both of them. The Baronessa offered cooking lessons at the second property during the summer months, using produce from their sustainable garden.

My husband and Heinrich hit it off and traveled a little ahead of the rest of us. Little Heidi was twelve and stayed close to her mother, acting as translator.

The mud, and pungent smell of livestock, left no doubt where we were heading. I had not brought rain boots and had to watch my step. The muck was deep and slippery. It took a bit to get used to the odor. We were able to catch great photos of the buffalo playing in their own mud baths, and a couple of them did some great posing for us.

Everyone met Cecilia Bellelli at the farm that day. She showed us around the house, the kitchen used for cooking lessons, and explained the historical family oil paintings on the walls. She informed us the first manor we saw driving in, now damaged from an earthquake back in the 1980s, was used to house American Army Air Force soldiers during World War II. Cecilia explained how the planes were hangared near the beach. Those were the pictures my husband saw when we arrived.

Sharing this experience with our new German friends was enjoyable. Heidi was very fond of my husband. Her father, Heinrich, spoke English well, had a great sense of humor, and a warm smile. Although Heike could not speak English, it didn't seem to matter, we communicated through the family. Like her husband, she had an easy smile.

Following the farm, we toured the ruins of Paestum. The Greeks had named this fortified city near the sea Poseidonia to honor the god of the Sea. Portions of the walls around the city still exist and are considered to be the best preserved of ancient times. My husband and I noted how similar the buildings were to those constructed in

Athens 600 B.C. The beautiful mosaic floors inlaid with images of fruits and people are still evident, although the tiles have faded to reds, pinks, and white. Because there are less people and it's not widely known, the preservation seems as if it was spared being loved to death.

After an exciting day of exploring, we couldn't wait to share another dinner with the other guests and more of Nicholai's stories, but the dynamic had changed. The French couple were now speaking with Nicholai, no longer interested in the Americans. The guests from Iowa were absent. While the French conversation was on one side of the table, it allowed my husband and me to get to know the German family better. We invited them to stay with us should they ever visit Northern California. We gave them our email addresses and Heinrich handed us his business card.

The next morning, as we packed our rental car, Heinrich, Heike, and Heidi came to say their goodbyes. Heidi mentioned she thought of my husband as the grandfather she didn't have and gave us each a big hug. We enjoyed our time at the agriturismo and meeting this family. I hoped we would indeed hear from them again.

* * *

We exchanged emails at holidays and birthdays over the years. Two summers from our initial meeting, we had another surprise. Heinrich and family were heading for California. They asked to stay for a couple of nights. Yes, yes! We insisted they stay with us.

They arrived in July. Our first night we ventured to our favorite Italian restaurant, returned to our deck in the foothills of Sacramento and spent most of the evening sharing wine, stories, histories, and questioning why things happen in the world. It was the most inspiring and educational conversation, and I was pleased Heike had learned a little more English.

We enjoyed playing tour guides and took them to Lake Tahoe the next day. We started just above Inspiration

Point at Emerald Bay State Park. The sun was bright and warm, the sky royal blue with light billowy clouds, and a miniature waterfall flowed from a rocky outcrop above us. Our guests checked out the boulder formations and dead limbs in contorted, abstract shapes; all interesting photos. We took a lake tour aboard the Tahoe Queen sternwheeler before storming the shopping areas.

Closer to home, we visited Coloma and the Marshall Gold Discovery State Park. We followed in the footsteps of those seeking gold, through the park, the museum, and stone stores built by Chinese immigrants. We headed to Old Sacramento and explained how the buildings had been raised due to the early flooding, explored the Railroad Museum, and stopped for a beverage at the Delta King.

As we made our way to the wooden walkways of the shops, we were lucky to see actors in period costumes this time of year. It wasn't Gold Rush Days just yet. Heinrich and Heidi were thrilled with the chance to ask questions of those in costume. Heidi then found *Evangeline's Costume Mansion* and fell in love. We did not know back in Germany she enjoyed the performance art known as Cosplay where she dresses up as a favorite character from a video game. She was excited to find a long-haired pink wig. We had to drag her out of there.

From Old Sacramento we headed to *Vic's Old-Fashioned Ice Cream* on Riverside Boulevard and introduced them to a banana split. They had never seen or heard of one and asked for assistance choosing their three flavors of ice cream with topping, and had never considered eating ice cream with a banana. Heinrich loved it. They were also amazed Americans can eat so much ice cream at one time.

I served a morning brunch that included mini-cinnamon rolls and Danish. The sweets were a big hit for both Heidi and Heike as they don't usually have sweet foods in the morning. Although, Heidi confided, she loved a croissant with Nutella.

We introduced them to Mexican food and Margaritas

(not Heidi) in one of our favorite restaurants. Another success. It was an action packed three days, and solidified our friendship further. When it was time for them to leave, they invited us to stay with them if we were ever in Germany. Heike and I cried when we hugged goodbye. None of us wanted the weekend to end.

*   *   *

Fortune smiled upon us once again two years later when we decided to visit Europe. We contacted our friends and, of course, they insisted we stay with them. As is our habit, this was another location off the tourist track I never expected to visit. Having flown into Amsterdam, it was a three-hour drive east to Bochum, Germany. It was a cold, rainy day mid-April, and we were tired from the long flight. Walking through the airport to the car rental felt equally as long as the trip to get there.

We pulled off at a rest area so I could change shoes, shake out my legs, and grab a sweater. This was the first time I noticed the bathrooms at the rest stations were unisex with full doors and private sinks. In the States at the time, there was a big brouhaha going on about the transgender population and privacy. My first thought was this could be a solution. We got back in the car to continue the journey. I wasn't going to resolve the world's issues on one trip.

Approaching our exit, I pulled out the address and discovered it wasn't complete. We found ourselves somewhere near Bochum, with no idea where to go and neither of us spoke German.

We found an office supply store and hoped someone might speak English and help us. There was a gentleman lorry driver (truck driver) with Brothers, who had a massive white spaceship-looking vehicle. He spoke English and was able to make the call for us to tell Heinrich where we were. He was a friendly fellow, and we asked about his truck. He explained it was custom-made and there were contests in Europe for such things. Another opportunity to learn about how others across the pond live.

We made it to our destination and Heike and Heinrich had set us up in a lovely loft room with its own private bath and shower on the third floor of their home. The ceiling came to a point in the center so we had to be careful not to knock our heads getting out of bed. It gave us a beautiful view of neighborhood gardens and trees.

We listened to Heidi's piano playing and were educated on how the German school system differs from the United States. Dinner was an introduction to *raclette* grill cooking (typically used with fresh vegetables, cheese, and meats), more great white wine (between a Riesling and a Chardonnay) and German beer. Heidi was eager to show us how to play a card game called Wizard. This brought much laughter as we tried to learn.

Our first morning in Germany, Heinrich was as excited to show us the history of their town as we had been to show them ours. Bochum is situated in the Middle Ruhr Valley which is known for its mining. We started with the Mining Museum. I admit, I wasn't excited about this, but I wanted to be polite. When will I learn to stop underestimating things?

The museum was interesting and high quality in history, equipment, and technology. It included a mock underground mine depicting how the industrial equipment was used. Only Heinrich and I took the tour because my husband and Heike are claustrophobic. The tour made me think of all the products we take for granted that result from mining, and I now have an appreciation for just how dangerous underground mining is.

At the end of the tour, Heinrich and I took an elevator to the top of the building. Although it was windy and gray outside, the 360° view of Bochum was worth it. Dinner that evening was sharing *tapas* in a Spanish restaurant they favored. I don't remember the tapas so much, but I remember the excellent Sangria. So much so, I journaled it!

Day two was a trip to the *Gasometer*. This was a round, tube-like building that previously housed a gas pipeline for the surrounding industrial community. It is currently used for art exhibits twice a year. It also had a planetarium presentation of the world revolving from day to night, and our visit was a nature exhibit encompassing the lives of plants, animals, and humans.

The morning to say farewell had come, and there were more tears and hugs. How nice to know it is possible to have dear friends who live countries apart from us.

*   *   *

Six years had come and gone. Heidi, whom we met when she was twelve, had since graduated high school and wanted to visit California, and her long-distance adopted grandfather, for her graduation present. Of course, we would love to see her again. She was now eighteen and venturing to another continent on her own.

We picked her up in San Francisco on a Friday in August. She had arrived early enough in the day to be able to show her the Japanese Gardens of Golden Gate Park, and drive through Chinatown. She didn't have plans for anything in particular.

Heidi seemed to settle in easily, as if we were her home away from home. She did enjoy talking American politics and had a very good grasp on the concept. This came, though, with lots of questions neither of us could answer. I find it fascinating to get the political spin from all my friends across the Atlantic.

We had many deep conversations about how Americans do things. Questions like "Why do Americans need so much storage?" as we passed a U-Store-It location. "Why are pharmaceuticals advertised?" as she noticed a commercial on T.V. "Why do Americans need so many guns?" as she listened to a political ad. Meanwhile, America was gearing up for the mid-term elections, so her questions were timely. She explained to us how short and effective the German election cycle is.

A week passed before she asked to visit an American mall, and *Evangeline's* in Old Sacramento, again. We spent a day at the Galleria in Roseville. Heidi spoke excellent English and most of the clerks thought she was a native until she had to show her ID. She has a slight German lilt to her speaking.

We ventured up to Apple Hill, and Heidi informed me she was now a vegetarian. We stopped for lunch at a vegan restaurant in Placerville. Good thing I had picked up cinnamon rolls and sweet breads for breakfast. I did spring for a jar of Nutella too! Heidi was disappointed the drinking age here is twenty-one; back in her country it is nineteen.

This trip was about becoming extended family. We loved hosting her as a graduation present, and we've learned so much from her.

*   *   *

Heidi's back in Germany and serious about her studies in international law. Everyone is doing well, we still speak with them, and FaceTime occasionally.

Sometimes taking a small risk while traveling fills you with a wealth of unexpected joy and lifelong friendships, which in turn become extended families.

L. D. Markham is a member of Northern California Publishers and Authors (NCPA), Sisters in Crime, and the local chapter Capitol Crimes.

Her debut novel *Murder in Costa Rica* was published in 2018, her short story "Saving Coy" was published in the NCPA anthology *Birds of Feather* in 2019. She has written several short stories.

Ms. Markham is employed with the California Department of Justice (DOJ) where she writes curriculum and teaches desktop, professional development, business writing, and proofreading classes. She is also a contributor to the DOJ internal newsletter *Justice Journal.* L.D. Markham resides in Cameron Park, CA.

Her website is www.ldmarkhambooks.com. You can follow her on Instagram at LDMarkhambooks or twitter @ldmarkhamwrites.

KARMA:
THE REINCARNATION OF TARANTULA?
RONALD JAVOR

Thailand, Laos, Cambodia, Vietnam. These four ancient kingdoms of Southeast Asia now bustle with young and old people, modern and ancient buildings, and a hodge-podge of vehicles ranging from ox carts to motorcycles and trucks.

With fourteen other Americans from a wide variety of backgrounds, I traveled overseas to those countries, with high expectations of experiencing their cultures, as well as their ancient and recent histories.

Like many world travelers, before I left, I read about the countries and their people in order to better understand the thousands of years of history I was about to see firsthand, and the similar but unique cultural aspects of each of these places. Little did I know, while both culture and history would be important steppingstones in understanding and enjoying Southeast Asia, their foods and my exposure to Buddhism would take on even more importance in every busy day of this adventure.

Buddhism originated over 2,500 years ago and now is the primary religion of over 300 million people around the world. For many. it is a "way of life" rather than merely a religion. Buddhists practice living a moral, mindful, and compassionate life through all their actions, pursuing what best can be described as non-exploitation of themselves and others.

In Bangkok and other parts of Thailand, we were regaled with walking tours of reconstructed and crumbling temples, numerous and varied golden statues of Buddha, both huge and small, and teeming city streets. These walks included a stop at the Grand Palace of Thailand, a group of ornate temples, and other structures with exquisite statuary and towering spires. King Rama IV, who we now know as the king in the famous musical, The *King and I*, ruled from there.

Our routine obliged us to eat three meals a day, and we discovered Thai food was not only Pad Thai, but included sweet and spicy curries, tangy shrimp soup, mango and sweet rice desserts, plus other delicacies.

A highlight in Bangkok was eating at *Cabbages and Condoms*, an internationally celebrated restaurant serving a wide assortment of varied and delicious dishes, while concurrently educating about and financially supporting, improved family planning and AIDS prevention. Throughout the restaurant, we were surrounded by statues, pictures, models, and other items constructed of bright multi-colored condoms.

In Laos, we spent time in Luang Prabang and Vientiane, visited more Buddhist temples, and had a peaceful excursion along the Mekong River, known there as The Mother of All Rivers.

Each meal served to us introduced more fascinating food highlights, usually including chilis and mint, coupled with rice, meats, fish and fresh fruits. Fish laap, or larb, comprised of fried chopped fish with mint and cilantro, was a scrumptious introduction to Laotian food.

One special stop was a hosted group lunch in a small village; after a tour of its residences and school, and an opportunity to mingle with grade-school students, we were treated to "finger-food" appetizers of fried rice worms served with homemade rice wine or rice whiskey, or both, and then a massive stir fry with more than a dozen vegetables and condiments prepared in an enormous wok over a large fire. After eating, we waddled back to our bus and a continuing introduction to Buddhism!

Buddhist monks live an austere life, wearing their ochre or saffron robes, teaching and learning, practicing 227 commandments of the 84,000 Buddhist doctrines, meditating, and eating one meal each day before noon. They teach that free choice and intention are the most critical factors for complying with their precepts which, like the Western Ten Commandments, include abstaining from killing living beings, not taking what is not given, and avoiding false speech.

What do Buddhist monks eat and where does their food come from? In Luang Prabang, one day at sunrise we joined in an "almsgiving" or "almsround" (known as *pindapata*), when dozens of monks in their colored robes walked slowly and silently in single file along a road lined with hundreds of local families. Each monk carried a small food bowl, into which the local residents and visitors, including us, handed each a small amount of rice or other food. No eye contract was made, nor were words exchanged. In Buddhist tradition, there was no giver or receiver, just giving and receiving. The food we all provided then was prepared for all the monks in their monastery, and the serving and eating complied with various ritual requirements.

"Karma" often is confused with "fate" but is actually the opposite: "karma" simply means that actions have consequences and, in a Newtonian type of concept, "good actions have good consequences and bad actions have bad consequences". The concept of karma is governed by three primary precepts: avoid harmful conduct, pursue good conduct, and live for and with all beings. Participation in the almsgiving ceremony is an act related to karma, with the gifts being investments in the givers' faiths as well as their own souls.

Cambodia, our next stop, is best known for its massive temples, the most visited and photographed of which is Angkor Wat, a pyramidic stone temple built in the mid-1100's, lost to the jungle for many years, rediscovered in the mid-1800's, and still being restored while serving as both an active temple and tourist destination. To many people, it is considered the center of all spiritual and physical universes and the home of many gods. The residents include not only monks, but families of chattering monkeys who blithely and cunningly steal tourist food if not offered to them first.

Between temples and reminders of the post-war "killing fields" era of Pol Pot, food continued to be a daily adventure. Soups and fish dishes were the main staples, generally followed by fresh fruits. Cambodian meals encompass contrasts such as salty and sour or fresh and cooked, and are tangy, rather than spicy. We enjoyed fish steamed in coconut milk curry, served in banana leaves with sticky rice, as well as barbequed sausage served with rice and fresh vegetables.

While in Cambodia, our group leader did not introduce us to another popular Cambodian dish, sautéed beef with red tree ants, ginger, and lemongrass; some of our group already had their fill of little crawly things. Little did we know there was more to come.

Our last stop, in Vietnam, was Ho Chi Minh City, formerly known as Saigon. It was impossible not to think about food! The city bustles with a growing population, construction is everywhere, and every corner has individuals and families cooking and serving others from small pots and fires.

Every street seems to have open markets of fresh and prepared food for sale, and scattered throughout the city we saw McDonalds, KFCs, and other familiar American eateries as well as local restaurants serving phos (noodle soups), spring rolls, and a variety of banh mi sandwiches filled with vegetables, meats, and sauces.

Along the Mekong River, we ate a variety of river fish, prepared in unique but tasty ways, and Vietnamese beer kept our thirst quenched. Interwoven with exposure to relics of the twentieth century "American War," Vietnam was one more great food adventure!

"Rebirth" or "reincarnation" as a Buddhist tenet

generally is misunderstood. One does not die and come back again through countless previous and future lives as another person, an animal, insect, or other living thing. When one dies, only "energy" continues, and ends up in one of several good or bad realms, some of which are living things. The nature of the rebirth depends on a person's karma at the time of death.

As I look back, the ultimate food adventure occurred in Cambodia. On the way to Siem Reap and Angkor Wat, our bus stopped in a small village. There, a young local woman took us out into the jungle and showed us numerous burrows, not currently occupied by small mammals, but now serving as homes for tarantulas and scorpions.

She showed us how to catch those fuzzy creepy crawlers by looking for burrows with webs at the opening, pushing a stick into the hole, slowly moving it around, then gradually pulling the stick out, often with a tarantula holding on. She picked the tarantula up, carefully removed its poison source, and let me and the others who were brave enough, hold and pet it.

We brought the tarantula, and other spiders collected on the walk, back to the village. Since it was lunchtime, we were greeted with a large bowl of deep-fried grasshoppers to snack on, with endless cups of warm rice wine or tea.

Other members of her family stood over a hot wok deep-frying tarantulas and scorpions, which, after tasting them first, I helped serve to the others in my group. Surprisingly, yum! I then was asked to help cook the next batch, including the ones we had just brought back.

As I poured about two dozen tarantulas and scorpions into the hot wok, I could swear that one tarantula looked familiar, glared at me and pointed a leg as he disappeared into the oily mass. I think I felt a twinge in my karma, and wondered where, when, and how my rebirth would occur, if that's my destiny, and the effect on my future of that brief encounter of our minds and souls.

Should Buddhists be vegetarians? If one eats meat, one is indirectly responsible for the death of a creature, thus breaking the first precept of not killing another living thing. The Buddhist teachings say we are responsible for killing a living being when we eat meat, but the same is true when we eat vegetables. In fact, it is impossible to live today without, in some way, being indirectly responsible for the death of other beings. The monk asks, if our goal is to live a moral life, who is the better Buddhist: one who is a vegetarian but selfish and mean, or another who eats meat but is honest and kind?

Three weeks in Southeast Asia showcased the multitude of sights, sounds, and experiences that a fulfilling trip should include. But my memories include more than scenic pictures and new historical and cultural knowledge. The tastes, aromas, and textures of my culinary exploration into a fusion of East and West and its exotic foods, along with exposure to timeless questions and answers of Buddhist teachings, permeated this remarkable journey of discovery and supreme enjoyment, and left me with stories and pictures of these discoveries that I share at every opportunity.

Figure 1: Author Ron Javor shares a kiss with a tarantula.

Ronald Javor's professional career involved assisting people with lower incomes, disabilities and homelessness to have access to safe and affordable housing. He has written seven children's books on young people confronting and overcoming those types of barriers. Each book also addresses negative stereotypes and shows that all children, despite handicaps, have the same desires. More information is available on his books at ronaldjavorbooks.com.

Since Ron's "retirement" into volunteering, he also pampers his shelter-rescue home partners and travels abroad or in the United States. The trip featured in this story originally was intended to be an opportunity to experience the effects of the "American War" in Vietnam, Cambodia and Laos, and the tour achieved that along with exposure to current political and cultural issues. A shout-out to Overseas Adventure Travel and our local leaders for a trip balanced with learning, visual experiences, and great and unique food!

TAKING IT ON THE ROAD

DIERDRE WOLOWNICK

Book Tour. Magic, scary words, for an author. In May 2019, after my book was published, I began a book tour. I'd done small-scale book tours decades ago (in the '90s) as an independent publisher, in Northern California and Nevada, so I started this one with enthusiasm and some trepidation.

When I was in charge of my own company, I did everything. Finding the venues, calling to connect with the right people, arranging the event, requesting all the things I would need — everything was my job, far more time-consuming than writing and publishing the books!

This time, I was only the author. That makes a difference, but not as big as I'd imagined. And I found that each event I did helped foster more events.

The Telluride (Colorado) Film Festival was the most impressively scenic place I had the good fortune to appear in. The tiny silver-mining town of Telluride sits at three levels scattered up the mountainside, up to about 9,000 feet elevation, connected by a gut-clenching gondola ride. I did two speaking/signing events there, and met an author, who introduced me to another author, who introduced me to "some people" from the Kendal Mountain Literature Festival in England...and that's how the momentum begins.

The person from Kendal who had dinner with us was excited by the idea of my book, and when she took it back to England, the director of the festival fell in love with it and offered to host me at their festival, which takes place in the beautiful Lake District of England.

I'd heard all my life about that area (I grew up in New York City after WWII, surrounded by people from all over the world), but none of the stories lived up to how lovely I found it. As I flew in via Iceland, the snow-covered mountains of Scotland took me by surprise. I had no idea Scotland was such rugged terrain...or that England's Lake District, just below it, with its rolling hillsides and scattering of charming villages, hamlets, towns and boroughs would captivate me so, visually, geographically...even linguistically. The lilt of the region's English was a music that tickled and delighted my linguist's ear.

I spent four wonderful days in a tiny hotel next to the festival site. As is common with medieval buildings that are still in use, the stairs were crooked, covered by worn carpeting, and the hallways helped one appreciate the small size of our predecessors who didn't have vitamin supplements and fresh food to help them grow tall and large. My elbows reddened over the weekend from bumping into walls and doorways and other unexpected protuberances. It reminded me of the house my grandfather had built in Pennsylvania at the turn of the 20th century.

My grandparents were from Poland, and like in most historic places, things were much smaller-scale. The hallway in their house sloped slightly, and the walls curved slightly, like my hotel in Kendal. The folks from, or in, the 'old country' adapted to their topography. Made do. Used the stone, wood, slate or whatever the locality offered to build with, and built as best they could without machines, computers, and all the tools we deem necessary. Age did the rest, settling here, sinking there, shearing off in a corner.

Food was not a priority at a festival of such energy and motion. Between the non-stop events, I grabbed whatever I could find at the kiosks in the multi-level hillside site — and the surprise was how wonderful it was! All the vendors were local, family-run and made mostly ethnic foods. Lots of lamb, curry, stews with lots of veggies and sauces that always made me want more. Only once did we actually get out into the town, to a real restaurant, and although it was delicious, it could have been anywhere in the world.

England has never been known for its food...but like in the U.S., I believe the people from elsewhere help shape the distinctiveness of its cuisine. When I go back to Kendal — and I will, for the climbing and the festival — I'll sample more of what the town has to offer. This time was just an appetizer.

The director of the festival knows all the national media, and he arranged interviews for me with the BBC, the London Times, EpicTV, UKC News, and others. My slideshow and speaking presentation filled the medieval Town Hall of Kendal — hundreds of people from all over the world crammed into a medieval setting that could have been a historical movie set. The vibe was modern and international, but the locale was strictly middle-ages European, and although I've been traveling the world for five decades, that event made an indelible impression that will always warm my heart.

From there, I went to New York City, my hometown.

While signing books in a building in lower Manhattan, I could look down at the tombstones of 174-year-old Trinity Church, where Alexander Hamilton and so many of our original patriots are buried. New York's (European) history goes back almost 500 years...but NY pizza has only been around for a hundred and a quarter, brought there by Italians towards the turn of the (20th) century.

Whenever I go home, I indulge, big-time. And yes, it is different from any pizza you'll get in the west. I miss it. I miss *Frank's Pizza*, under the (elevated) subway on Roosevelt Avenue in Jackson Heights. I miss the tasty oil dripping down my hand, the foldable slices, the waves of fragrant heat, in the winter, from the pizza ovens constantly being yanked open. I miss Frank and his boys, a friendly, sweating presence as they operated the ovens right behind the counter. A pizza parlor is a builder of community, a foot-traffic kind of eatery, but there's no foot traffic on streets in California.

I miss that, too.

While in New York, I also did a book event (slideshow/signing) at the *Central Rock Gym* in midtown Manhattan. I walked there from my hotel, about a mile and a half uptown along storefront-lined Ninth Avenue, paralleling the Hudson River, and all the way I wondered at the transformation just a few decades had made.

My father grew up in Hell's Kitchen, where the climbing gym now sits surrounded by high-rise apartment buildings and exclusive car dealerships (Audi, Mercedes Benz, etc.) and small green parks and playgrounds. In the early 20th century, when my father was a kid growing up on West 50th Street, Hell's Kitchen was the roughest, toughest part of New York. Many of his friends wound up in Sing Sing (Prison). Gangs were rampant, Irish gangs who preyed on all the other immigrants (one of the few groups of immigrants who spoke English, they had the upper hand).

My father's stories were the stuff of movies — but he had lived it. And survived. And I survived my whirlwind tour of California, Colorado, England and New York. What a ride it's been! I met television producers and writers, explorers, festival directors, entrepreneurs, movers and shakers in business and in the media — and they all connected me with others equally talented, fascinating and multi-faceted.

Had I not gone to Telluride I never would have gotten to see Oprah (she spoke there, too).

The director of the Kendal Mountain Literature Festival would never have heard about my book and I wouldn't have wound up signing books in the medieval Town Hall of Kendal.

I wouldn't now have all those new friends to go climb with all over England.

EpicTV would not have done a special interview with me for their channel.

I could never have dreamed up the characters I've met, the invitations extended to me, the new friends I've made. That's probably the most valuable benefit of touring with a book.

This kind of momentum is a crazy, wild animal you need to grab onto and ride everywhere you can, even the most unlikely places. For many months, I turned no offer down — film and literature festivals, senior centers, climbing gyms, schools, science centers, historical societies...and of course, some bookstores — and each one was a surprise in some way.

I know I'm not nearly as good at marketing and promotion as I need to be. But I'm learning. And one thing I've learned is that none of this would have happened if I hadn't written that book.

So, take your book idea and make it something you can share with the world. You never know where it might take you.

Dierdre is past President of NCPA, author, language professor, conductor, musician, marathoner and rock climber. Her 2019 memoir, The Sharp End of Life, about climbing El Capitan with her son at 66, took her abroad as a speaker, and her latest textbooks, Allez! — Foundations of Beginning French and English for Foreign Language Students are taking her revolutionary language-teaching method all over the US. Besides writing full-time and rock climbing, she's currently the Senior Spokesperson for La Sportiva and other companies, encouraging seniors to get outdoors to get healthy. Her next non-fiction book, about how to raise children to be stewards of our planet, is scheduled for 2021, and she has several novels in progress.

KNIGHTLY NACHT, THE WANDERER

ROBERTA "BERT" DAVIS

Freaking pigeons! They were everywhere, cooing, fluttering, and shuffling around him every day. Pigeons, ugh! They weren't even great for eating. He couldn't even enjoy eating them. If one pigeon turned into dinner, then the others would throw a fit. Some even watched with wide eyes while he chomped away on their distant cousin. When they weren't scavenging for food, the feathery flock chased each other shamelessly, trying to make more baby pigeons.

Humans weren't much better. Many of them shuffled around like pigeons, lost in their own self-amusement and quest for food. Not many of them cared enough to give handouts.

Worst of all, Nacht had ended up in a city surrounded by water. That's fine for a duck, but what's a self-respecting cat to do? Being a cat, and a black one at that, he couldn't hide among them. He stood out; his black fur too dusty to cast the normal radiant shine in the first rays of morning sunlight. More annoyingly, his stomach gnawed at him.

Nacht sighed as he shoved his way through the obnoxious birds. When a few pigeons dared to peck at him, Nacht bared his formidable fangs and claws. The birds flapped their wings angrily, snapping their beaks and hissing back at him. He charged at the nearest birds, swiping a few, and sending feathers flying. Grey, white, and dirty-brown feathers fluttered to the ground in their wake. The pigeons scattered, ramming each other aside like bumper cars.

Too bad the tiny victory was short lived, for minutes later, the tourist-trap chickens cluttered around him. Maybe they knew he ate their cousin yesterday, and wanted revenge.

There was better food here than pigeons, anyway. The smell of sea water and birds were strong to his senses, but he'd attuned his senses to hunt better things, like comfort food from nice humans.

Tantalizing aromas drifted from the local cafes as lights came on and merchants started baking and cooking. Oh, the delicacies! He salivated at the scents of eggs, fresh bread with cheese, wondrous sausage and fish, and other yummy smells that were confusing, yet intriguing. Maybe the fishermen would be nice to him again. He didn't always get fish or meat. Sometimes, he enjoyed leftovers, from boiled potatoes, or pasta with zucchini and finely shredded cheese. He climbed up some crates, jumped onto one ledge after another, and climbed to a rooftop of one of many cafes.

Ah, Venice. People walked around as if they were enchanted children, or lovesick romance hunters. Nacht didn't see what the big deal was, but he adjusted. A savvy cat, he knew how to play humans. Be teasing, yet friendly, meow, and give them big, hungry, eyes.

He traveled by rooftops to a few relatively safe havens; docks or shops where merchants or locals were nice to street cats. It sufficed. Still, he was never quite full or relaxed.

He didn't understand how his humans could lose him. He gave up searching for his people quickly, for surviving took priority. He learned from local cats where to find food. A few nice cats let him follow them to the friendly vendors in town, but the pigeons competed for food.

And then there were tourists. Big, small, self-absorbed tourists flooded the town most days, tripping over the land-rat birds, or even their own feet while staring upwards, holding strange gadgets, taking pictures. Thankfully the hustle and bustle only lasted through the daylight hours.

At night, Venice morphed into a charming place of serenity. Most of the humans departed the city by boat or ferry, leaving a quiet nightlife of far fewer tourists, and real

Venetians. After the mass exodus, there were few to no boat motors, no gigantic cruise ships, no ear-barraging clamor of thousands of feet and voices, only locals and visitors, and of course, cats.

Sunset would cast a magical sheen over the darkening water. Nightfall felt blissful. On clear nights, the moon and stars dotted the sky, while nocturnal businesses lit the ground level with softly glowing lights. There were fewer boats on the water beneath twinkling starlight; several gondolas giving special rides to romantic customers. Music was more beautiful without the clamor of crowds. Locals would take walks and enjoy their home town. Of course, some tourists stayed the night in apartments, shopping or eating late, but far fewer than by light of day.

Now the cats could prowl for leftovers and handouts if not lucky enough to have an apartment to take refuge. Even to a wandering gypsy such as Nacht, the night was serene. He could roam without fear of being tripped over, and explore the unattended docks, boats, and gondolas. Without the hustle and mobs, locals were often more generous to him. A gentle breeze usually whispered through the city, now audible in the night's calm. Many lights shimmered off the calmly rippling water like fireflies and starlight. Small gatherings of humans would listen to musicians, or talk and drink, often sharing bar food with the cats.

And, thank goodness, the blasted pigeons sought places to roost and left him alone! Nacht sought out his few, new friends for food. After mooching a late evening snack, he would curl up on a gondola's soft cushion, and be gently rocked to sleep

Even with his luck at surviving thus far, Nacht was grumpy. He missed his elusive family, a warm bed where he could roll in tousled blankets, and regular meals. This particular day started out a bit rough. The boat's owner showed up earlier than usual, shooing Nacht away from his comfortable bed on a tourist chair. He hopped from gondola to gondola until his paws found the sidewalk. Of course, the pigeons were there to greet them. Nacht hissed at the pigeons as he lithely leapt and bounded away from the boats. Upon reaching an alley, he sat down to lick himself in his favorite position that humans couldn't do.

The scent of fish drifted from the open market. Despite himself, Nacht was tired of fish. Maybe his luck would improve. Moving on, he found routes up to the rooftops while the morning's coolness lingered. High above the ground, he viewed a typical morning scene.

Saint Mark's Square was quiet, but not for long. Boats approached the docks. A human would pay big bucks for this view. San Marco Cathedral cast an ambiance of its own, a plethora of ancient sculptures and majestic arches and peaks. Not good for a cat, though, too high, and too sunny. Nacht gazed longingly at a rock carving of a lion with wings. He wished he had wings right now, to fly away from this place. More puzzling were carvings of humans with wings. He wondered if humans had a thing with pigeons. Gross!

Nacht was so tired, he had overslept. He returned to ground level to search for breakfast. He had barely mooched some lunch meat from a nice local when the daily swarm began. The first ferry arrived, and with it, came the usual flood of boisterous tourists. One large man stomped off the first boat to town with a wife and two kids in tow. When the youngsters giggled and pointed at the black cat, the father pulled them away. "Don't touch him. He looks sick!" And off they went, the kids sighing, and the woman indifferent.

Nacht glared after at the man, grumbling, "Oh, like you're a picture of health. Have some more rat-burgers, fat boy."

All the people heard was sultry growling of a disheveled, disgruntled cat. While some people, often ladies or children, gave him curious or sympathetic looks, most of the public ignored him, no doubt, presuming he was fine.

Nevertheless, his newly found freedom had its perks.

Nacht shared the alleys with other cats, learning which ones to befriend and which cats to avoid, where to mooch a meal, and where to sleep. He sometimes followed tour guides and saw the wonders of all of Venice. At least there were no cars to run him over, no wheeled transports at all, only feet and boats. He returned to his favorite café, the one with a nice lady with feline-friendly snacks rummaged from the kitchen. The orchestra would start later, usually a quartet playing soothing, classical music for the outside patrons. He found his usual nap spot behind a couple of large planters and sat down where he could peek through the decorative foliage.

Tourists came and went, like any other day. A group of five shoppers hustled by, most of them, mesmerized by the sights. Among the harried group, one woman lingered behind, arguing that they should sit down and listen to the music. The others refused, saying it was too expensive.

Something about the lingering woman drew Nacht's attention. She was calmer than the others, more grounded. She wore shapes of little animals around her wrist, and Nacht caught a whiff of feline and canine on her. Smells like a pet lover, maybe even a cat lady.

"Everything's expensive," the cat lady replied with thinly veiled patience.

The others returned and rattled off a chaotic list of other places they needed to see, basically, all the tourist traps in the city. One of them argued, "Come on, Celeste, we're on a schedule."

"You can't do it all in one day," came the defense.

The others hem-hawed and shook their heads, hurrying on. Rolling her eyes, the cat lady shook her head at the approaching waiter, and flippantly gestured to her companions. She hesitated a bit longer, noticing the black cat watching her from the shadows. She didn't stare, like most humans would, but instead, smiled and slowly blinked at him, cat style.

Nacht froze, unsure of what to do.

"Hey kitty, you've got the right idea," she said softly. "Sorry, this is all I have." She reached into a to-go bag, eased closer, and left a couple of chicken tenders for him.

One of the hurrying shoppers called back, "Come on! We don't have all day."

"Yes, we do," Celeste argued.

"Oh, a cat," one of the companions said, pointing at Nacht, who leered back. "That figures. You want every cat you see."

"You should try it some time," Celeste said defensively, catching up to her group.

Nacht watched her go. He snuck out of hiding, grabbed the meat, and ran victoriously back to his shady spot. Nom nom nom. Chicken.

It wasn't long before the same group went past the café again, carrying more bags and snapping pictures, giddy in their quest of power shopping. Celeste was only half-heartedly engaging in their chatter. She halted to take pictures of the grand cathedral and all the surrounding arches, mosaics, statues, nearly ancient beauty all around them. She was taking her time enjoying the scenery when she almost lost the pack of fools yet again. Rolling her eyes, she followed her unlikely companions.

Except for cat lady, the other four shoppers were bustling through the crowd much like pigeons, making odd noises and hurrying with no specific place to go. Celeste even took pictures of them when a bag ripped and her friends hurried to pick up the fallen oddities,-a few of them joking, the others complaining. Celeste glanced back toward the cafe, where Nacht was hiding.

The group went into another shop, and this time easily left their lingering friend behind. Celeste emerged in a leisurely stroll, smiling as she held a new bag under one arm. Then she halted, frowning as she looked all around. Nacht had seen people mouth the words she uttered, and they were not pleasant ones. Scowling, now, she trotted up one way and down the next, even towards the docks. For a short while, she was lost in the crowd. Nacht curled up for a nap, his slightly crinkled whiskers drooping. He tried to sleep, but couldn't. It was too noisy, too hot, and the crowds annoyed him even more than usual.

By the time Nacht rose to try and find another friend, the cat woman came into view again, headed his way. She was smiling, strolling along as if time no longer mattered. She detoured into the majestic cathedral, ultimately basking in the radiant beauty of gold, gigantic, high arches, and timeless artwork. Nacht kept watching, his tail twitching, the flavor of chicken lingering on his mind.

After a short while, she sauntered toward the café, Nacht's café. Her expression was ponderous, yet no longer dark. A quartet nearby was playing Phantom of the Opera, a recognizable, enchanting melody. She strolled closer, finally able to enjoy listening without a group of human-sized pigeons pestering her to run along. She chose a table nearest the planters and ordered a *Caffè* with milk on the side. The harried group was gone, and all was wonderful.

"Hey, kitty," she called softly, "I see you. Why don't you come see me?"

The waiter brought her Italian coffee, and smirked, overhearing her talking to the cat. "That is a new cat." He had a thick accent. He rambled something like, "Someone will be trapping him soon, to see if he's friendly or feral."

"Ferals aren't this brave," Celeste replied. "This cat's tame, to be this casual."

"Hope he gets lucky," the guy said, moving off to serve others.

Celeste frowned in thought for a moment. She sipped her coffee, enjoying the music. After gazing at the cat again, she fished a water bottle from her bag. She took the saucer from beneath her cup, set it on the ground beside her chair, and poured some water into it. When Nacht still hesitated, she poured the water out and filled it with milk instead. That worked. The cat crept over to her.

"It's not that good for you," she chided quietly.

Slurping the milk, Nacht didn't care.

Another coffee and an appetizer later, Nacht let her pet him. He didn't know why, except it felt right. This human was different. She was a loner, like himself. Nacht followed her when she left the cafe, feeling safer as the day slipped by. Nacht finally walked by Doge's Palace at ground level, and saw that it wasn't really a palace of dogs. Torre dell'Orologio stretched out along the main plaza, bold in its Renaissance beauty. Gondolas gracefully carried passengers through the canals, and the many boats each had a different personality, from meager, to workhorse, to ornate. The bell tower appeared to watch everyone around it as it loomed over surrounding buildings. They paused by a cozy glass shop, where a skilled craftsman turned hot glass into adorable animal shapes.

Celeste led him to the quieter, less touristy side of Venice, past museums and old-world cafes. They strolled together as kindred spirits. With some effort, Celeste sweet-talked directions to the local meat market, where she shopped mostly for the cat. She even magically found a pet boutique. They saw apartments of locals, with balconies adorned by flowers of rich hues in the soft, evening lights. A gentle breeze whispered through the city.

By the time sunset drew near, tourism slowed down for the day, and shop owners prepared to close. Celeste sat down on a park bench, not too surprised when Nacht hopped up beside her to accept pieces of fresh meat and bottled water from her palm. Soon, the horizon would be twilight, where the colors of sky and water appeared to mesh together.

"It's getting late. We need to get going," Celeste admitted. She nodded toward people migrating out of the city. "I can't see leaving you here and hope you get lucky. Do you really want to stay here on pigeon island?"

For the first time, Nacht meowed at her, reaching for her hand with the food.

She gave him another piece of meat before closing the bag. "You want more goodies, come with me."

They made their way along with the tired tourists, a weary crowd now, grumbling about the weather. Sure enough, it did rain, quite a boisterous shower. Most of the crowd gathered quietly under awnings and bridges to wait it out. Celeste and Nacht followed suit. It was a humid rain, but not that cold. The wait was surprisingly pleasant, wandering adrift among strangers, everyone getting along even though many spoke different languages. It was a good chance to relax and rummage through newly purchased trinkets.

Nacht kept close to this human, who enticed him with treats and spent quite some time haggling with people for directions, and means, to keep a cat safe. By the end of the day, she whisked him away in a large tote bag cuddled against her body, on a train where Nacht watched the world sweep past him in a blur. He complained until fatigue, boredom, and a full belly lulled him to sleep. He awoke being carried into a modest house with enticing beds, treats, and pampering. That night, he curled up beside his new human for the best sleep he could remember, purring and kneading in his new, fuzzy bed.

Celeste rubbed Nacht's head, whispering, "Sweet dreams, Knightly Nacht."

Nacht proved to be an adventurous cat, cautiously social to people and other cats. Braver than many felines, he learned to love car rides, once he realized it was so much better to be inside, than to be in front of them. One thing for sure, he didn't miss pigeons, not at all.

Roberta "Bert" Davis has written fantasy and science fiction since childhood. She's a former aircraft mechanic and historian. A graduate of Embry-Riddle Aero U, her thesis was on Human Factors in Aircraft Maintenance. She works as a lead technical writer by day, and writes sci-fi/fan by night. Roberta's first novel is in final edits by her and her editor (should be named the "100 Year Book" for taking so long). She's published in the first two anthologies of SSWC, *The Moving Finger Writes*, and *Thinking Through Our Fingers*, and in NCPA's 2019 animal anthologies, *Birds of a Feather*, and *More Birds of a Feather*. Roberta is a lifelong animal enthusiast, learning from trainers and behaviorists much of her life. She is a vivid advocate for animal welfare and care/TNR of feral cats.

Facebook: https://www.facebook.com/Dragonscriber.
Facebook: https://www.facebook.com/Dragonscriber.

MY WORST AND BEST TRAVEL EXPERIENCE

TOM KANDO

February 26, 2004

This was more stressful than any other international trip I have ever taken, worse than losing luggage, worse than being bumped from a flight, worse than having to spend an extra night at an airport hotel, worse than being pick-pocketed.

This is what happened:

Today, I am flying back home to San Francisco from Holland. It's rather complicated: I am staying in a place about 40 miles north of Amsterdam International Airport (named *Schiphol*): I have to take a taxi from our flat in *Bergen* to the railroad station in *Alkmaar*, then the train from there to the Schiphol Airport. However, the train ride requires you to go into a suburb of Amsterdam (*Sloterdijk*), and transfer there onto an outbound train to the airport.

Everything is set: My flight to San Francisco leaves at 11:30 am. So, I reserved the taxi for 7:15 am, and got my train ticket in advance for 8:00. That should get me to the airport no later than 9:30, i.e. two hours before the flight.

I have one small carry-on suitcase and a monstrously large red check-through suitcase. Both have wheels of course, but things promise to be a pain at transfer points, especially the small local railroad stations, which frequently lack elevators or escalators, and thus force you to haul heavy luggage up and down the stairways that lead to the train platforms.

At 7:00, I begin by going downstairs and outside the building to await the taxi. Already, hauling the red monster starts me sweating.

Outside, it's still dark, and – for the first time since I got to Holland nearly a month ago – the entire landscape is blanketed with a beautiful, thick, pristine snow cover. Wow!

The taxi arrives punctually but – living up to the image that 10-15% of Dutchmen are jerks – the driver promptly tells me he can't take me because rules only allow one piece of luggage per passenger.

A short "discussion" ensues:

Me: "Why?"

Him: "Because there isn't room for all the passengers with several suitcases"

Me: "How many people you got this morning?"

Him: "Just you."

Me: "So what's the problem? If you don't take me, I'll miss my flight."

Him: "The rules, blah blah..."

Me: "I'll pay you extra. Let's go."

Him: "Okay."

On the way to the Alkmaar railroad station, all stop lights are broken. Intersections are dangerous and difficult to negotiate. The radio informs us that due to the freak overnight snow storm, much of the country is paralyzed. Trains only run sporadically, there are 891 kilometers of "files," i.e. traffic jams.

Alkmaar railroad station: I haul the red monster up and down a couple of stairways to the appropriate platform. Sweating like a pig, I get on the train with 30 seconds to spare. Feeling good, though. First hurdle overcome. I sit down and relax. The train leaves, Amsterdam-bound. It's dawn and I watch the snow-covered landscape whizz by. I am the only passenger in the entire car.

The train stops in various small towns, Dutchmen start pouring in at the consecutive stations – early morning commuters to Amsterdam.

Then, the really, REALLY annoying intercom announcement: "Ladies and gentlemen, we are told that all train traffic into Amsterdam has been halted due to the snow storm. All trains stop at *Zaandam* (a remote suburb). All passengers must get off."

I think: *I am screwed! I am going to miss my flight for sure. My ticket is non-refundable and it has so many conditions I might as well buy a new one. What am I going to do?*

We arrive in Zaandam. It's surreal: All trains have stopped, literally thousands of passengers have poured out onto the platforms. The crowd is so thick you can't move one step in any direction. I toss the red monster and my small suitcase onto the platform, and I am imprisoned by the throng, unable to move anywhere. It's utter pandemonium.

Okay, now what?

I begin to shove my way toward the exit. Maybe if I get down to the street (the train platforms are elevated), I'll find a taxi (fat chance, with 10,000 other commuters competing for them!), or maybe there is a bus going to the airport (about 30 kilometers away at this point), or something.

I push, shove; the wheels of my red monster run over many feet. Of course, there is no elevator in sight, so I drag the suitcases down the stairway.

Now I am outside, in front of the station, in the snow, with 10,000 stranded commuters. No taxis. No bus connection to the airport. It's a quarter to nine. I have 45 minutes to get to my flight on time. Hopeless.

Maybe there is an information office. Where the hell is the train ticket office anyway? That's where I have to start, right? At least begin to ask some questions, like: "When are the trains gonna start running again?" etc.

Well, that's back up on the elevated level. Damn! I haul my monstrous luggage back up, through the crowd. It's like American football: You hit people as hard as you can. It's best to use your shoulders. One big Dutchman, trying to fight his way downstairs, hits me so hard my glasses fall on the ground. I grab them up just as someone is about to trample them.

Now I am in line at the ticket/information counter. When I finally get to ask my questions, they have no answers whatsoever.

But now, the Dutch start to show me their unbelievable class:

First, a guy who heard my predicament taps me on

the shoulder and points me towards a KLM flight attendant who is also standing in line. So, I go talk to her and exchange notes, so to speak: "You got a flight to catch, too? To Miami at noon? I see. So, what are you going to do?"

Suddenly, someone tells the flight attendant they found a taxi. It's waiting outside, downstairs. So, I beg her: "please, let me share the cab with you!?"

"Okay, follow me," she says, and we start fighting the crowd to get back outside, downstairs.

She has little baggage, and I almost lose her. She disappears in the crowd in front of me, but I redouble my efforts, hitting and tackling people, shoving my red monster into their bellies, rolling over their feet.

Outside, I find her, loading up into a minivan cab – along with half a dozen Dutchmen also desperate to get to the airport. I present myself and my baggage, but there is no way I can fit in.

The cab driver is also talking to a second car parked behind him, which is trying to absorb some of the folks for whom he has no room. I walk to the second car and beg: "Please, I MUST make my 11:30 flight."

The lady driver of the second car grabs my red monster and together we begin to shove it into her trunk. The two drivers figure out who is going in which car, allocating people and baggage as best as possible. I almost end up being separated from my baggage.

Finally, both cars take off towards the airport. There are five of us in the second car, a small sedan. My black suitcase is on the knees of the elderly lady in the front seat. I am wedged between two large Dutchmen in the back. These folks are all flying to places like Miami, Suriname, etc.

A sense of hilarity and euphoria reigns. We are going to make it after all. I ask the lady driver how much I owe her. Turns out, she isn't a taxi driver. She is a Senator for the Province of North Holland. Her name is Dr. Lydia Snuif-Verwey, and my fellow passengers are friends of hers who are government officials going to Suriname on a state visit.

Jesus! And a moment before, I let Senator Verwey lift my monstrous suitcase into her trunk, offering her a tip!

From that moment on, all we do is laugh, roaring-laughter, talk and have a ball all the way to the airport. What a people, the Dutch! This is how they behave in emergencies. Whether it's World War II or a freak snowstorm, these people are there for you when it counts! Fantastic!

The roads being as they are, it takes us an hour and a half to cover the 30 ks (20 miles) to the airport – a fun, lovely hour and a half of bonding and laughing. Then, we quickly separate, after I make sure I get Senator Verwey's business card so I can send her a lavish gift.

I run to one of the KLM counters to begin the check-in process. I've got less than an hour. My euphoria is premature. I am not out of the woods. My line is immense, and it's not budging. I observe and compare my line with another one next to me, and I swear, we go through a 45-minute time span without one single party moving forward to the check-in counter.

Twice I approach one of the security people in charge, telling them our line is clogged, that all other lines are moving at a reasonable pace, but not ours. Each time they give evasive answers and nothing happens.

Finally, I take matters into my own hands. It's amazing how sheepish, sullen and obedient travelers are. No one else does anything. I have been called a nervous Nelly, but you know what? If I hadn't taken it upon myself to play traffic cop, I would have missed my flight. What I end up doing next could have had me arrested, in our paranoid post-September 11 world:

I walk over to the front of our line and find out what the problem is. There is another line feeding into ours, and every single passenger who has moved forward over the past 45 minutes was from that other line, while no one from our side did. The idiot airport personnel have not been paying attention, that's all.

So, I approach security personnel again and tell them what they are doing wrong. I do more: I stand at the point where the other line merges into ours, and I tell the people there: "Look, you MUST ALTERNATE people from the two different sides. Otherwise, the 100 people on our side will all miss their flights!" I do more: I talk directly to the passengers in the other line and order them to wait and let some people from our side advance, as no one from our side has advanced in nearly an hour.

I didn't get arrested. Better yet, I had run out of time, my flight was leaving in 10 minutes, and my gate was half a mile away. So, I told the airport security guy who had messed up so royally: "Look, I don't care anymore what you do with the clogged-up lines, but you MUST let ME through NOW."

And he did. I checked the red monster, the woman at the check-in counter gave me my boarding pass in less than two minutes, she called the gate to tell them to wait for me, and I started running to the gate.

And so, I got to go home.

So, here are the lessons: (1) Shit happens; (2) People in general – and the Dutch in particular – can be awesome. There is something truly redeeming about human nature, people helping people in emergency situations; (3) You got to take some damn initiative, sometimes. Things aren't gonna happen for you if you don't do some things yourself. Most of the trouble with the world today is that people have lost the initiative. I hate to moralize; I am usually no hero. But I'll tell you one thing. On this occasion, many things did fall into place the right way.

Tom Kando, PhD, grew up in World War II Europe, spending his formative years in Paris and Amsterdam. At eighteen, he came to America as a lonely immigrant and a Fulbright student. He became a professor at major universities, taught in prisons, and lectured worldwide. His memoir, *A Tale of Survival,* describes his far-flung and sometimes harrowing experiences.

He has authored articles about crime, psychology, sociology, sports, terrorism, and travel, in the *Wall Street Journal*, the *Los Angeles Examiner, the Sacramento Bee* and scientific journals, plus nine books, including *Leisure and Popular Culture*, *Social Interaction* (C.V. Mosby), *Sexual Behavior and Family Life* (Elsevier), *Readings in Criminology* (Kendall Hunt) and Humanity's Future: *The Next 25,000 Years.* Tom just completed a travel book, *Tried and True: The Best Travel Experiences in Europe.* He is fluent in four languages, and lives in Gold River, California. His website is www.TomKando.com.

MY NEW SPANISH LOVES

KIMBERLY A. EDWARDS

I ambled from salon to salon in Barcelona's Picasso Museum, my ears squeezed between headphones, listening to a voice narrating a self-guided tour. Not long into the tape, my eyes fell upon two paintings that differed from the others. They were small and unassuming. Both featured a line of trees. In one, the trunks stood abreast from left to right. In the second, the same grove of trees, portrayed from the side, cast progressively short shadows over a path narrowing in the distance.

What held my gaze was not the scene that each painting rendered, but the fact that two distinct angles projected the same moment: two vistas transmitting a single peg in time. The taped voice coming through my earphones faded as bells chimed in my head, heralding an epiphany greater than any lecture or book I had ever read on writing. These two little paintings demonstrated "Point of View."

Point of view, that oft-elusive literary device! Nobody had ever explained it better or more efficiently than a deceased Spaniard genius communicating from the past on a Wednesday afternoon in Barcelona.

I leaned into the wall to read the date of creation: 1896. My mind thrust into calculation gear. Picasso would have been fifteen at the time. Fifteen! Here I'd come to Spain to relax, not to be insulted by the reminder of a 50-year delay in my own artistic development.

With museum visitors pressing at my back, I left the two paintings to proceed through the museum. I begrudgingly trailed Picasso enthusiasts ogling the works ahead. No other design or rendition incited in me the same palpitation as those two little discoveries.

How is it, I pondered, that brushstrokes birthed by the

twist of an adolescent's wrist could ignite a light bulb in an onlooker's brain (mine) a century after creation? I recalled reading that Hemingway told Lillian Ross in a 1950 *New Yorker* profile that he learned to write by studying paintings by a departed artist. Was my infatuation with the two Picasso pieces another example of a long-gone prodigy teaching a writer?

Like a Mediterranean sea turtle drawn back to its home, I reversed my course in the museum, elbowing my way against the flow of the crowd to view the little paintings again to verify they were as inspiring as I remembered. And they were, a set of unheralded gems calling little attention to themselves. They emitted no smoke or scent, no phonemes, or syllables, but my instincts sensed profundity, that rare occasion when comprehension leap frogs over the brain to burrow directly into the soul, as Tolstoy once described.

In fact, by now these two pictures were mine, whispering to my writer's heart, that place where we hold our greatest intimacies. I stood with the paintings a few more minutes, then left for the museum gift shop, hoping for a reproduction on a bag, a bookmark or a coffee cup to carry back to the States. Alas, no trace of them anywhere in the gift shop.

That night in my hotel bed, I lay awake wondering how I could ever see them again. Sadly, I had to leave in the morning, heading south by train to Seville. Yet the memory of the paintings dominated the terrain as we chugged past orange groves, shadows of moving clouds across the hues of the land, the towers and tile of White Towns rising over the slopes into vastness.

Upon arriving in Seville, I emailed the Barcelona Museum. In my best pleading Spanish, I explained that two paintings exhibited there spoke to me and I was desperate to see them again to teach others about point of view. The curator emailed back, "Which paintings are you asking about? More details needed. What did they look like? Which salon were they in?"

I sat back, blinked, looked away from the screen. My

memory, so taken with the paintings, now vanished. Were the paintings in the first gallery? The second room around the corner? Were they partially hand-sketched? What were the pervasive colors? Exactly what size were they? The more I pressed myself, the less I remembered.

I had written nothing down, made no record of specifics. In that moment it was clear I was just a pedestrian writer; the masters always took notes. Thoreau measured. Da Vinci diagramed. Maugham detailed. Wharton outlined. I had failed to document basic information about masterpieces I considered so precious.

The next day, at a moment least expected after visiting the Alcazar Castle, the paintings surfaced on their own. They came slowly, starting vague and sharpening into focus like images on a light table: about eight trees, brown, on a far wall, in an early-period salon, before the Blue Room, displayed with larger paintings to the right.

With these strands of memory conveyed to the Barcelona museum curator, she found the paintings. Hallelujah! And she sent them to me in digital format.

Today, back in the States, I am still rejoicing. I cherish the paintings that crossed centuries, generations, and time zones to come live with me. They're the lovers who gave me a second chance. They taught me that noticing particulars is important. Those invisible arms that reached out from a wall in Barcelona vowed, "Now that you see us, we're with you wherever you go, whatever you write."

Kimberly A. Edwards loves writing about curious things, including inequities, she observes along life's path. These subjects offer levels of interpretation that take her years to figure out, and even then she continues revising to illuminate new discoveries. Her travel often serves as the backdrop for stories. Marginalized communities and the lessons they have taught her appear in many of her pieces. For decades she has written articles, but literary nonfiction is her favorite genre. Currently she is working on a book for the History Press on early Sacramento motorcycling in the first half of the 20th Century. She is an alumnus of Squaw Valley Community of Writing (Fiction), and the Kenyon Review Writer's Workshop (Non-fiction and Hybrid). A long-time NCPA member, she also serves as president of the local branch of the California Writers Club.

OMENS, MEDICINE MEN and MYTHS
PATRICIA E. CANTERBURY

OMENS

My only trip to the continent of Africa was in 1985 as a Delegate to the United Nations Conference on Women, to be held in Nairobi, Kenya.

My friend, Bettye O Williams asked if I'd like to be her roommate on a trip to Africa. Of course I jumped at the chance, even though I was saving for a trip to Mongolia and Northern China. However, the chance to tag along with Bettye O and see Africa was too tempting.

I couldn't travel all that way "just because", so I asked then-California Assembly Speaker, Willie Brown if I had his support to deliver a speech on Women and the Family Farm. After all, I had been a member of 4H and raised lambs waaaayyyyy back in the day.

I received The Honorable Willie Brown's endorsement; plus, I would be traveling with the esteemed Dr. Dorothy Height, president of the National Council of Negro Women. By *traveling with* I mean Bettye O and I were two of thirty-four folks from the United States who accompanied Dr. Height as she met with diplomats, ambassadors and future kings in five countries.

A third of the women in our tour spoke French, as well as English, which helped a lot when we landed in Senegal; none of us learned *Wolof*, other than to say hello and good bye. The majority of our tour were women, and three brought their husbands with them. Two of the men were doctors.

Bettye O and I flew from Sacramento to Los Angeles, and on the way to the airport we saw a car fly off the highway and land sideways on the side of the road. Bettye O said, "I hope that's not an <u>omen</u> of how our trip's going to be?"

We arrived at LAX unhurt and on time. We boarded the plane which would take us to New York, where we would fly directly to Dakar, Senegal. After an hour on the tarmac in L.A., the pilot came on to say we would have to exit and take another plane. Our suitcases would be waiting for us in Dakar, and for us to LEAVE our carry-on in the overhead bins. The maintenance crew would make sure they were put on the next plane leaving for Senegal.

I had my carry-on resting at my feet, so I took it with me when we left the plane. After spending 1968 traveling by car through Europe and the old Soviet Union, I was used to packing light.

I was wearing a ten-pocket REI travel jacket which contained my passport, funds, malaria pills and a small notebook. Bettye O left her carry-on with our original plane. We arrived in New York and met the rest of our group, which had arrived from eastern and southern states.

We had an uneventful flight to Africa, arriving early in the morning in Dakar where our tour group took several cabs to our hotel. I have no sense of direction whatsoever. Yet, somehow, I knew my way around Dakar. I kept telling the cab driver where to turn to avoid the crowds. To this day, I have NO IDEA how I did that as I STILL get lost in my hometown of Sacramento. (Omen?)

The sounds of Dakar were different than those of Northern California, with diverse noises, the French, Wolof and Arabic languages, as well as the call to prayer from large mosques. Once checked into our hotel, Bettye O and I met our guide, Mikle, who happened to be the same guide Bettye O's daughter, Kathy, had when she visited Dakar three years earlier. Kathy was in another hotel across town. (Another omen?)

After lunch, the entire tour group took a large boat to lle de Goree, which is famous or infamous, as one of the last places on the African continent, that slaves, headed to the new world, saw before beginning their journey on the middle passage. As the boat came ashore, our party climbed onto the small dock where I immediately fell and sprained my ankle so badly it nearly doubled in size.

MEDICINE MEN/MYTHS

I couldn't put any weight on my ankle. Both doctors (Medicine Men) rushed to my side, wrapped my foot and ankle and told me to stay off my foot! Two friends, one on each side, walked with me as I hobbled through the museums and places of interest on the island. They helped me return to the boat, and waited as a cab took us to our hotel. One of our doctor friends said he would go to a local hospital in the morning and see if they would loan him crutches, as I would not be able to walk safely for a least six weeks!!!!!

I was only going to be in Africa for six weeks. I had five other countries to visit; and a speech to give in Nairobi. I couldn't hop along for six weeks.

Bettye O and I retired to our hotel room where our guide, Mikle, met us. He asked why my foot and ankle were bandaged. Bettye O explained everything to him, because I was in too much pain to talk. He said he needed to get some mud for my ankle and would return in an hour. Bettye O and I had dinner in our room.

Mikle returned with a jar of dark mud, immediately removed my bandages, and rubbed my foot and ankle with the mud. My ankle was turning an ugly blue as Mikle rubbed the mud over it. I don't remember the mud having any odor whatsoever, not even the smell of dirt. He said not to wash the caked-on mud off until my morning shower and I'd be able to walk by 9 am. (Myths).

Mikle was going to take Bettye O and me to his village, which is off the tourist trail, and where we could go shopping for baskets and fabric to bring back to America. I slept peacefully and did not give my ankle any thought the next morning as Bettye O and I took the elevator downstairs for breakfast.

Both American doctors saw me in the dining room, took a look at my now normal- looking ankle, noticed I wasn't limping, and asked what happened. I told them

Mikle put some mud on my hurt ankle and now it felt great.

Bettye O and I had breakfast as the two American doctors and Mikle spoke together for nearly an hour (<u>Medicine Men</u>). The rest of our four days in Senegal were wonderful, even though Bettye O's and all of the California tour members' luggage didn't arrive for three days.

We were still able to have dinner in ambassadors' homes (because we were part of Dr. Height's delegation), go on trips to rural hospitals (because we had American doctors with us), and local trips on marijuana-filled small buses (10 people) full of chickens and tiny, pregnant pygmy goats. One ride took us to Mikle's village where we were able to bargain for colorful home-dyed fabric.

I was able to bring the jar of magical mud back home with me. When asked if I had anything to declare I did mention I had a jar of Senegalese mud, but I was waved through customs by a bored customs' agent. The mud lasted nearly five years.

Patricia E. Canterbury (Pat) is a native Sacramentan, political scientist, art collector, retired State Administrator, author of seven novels: children, mid-grade, young adult and adult, as well as a world traveler.

One of her young adult novels, *The Case of the Bent Spoke*, won an Honorable Mention at the 2019 NCPA Awards. She has been accepted in over 26 anthologies including the 2018 Brom Stoke Finalist, *Sycorax's Daughters.* Pat, her husband and elderly cat live in Sacramento. She can be reached at www.patmyst.com or patmyst@aol.com

The Busboy's Secret, Due October 2020 Obsidian Anthology
The Secret of Sugarman's Circus A Poplar Cove Mystery
The Case of the Brent Spoke, A Poplar Cove Mystery
    *2019 NCPA Young Adult Honorable Mention
Sycorax's Daughters 2018 Brom Stoker Finalist-- Anthology
The Geaha Incident, An Afro-futuristic mystery
The Secret of Morton's End, A Poplar Cove Mystery
Carlotta's Secret, A Delta Mystery, Option for a motion picture

MY BIG RED SHADOW
ROSEMARY COVINGTON MORGAN

It was an honor and I was thrilled. I had been selected, along with twenty other people, to be part of an international study mission to Europe. I would travel to Italy, Germany, Switzerland, and France to evaluate transit innovations. It would be a three-week adventure.

I love to travel. I love everything about exploring new places, eating different foods, meeting new people, just the experience of being someplace different. What I like best about traveling is wearing clothes. I wouldn't call myself a clothes horse, but store clerks greet me by name.

The itinerary for this trip promised many, many opportunities for me to look fashion-forward. I would visit monuments, have lunches and dinners at elegant restaurants, attend high-level meetings at official buildings, and travel on almost every kind of train and bus in Europe.

However, I could only bring one bag. There was no way I could travel for three weeks with one bag.

My husband, with whom I shared the clothes obsession, decided to solve my problem. I came home from work one day to find him grinning like the afternoon sun in summer, standing by the largest suitcase I had ever seen. "It's red. You won't get it confused with anyone else's luggage." He had even tied a red bow on the handle.

"Plus," he added, "you'll have extra room for shopping. Maybe you can buy something for your husband." He winked and hugged me before opening the bag to show me all its features. He was so proud. How could I tell him it might be too big?

The day came for me to leave and he dropped me and the bag at Dulles, the International Airport for the DC area, to begin my trip. The travel agency had arranged a room at the airport for our group to meet for a briefing. I walked in with my big red bag. Conversation stopped; I became the center of attention. Or rather, my bag became the center of attention.

Our travel coordinator greeted me. I was prepared for her to tell me I'd have to get a smaller bag. Instead, she said, "Hi. My name is Nancy, and what a lovely red bag. You certainly won't miss that at baggage claim."

I looked at the other travelers. Most of them had large backpacks. A few had small suitcases. Nancy made sure all our luggage was tagged and placed on a cart to be loaded on the plane. My bag certainly stood out.

First stop, Rome. First problem, my bag wouldn't fit in the cab. I wanted to scream. The Rome pick-up area was busy and filled with loud, tired, and crabby travelers moving between cars to get their rides. I stood there, embarrassed, while the driver tied my bag onto the vehicle's roof as cabs, scooters, cars, and people maneuvered around, honking and yelling at him. I didn't need to speak Italian to understand the screaming curse words.

The hotel was very charming, very Italian, and without a bellman. There were ten steps to the door of the hotel and another twenty to my room. It was not easy, but I made it.

For dinner I selected a lovely, flowing dress that seemed perfect for an Italian evening – until the temperature dropped and I was freezing. Everyone else was in sweaters and slacks, except for the one other woman on the trip. Carol was still living in the seventies. She wore a bulky sweater over a long wool dress, and Birkenstocks, the entire trip.

The next three days were filled with meetings. I wore black dresses and suits throughout the visit, very Armani, very cool. I was pleased the large bag provided me with several choices for my monochromatic look.

On the fourth day, we traveled to Trieste, Italy. Nancy arranged for a bus to take us to the airport.

The airport at Trieste was small but modern and, most importantly, accessible to the disabled. And people with giant suitcases. I was lucky the hotel was also modern and accessible. There was no bellman, but the elevator was nice and large.

My meetings went well. We had two formal dinners with Italian transportation officials. On the last evening our hosts took us to a charming restaurant overlooking the Adriatic Sea. The dinner was wonderful. I had seafood pasta followed by dessert, and my first excursion into the blessing that is *grappa*.

I had appropriate clothing for each event and received several compliments on my fashion sense. I began to think having a large suitcase may not have been a bad idea.

Before we left, we visited a church that had been a place of worship since before the Roman Empire. While Its religions changed over time, the church remained. I was humbled by its simple beauty. We were leaving Trieste after the church visit, so the suitcase visited, too. It was a little awkward on the cobblestones, but no major problem.

My travel companions had given my bag a name, Red. By the time we left Trieste, Red was a mascot with a gender, male. Red became the favorite object of not-so-funny jokes from my travel companions.

"That bag has lost a little weight, hasn't it?" "A bag that big should be able to carry itself." "Will your bag be joining us for breakfast?"

Next stop Geneva, Switzerland. Getting to Geneva meant flying over the magnificent snow-covered Alps. The journey was amazing. The interior design of the plane was comfortable, and the service outstanding.

I was well-rested as I retrieved Red and walked to the vehicle pick-up area. As part of a marketing effort, the bus manufacturer, Mercedes Benz, sent a fleet of Smart cars to take us to our hotel. They were the first I'd ever seen. After the experience of loading Red in a Smart car, I never wanted to see one again.

It was a group effort, with my travel companions and some of the fleet drivers (all male) helping. It took a half-hour of anguish to load it; everyone had an idea.

"Try the passenger door."

"No, sideways through the driver's side."

"Will it fit on the roof?"

"Too big."

"What about the hatchback?"

"Too long."

Red could only get through the hatchback, if tied to the front seat, with me holding the handle. I had to sit sideways in the seat with my knees to my chin while holding the bag.

When we arrived at the hotel, several of our group pitched in to help get Red out of the soup can vehicle. Then they had to help me get out of the seat.

Once again, the hotel was quaint. Once again it had many steps. It also had an elevator, just large enough for me, an average-sized American, and Red. So, being polite, I waited for everyone to go up before me. Sitting on Red, I looked around the lobby, admiring the marble floors, the dark wainscoting surrounding an exquisite mahogany check-in desk with milk glass pendant lights, providing an air of romance. I expected Cary Grant or Audrey Hepburn to walk in and ask for one of the keys hanging behind the desk.

When it was our turn, Red and I squeezed into the elevator. We stopped at a dimly lit hallway and walked into a room so small I had to climb over Red to get inside. The bag laid on the floor by the door. I spent the entire visit crawling over it to get in and out of the room.

I fell in love with Geneva. Lake Geneva sparkled in the sunlight as if stars had landed on its surface. The city sparkled, too. It was spotless. The shopping was marvelous. The food provided delights. *Pommes Frites* were new to me. I let their deliciousness melt in my mouth with every meal. Swiss chocolate became my drug of choice, and every dessert was chocolate.

After five days, I needed to get out of town before I exploded. On our travel day, I woke early, dressed casually, packed Red, and went to the lobby to wait for my travel companions. After having crawled over Red in that small room for almost a week, I couldn't wait for him to become checked luggage and out of my sight.

The always-smiling Nancy came to the lobby with a surprise. She had arranged a wine and cheese tasting in Lausanne for our breakfast. "You'll love it," she gushed.

I walked outside to have some extra time to get Red in the Smart car. There were no Smart cars. There were no cars at all. Nor was there a bus.

I was standing at the top of the stairs waiting for an explanation, when I heard Nancy say, "There is a train that travels directly to Lausanne. We can walk to the station from here. It's only a fifteen-minute walk."

Did I mention that I'm not the most physically fit person? Well, the rest of the group may have made it in fifteen minutes. Let's just say, pulling Red, I got there before the train left.

Like everything else in Geneva, the train station was immaculate and accessible. I took the elevator to the boarding platform and within seconds, boarded a modern, gleaming rail car filled with a crushing load of people. I found a space where Red and I could stand for our fifty-two-minute trip.

I was holding onto the railing when I looked down and saw two young men sitting on Red. I was perturbed. Should I ask them to move? After dragging that thing all morning, I didn't give a f—.

Within a few stops, the train nearly cleared out. The squatters left. Red and I found a seat. The ride was worth it. The train moved smoothly, allowing me to relax and observe the lovely views of the mountains which on this day, were hugged by low hanging slate-blue clouds. I looked across the aisle to gaze at the hypnotizingly blue waters of Lake Geneva.

I arrived in Lausanne relaxed. We disembarked and I was confronted by what looked to be a hundred steps. Luckily a rail employee saw my dilemma and led Red and me to a service elevator. Several in my group followed me, rather than tackle the steps. Of course, there are always the overachievers, God bless them. They could hardly breathe when they rejoined the group.

A brightly painted new bus met us for the trip to the winery. Red was placed in the luggage compartment. I didn't get to see much of the city, but what I saw made me want to return for a longer visit. Lausanne was a city with many intriguing historic places to explore.

The wine tasting was in a cave. We walked through its arched entrance of gleaming natural rock. The vintner explained the cave was centuries old, perhaps prehistoric. The arch had been originally carved by some of its earliest inhabitants and developed its striking blue/brown patina through many centuries.

A gigantic round oak table offering a bounty of fresh fruits, freshly baked loaves of bread, and various cheeses, occupied the center of the tasting room. The fragrance was heavenly.

The tasting began right away. I preferred a light fruity Rosé that paired with everything but the cheese. For that, I tried a deep red Bordeaux. A perfect morning.

We were offered a tour of the winery but there was a problem. A different bus was coming for us and we'd have to unload our luggage and take it with us on the tour. I skipped the tour, content to sit with Red and taste wine until they returned.

After a while, I was having such a good time wine tasting with my companion, Red, that things became a bit blurry. I vaguely remember struggling to get Red in the luggage compartment of our new bus. I must have immediately fallen asleep upon boarding. I didn't wake up until our arrival in Dusseldorf.

There's not much to say about Dusseldorf. It has an innovative transit system, lovely trains and buses, and I understand that at Christmas, they have a wonderful fair. We were only staying overnight so I didn't bother unpacking. For the first time on the trip, I didn't dress for dinner. We ate at a monastery from the middle ages that was now a restaurant. Dinner was beef, potatoes, and some kind of vegetable. After Italy and Switzerland, German food was pretty bland.

This was the night the group decided to bond.

Someone had German background and offered to lead us in several songs. Before long, there was singing throughout the room. This was also the night Nancy wanted us "girls" to get to know each other. So, there I sat surrounded by people singing in every off-key while Nancy and Carol talked about their lives, screaming above the singing. I had nothing to offer. I just wanted to get back to Red and the aspirin I'd packed in his side pocket.

Red helped me get dressed the next morning. I zipped him open and grabbed whatever was on top. There were a few lectures before we left Dusseldorf, so there was more food. Sausages and eggs for breakfast; sausages and pretzels for lunch.

We were taking a train to the airport, then flying to Rouen. Once again, the train station was old and not accessible. I bought my ticket upstairs and sought out the rail platform. Access to the platform was by staircase. A staircase so long and so steep, my treadmill, at its highest incline setting, would be intimidated.

My new friend Carol, with her long skirt and Birkenstocks, came to help with Red. "If we work together, this should be easy," she pronounced.

"Thank you," I replied, desperately looking for a redcap.

Carol was a healthy girl. She looked like she might mountain climb and chop her own wood. Before I could say anything, she grabbed Red by his back handle, and, with the bag between us, we proceeded to tackle the steps.

We made it about five steps before Carol had to stop and adjust her skirt. About eight more steps before one of her shoes slipped off. A guy passing by suggested, "Turn the bag around and lead from the back handle."

While my inner, smarter, more assertive voice yelled, *"Don't do that, it's a stupid idea,"* Carol and the random guy were maneuvering Red in front of me. I was holding the handle with one hand trying to keep my balance as I stood in the stairwell with the bag's weight in front of me, as Carol profusely thanked the random guy.

At first, Red just kind of dropped a step. I pulled him

back. Next, he jumped a couple of steps. My arm was beginning to stretch. He was slipping. I grabbed his handle with both hands and he only slipped a step. Then, he started bouncing down the steps with me behind him. He kept going faster. I was trying to keep up. He was dragging me. Carol was screaming. I couldn't keep up. I released the big red bag and watched him tumble down the steps while gravity knocked me on my Eileen Fisher clad butt as I yelled, "WATCH OUT!!!"

I really didn't need to yell. The bag was so loud and so red that people began scrambling before I let go. I ran to grab my bag, glancing at the people to be sure they weren't hurt. Carol was following me with her skirt gathered in her hand. The random guy had disappeared.

I grabbed Red at the bottom of the staircase and we reached the platform just in time to board the train with our group and arrived at the airport only to find our flight had been canceled. Nancy called the travel agency back in the States. She found someone who booked us on another flight, but we'd have to run.

One of Red's wheels had been cracked on his fall. As I ran with Red, he swung around in circles like he was trying to square dance all the way to the gate. The flight had closed its door.

There was one more chance, but that flight was leaving soon, and was on the other side of the airport. Once more we were running, all twenty-one of us, with Red and me dancing behind them. We made it. I said "good riddance" when I gave the suitcase to the flight attendant to check.

Red didn't make it to Rouen with us. He was lost. I finally got him back after he had spent 24 hours on the tarmac in the pouring rain.

He looked sad and sorry, dripping water, his color fading when the airline employee brought him to me. But Red had become like a bad boyfriend and it was time for him to go. The hotel dried my clothes and folded them in a box. The box was mailed home. I felt liberated if underdressed. I only saved blue jeans and tee-shirts for the rest of the trip.

My group eulogized the loss of Red with a six-hour lunch in the historic hotel overlooking the plaza of Joan of Arc's execution. It seemed appropriate.

It was our last city, our last travel day and the best day of the trip. The French treated us well. We indulged ourselves with ten courses of spectacular food and perfectly paired wine. I was feeling good, comfortable that Red had become a gift to someone in the hotel's housekeeping department.

I was sure my husband would understand.

RoseMary Covington has just stepped on stage for an encore. After a 40-plus year successful career as an urban planner, the curtain is rising on a new challenge as an author.

Writing is not new to her. Born in St. Louis, Missouri, she started creating stories using her dolls and plastic action figures while in elementary school. Her interest followed her through high school, to the University of Missouri- Columbus and Washington University-St. Louis.

Her early career included investigating civil rights cases, housing development, reviewing grants, and developing community-based programs. She then began the development of major public transit projects, becoming an executive manager and an acknowledged expert in her field.

She has led transit projects in St. Louis, Cleveland, Washington, DC, Sacramento, and other cities as a consultant.

RoseMary has published a short story, *The Song* in the anthology *Storytellers-Tales from the Rio Vista Writers' group.*

NCPA * OUR PURPOSE * WHO WE ARE * WHAT WE DO

Northern California Publishers & Authors (NCPA) is an alliance of independent publishers, authors, and publishing professionals in Northern California.

Formed in 1991 as Sacramento Publishers Association, then expanded to Sacramento Publishers and Authors and eventually to NCPA, our purpose is to foster, encourage, and educate authors, small publishers, and those interested in becoming authors and publishers.

We support small indie presses, self-publishers and aspiring authors at our monthly meetings by covering topics such as self- and traditional publishing, editing, book design, tax & legal issues, and marketing.

Service providers who cater to the publishing industry – illustrators, cover designers, editors, etc. – are also invited to join NCPA as associate members.

In addition to our annual NCPA Book Anthology, for *members only*, which started again in 2019, NCPA holds an annual Book Awards Competition for both *members, and non-members.* The NCPA Book Awards Competition celebrated our 25th year with the entry of 38 books published in 2018.

NCPA also gives back to the community through proceeds from a Silent Auction during our Book Awards Banquets in the forms of: $1000 scholarship to a college-bound, local high school senior intending to pursue a publishing or writing-related degree; 916-Ink, which empowers youth through the published, written word; Mustard Seed School for underprivileged youth; and Friends of the Sacramento Public Library who provide books to the homes of underprivileged children.

Check out our website www.norcalpa.org for information on our next Book Awards Competition, the next anthology and information on how to join NCPA.